MULTIPLE MIND

MULTIPLE MIND

Healing the Split in Psyche and World

GRETCHEN SLIKER

SHAMBHALA · Boston & London · 1992

Shambhala Publications, Inc.
Horticultural Hall
300 Massachusetts Avenue
Boston, Massachusetts 02115

Shambhala Publications, Inc.
Random Century House
20 Vauxhall Bridge Road
London SP7 8BP

9 8 7 6 5 4 3 2 1

First Edition

Printed in the United States of America on acid-free paper

∞

Distributed in the United States by Random House
and in Canada by Random House of Canada Ltd.
Distributed in the United Kingdom by Element Books Ltd.

Library of Congress Cataloging-in-Publication Data

Sliker, Gretchen, 1938–
Multiple mind: healing the split in psyche and world / Gretchen
Sliker.—1st ed.
p. cm.
Includes bibliographical references and index.
ISBN 0-87773-634-0 (pbk. : alk. paper)
1. Psychosynthesis.   2. Psychosynthesis—Social aspects.
I. Title.
RC489.P76S57 1992
155.2—dc20   91-52526
                                                          CIP

To my family,
the first teachers of my psyche

CONTENTS

Contents

Contents

PREFACE

In 1982 I became aware that the psychotherapy process that I observed in my clients, and some clients of those I supervised, was clear, deep, fast, and transformative. As I considered the work of colleagues, whether it be my own consultation group or the presentations of experts at conferences, I had to acknowledge a more comprehensive process being accomplished by my clients. I was observing the dramatic impact produced by one therapeutic approach, namely, the concept of subpersonalities.

Because of the degree of effectiveness of this approach I finally had to make a commitment to write about my observations. At first sitting with the project I wrote down titles for eight articles intended for professional journals. All seemed equally important to a comprehensive understanding of subpersonality dynamics. The titles themselves read like the progressively deepening subject matter in the chapter titles of a book; thus the project became a book. To my surprise, after describing the initial introduction to subpersonalities and their basic dynamics, I found with every topic I was in new territory of my own learning. In the research I found that observation of subpersonalities was part of the early work at the beginning of the field of psychology and that it was lost as Freud's theories became popular. Giants like Pierre Janet and William James all acknowledged in their broad systems that subpersonalities are an essential aspect of the psyche, but without detailing at that time their practical importance in the healthy mind. I have been particularly fortunate in my work that the clients who have been attracted to working with me are talented individuals who function at a high level and who manifest light, transitory pathology; hence the work quickly becomes a study of their own potential. The system of subpersonality work is an efficient way to look at problems ranging from light to heavy, but it is even more significant in enabling an individual to understand the structure of his own normal psychological process and to initiate growth. There is also a realization of the uniqueness of each individual, which is portrayed vividly in his set of subpersonalities; in every case, a brilliant invention in the face of survival needs. The result is that the subpersonalities—the knowledge, management, and deep polishing of them—inevitably lead the individual into expanded development. In fact, subpersonalities are a bridge between traditional psychological understanding of development and more advanced development which in the past was described in religious systems and more recently in the field of transpersonal psychology.

At the time I was working on this deep study of the psyche in order to write about it, I spent a day with a family from my childhood, a mother and her sons whom I had not seen since we were adolescents thirty years ago. In that meeting one of these men said to me in essence: it is all well and good that you work on understanding the individual, but what about relationships with other people, what about the world? The last three chapters of the book were thus born. Stepping out of the field of psychology altogether, stepping out of the individual psyche into the world, the subpersonality concept still applies; the psyche, with its family of subpersonalities, projects its own structure onto the community, and vice versa, allowing the imprint of that community on the psyche: the family, the aspects of the single culture, the many cultures, the aspects of a nation, and the many nations that make the world. The world is literally a mirror of the mind of humankind.

Apparently, I have been working on this study all my life. When I was seven I remember that I discovered my mind through watching it compartmentalize: when I was thinking about pears, I was not thinking about apples; and when I was thinking about apples, I was not thinking about pears. My disappointment was genuine when no one around me thought that was amazing. Another childhood experience I called listening, I now recognize as what is referred to in this study as *Center*, an essential mental shift to disidentify from (move out of) the dominance of subpersonalities. In a dream from my early adult years I was marching up a mountain with the parts of my body in a bag on my back. Even then it was obvious to me that I carried the parts of myself. My doctoral dissertation on egocentric thought in creative adults, although I did not realize it at the time, was about egocentric subpersonalities. It was not until several years after I had finished graduate school that I discovered Jung and Assagioli. I wondered why they had not been part of my formal studies, for they affirmed and celebrated the richness of the psyche and the dynamic process of growth.

I am aware that in many cases in this book I simply skim the surface of very rich topics. I invite others to take up where I leave off and follow the enticing research paths that beckon on practically every page. Would I had more hours in my lifetime. *Ars est longa; vita brevis.*

ACKNOWLEDGMENTS

I give many thanks first to my amazing clients and supervisees, from whom I learn infinitely; to my colleague, Marie Fay, for her keen editorial comment and her enthusiastic pursuit of the ideas; to officemates John Lee and Bob Diehl, for careful reading, stimulating discussion, and unflagging vitality and cheer; to other Jungian colleagues Clyde Reid, Laura Dodson, and Susan Wolkerstorfer, who have taught me; to consulting psychiatrist Joel Miller, who kept me in touch with the breadth of the psychological community; to psychosynthesists Piero Ferrucci and Massimo Rosselli in Florence, Italy, Tom Yeomans, Martha Crampton, Jane Vennard, Astrid Koch, and David Kolb in the United States, and to Jungian analyst Don Williams, for their invaluable varied contributions; to Ken Wilber, who, receiving my unknown manuscript, gave encouragement and direction; to Jeremy Hayward, Kendra Crossen, and Lenore Thomson Bentz for their skillful editing and shaping of the book, and especially to Jeremy Hayward for championing my work; to Dennis McGilvray, for his suggestions in the anthropology study; to Julia Amari for her vibrant Italian translations; to Karen Sbrockey, for her encouragement and for initiating me into the ways of the writing world; to Jim Shaud, for bringing me to task on behalf of "others" and the "world"; to Bill and Marge Riddle for practical guidance in computer skills; to the staff of Cover to Cover Bookstore, Boulder, Colorado, especially Steve Graham, who found obscure source materials; to Jo Tom, for meticulous word processing early in the project; to my husband Todd and daughters Cynthia and Kathryn for their unwavering, unquestioning support, and to the girls, especially Cyndy, for secretarial help in preparing the manuscript.

MULTIPLE MIND

1

FACETS OF
THE PSYCHE
Subpersonalities

"I do not understand my own actions. . . . I can will what is
right, but I cannot do it. For I do not do the good I want, but
the evil I do not want is what I do."   —*Romans* 8:6

Two thousand years ago, Paul of Tarsus spoke of the "part of
him" responsible for a particular frame of mind, the "other
part," whose behavior was beyond his conscious control. All of
us can identify with his dilemma. To name and characterize the
poles of thought within us, and thus to isolate the unique clusters of dynamic psychic energy, is an easy natural process. The
delineation of subpersonalities is merely an expansion on this
normal understanding of mental mechanics.

Everyone is aware of subpersonalities in themselves. The first
evidence is natural dialectical thought. When one is faced with
the need for a decision, thought moves into specific dialogue,
one pole answering another, each pole contributing consistently
its separate evaluation of the best decision.

The many roles we play in the world are subpersonalities. In
one setting my behavior is that of the polished, dignified, and
capable professional; in another setting I am the kind, gentle,
and joyful parent celebrating the delight of my children. My
body posture and movement, my voice and vocabulary are
different as I play each role. Yet these roles are not external to me,
they are who I am.

1

Each personality is an aggregate of styles that comprise respective behaviors, experience, and memories. The styles may flow gracefully or awkwardly from one to another, but they remain distinct down to the body posture and the characteristic severity or twinkle in the eye. The diverse styles do not become homogenized into one style, one unitary personality.

Indeed, the subpersonalities of an individual are far more than generic mental "parts." They are a unique portrait, a configuration that embodies not only the actual behavior of a person, but her [1] potential; not only the surface, conscious qualities witnessed in daily life, but the deepest motivational archetypes—those harbingers of the future. The Renaissance man, by definition, is a person of multiple subpersonalities. Such a person might be, for instance, a scientist, a playwright, a musician, and a lover. These components are mental polarities, each using different mental skills, each encompassing a different body of knowledge and experience. The very right to possess these distinctive designations means that the subpersonalities have been developed to their potential.

We can see the development of subpersonalities as early as the first few months of infancy. At first, the core needs of a new baby—feeding, touching, comfort, and so forth—produce random behaviors. However, by the time a baby is a year or two old, embryonic subpersonalities have been organized, and there are specific characteristic behaviors connected with each need as it functions or emerges. Through the years these subpersonalities become complicated aggregates layered with experiment, experience, and memory, so that by adulthood the healthy mature personality has many diverse forms, styles, and roles. On the one hand, the subpersonalities are the sharpened tools for dealing with the world, and on the other hand, they are a reflection of a person's unique beauty, the facets of the jewel that is her psyche.

Just as the light plays between the facets within a jewel, there is in the psyche an energetic dynamic between the subpersonalities. Polarities of thought, whether words or images,

2

whether conscious or unconscious, are the play of the energy between the facets of personality. The quality of this dynamic pattern is unique for each individual.

Let me offer a simple illustration of subpersonalities from my own experience. Many years ago, when my career was first beginning, I made a spectacular leap from an entry position as a team school psychologist into an administrative position. On the basis of a few A's in graduate school statistics, I was chosen to develop a statistical management program for all special education classes in a large school district. The ensuing stress sent me to a psychiatrist, who was of little help.

As it happened, I had subscribed on a whim to a scholarly publication called *Synthesis Journal*,[2] and the first copy arrived during this confusing period of my life. The journal outlined the rudiments of subpersonality technique, and I proceeded with great fascination to put my conflicting thoughts in the form of a dialogue. As the two poles spoke to each other, it became increasingly clear that one part of myself refused to respect the efforts of the other to fulfill the requirements of the new job. For the sake of clarity, I named one pole Camille and the other Dagmar. Then I stepped back from their dialogue and wrote down what I heard them saying. When I reread what I had written, I was amazed at the antipodal quality of my stressed thought.

CAMILLE: Why did you take a job for which you had no training?

DAGMAR: Because I thought I could easily learn whatever I needed to know. After all, I have been very successful in my work. It seems that I can do anything at least as well as anyone if I simply put my mind to it. I thought I could have a positive influence on the school district, perhaps even establishing new programs. I like the prestige and power of this job. It gives me a good feeling about myself. I believe I am influencing the highest powers in the administration.

CAMILLE: I think you are talking about manipulation. Besides, if you have influence, it is my charm that is doing it,

3

given the fact that you don't have real competence in this job yet.

DAGMAR: Do you think it was a mistake to take this job? Are you blaming me? You had a stronger influence in this matter than I did. Romantic nonsense is what I call it. You and that Samuel person both act like fools. You thought surely you could get close to him; you thought that was why he asked you to apply for the job. You forget that it was my reputation that made him think you could do the job. Now you are disappointed because you see he just wanted some ego gratification. And I've pretty well put a stop to that.

CAMILLE: I am disappointed. I have stopped trying to get his attention. I thought I could learn from him. And I thought the playfulness was doing no harm.

DAGMAR: You imagined a lot of nonsense. Oh, you are so young and such a dramatist. You need practicality. Do you realize that because of your idealism and silliness, I am having a great deal of difficulty meeting my responsibilities on this job? You object to the discipline of sitting all day and facing real work. It's a job that has to be done, and I have agreed to do it. You're a kid, always backing away. You'll do anything to get out of work.

CAMILLE: This is not healthy work. I cannot give my precious life hours to work I do not believe in, and I see as actually impeding my creative work. This work depresses me physically and mentally so that my creative spark is disappearing.

DAGMAR: I believe that this information I collect will help people work more effectively.

CAMILLE: I worked well before, and I did not have this information. I don't think any of these numbers will make any difference as to how I function. I walk in and do the job that needs to be done, irregardless of anybody's guidelines or published reports. And you will remember that I was called the best and an expert.

DAGMAR: No, that was me. My polish and organizational skill won that praise. I know how to deal with people in an organizational context. You may read people, but I plan goals and work through the organization.

CAMILLE: Do not minimize the fact that I understand people. That's what it's all about, lady, and that is exactly what is wrong with this job. It's irrelevant to people's needs. Given a simple structure within which skilled, dedicated people can function, there is no need for elaborate managerial superstructure.

The notes ended here, but the dialogue went on. Six months later I left administration to become a therapist for a classroom of emotionally disturbed children. I analyzed my notes repeatedly in succeeding months, and saw clearly the stark contrast between and apparent irreconcilability of the two life positions. The voice of one pole of my thinking was business-oriented, talented in organizational skills, and concerned about participating in society in a traditional way. The other pole had a radically different orientation: sensitivity, intuition, romance, empathy, and charm. The two separate constellations of thought functioned side by side in my personality.

Even in the initial dialogue the complex interaction between subpersonalities is evident. In the first words it is clear that these subpersonalities have different developmental goals. They display psychic specialization focusing on the fulfillment of different needs; they play separate roles in the world. Each has both positive and negative aspects. Each subpersonality has an opinion on everything, and the particular perspective and point of view expressed by each remains consistent. Further, each personality part has a characteristic vocabulary, a jargon that is a consistent expressive mode. All these facets of a dynamic psyche are presented in a few words of mental dialogue.

As I continued my exploration, the natural tendency to form pictures around dialogue led me to form vivid images of my two psychic poles. I saw Dagmar as a round, middle-aged woman dressed in a brown tweed suit, her body movements awkward and stiff. The expression on her face was wary, determined, and frowning. Camille, on the other hand, I saw as a young girl with quiet clear eyes. She had a listening attitude. Her clothes were soft and full, appealing in warm color and texture. She smiled. Her beauty was healthy and simple. These portraits amplified my understanding of the conflict and turmoil the two points of view were creating in my life.

The very attempt to stand back, listen to, and observe these two subpersonalities is the first step toward the skill of centering—finding a neutral psychic space that does not identify with any of the subpersonalities. I began to notice, among other things, how the dialogue was a microcosm of many social conflicts peculiar to our culture. The two entities represented different generations, different views of social responsibility, different ideals—traditional competence versus creativity, social acceptance versus individualism.

Simply learning to visualize my inner conflict gave me some objectivity. My own personality was standing before my mental eye. Because I could actually see the aspects of my personality, I had direct opportunity to disidentify from them and to change their behavior—to better "utilize" them to accomplish the goals of a yet "higher" self. This is a complex organic process that happens over a period of time. On the other hand, it is a process that is natural to us and begins with constructing the initial dialogue.

The direct antecedents of subpersonality theory are well outlined in John Rowan's *Subpersonalities* (Routledge, 1990). It is worth recognizing, however, that the idea of subpersonalities is already implicit in Freud's central problematic—the mastery of the unconscious mind by the ego. It becomes explicit in the work of two men who moved beyond Freud, Carl Jung and Roberto Assagioli. Although their careers overlap, Freud, Jung, and Assagioli quite literally represent three generations of thought on subpersonalities. In 1907, the year they all met, Assagioli was nineteen, a brilliant Italian medical student; Jung was thirty-two, a fast-rising star in the Swiss psychiatric community; and Freud was fifty-one, an internationally recognized psychiatrist in Vienna, upon whose theories the school of psychoanalysis was being founded.

Freud had hoped Assagioli would become the authority on psychoanalysis in Italy, and at first Assagioli did champion Freud's work. Ultimately, however, both Jung and Assagioli saw Freud's theory as only a partial description of the dynamics of the psyche. Each set out in his own way to develop a more accurate, complete theory. From the start, much to Freud's consternation, Jung freely improvised on the tenets of Freud's theory according to his own views.[3] Assagioli, on the other hand, maintained the integrity of Freud's and Jung's theories, but then developed a framework that expanded beyond both.

For Jung, of course, the ego's task was not mastery of the archaic unconscious, but integration. As a child, Jung already saw that he had two separate selves. "I always knew that I was two persons."[4] He recognized one subpersonality as the nervous, difficult child that he was in the world. The other subpersonality, which functioned initially only in his mind, was a prominent, intellectual man of the eighteenth century.

In his middle years, as he began to explore his own psyche, there emerged from his unconscious several more subpersonalities. He did not until later in his life acknowledge these figures as parts of himself.[5] Salome, a beautiful blind girl, the feminine side of his personality, appeared always in companionship with Elijah, a wisdom figure. Elijah evolved into Philomen, and eventually into Ka, all ever higher aspects of his psyche. Through painting and dialogue Jung enlivened these images as impetus to his own development.

Indeed, the deep encounter with these numinous figures led Jung to some of the basic principles of his psychology. Initially, he saw these subpersonalities as the product of archetypes, clusters of energy in the psyche that give rise to conscious imagery of specific basic form. Jung considered archetypes to be the rudiments of psychic experience. His encounter with his subpersonalities also led him to develop the dialectical process that he calls active imagination, a form of dialogue between conscious and unconscious psychic elements.

Jung taught his patients to dialogue with the images in dreams, allowing the dream to further unfold. In this process unconscious parts of the psyche that are not ordinarily available become directly accessible to the field of consciousness. Jung was fascinated by the psychoactive quality of symbols. He observed that a dream can contain a single symbol that can affect the entire life of an individual. His own experience with the psychic figures that he eventually acknowledged as subpersonalities stimulated deep creativity in him, the fruition of his mind. Gradually, he saw the ego as a set of subpersonalities subordinate to the Self, which is both the totality of the psyche and its functional center.

For Jung, knowledge and control of the ego, the conscious social aspects of a person (the aggregate of subpersonalities) is not the end of psychological work, but the primary step that allows for further development. Jung understood this development as a process of unfoldment, which he called individuation, wherein the ego is brought gradually into line with the purposes of the Self. In his system the Self is not attainable as such. Roberto Assagioli, on the other hand, wrote about subpersonalities as an entry point for *active* movement to higher development and contact with the Self, which he considered the ordinary course of human potential. He called this process psychosynthesis, the harmonization of the parts of the psyche. It might be said that in Jung's system, individuation happens to a person, whereas in Assagioli's system, psychosynthesis is a skill to be learned.

Assagioli cautioned, however, that one does not enter upon high development without enormous preparation. He likened it to an arduous mountain climb that no one would undertake without first attaining a high level of fitness and skills and obtaining the best equipment, the equivalent in psychological terms of conditioning the subpersonalities. In this respect,

Assagioli saw the inevitable emergence of transpersonal psychology. For him, the unconscious had equal importance to other parts of the psyche, and the practical use of the mythopoetic function of the mind with a natural development of mental skills.

Combined, the work of Jung and Assagioli presents the importance of subpersonalities. Jung focused on the inner experience of constellated psychic elements, whereas Assagioli was concerned with the conscious management and development of inner potential. It is the context of Assagioli's work that puts subpersonality work into proper perspective. Because of the ceiling of Jung's own experience, Jungians have a tendency to become bogged down by the endless images of the unconscious subpersonality fragments. Because of the expanse of Assagioli's vision, Assagiolians tend to give cursory attention to subpersonality foundation work in favor of moving rapidly into higher development. To live in the whole building of the psyche, however, the foundation must be solid and strong before adding and inhabiting higher floors. A building without adequate foundation is dangerous. A building with only solid foundation and no higher floors misses the scope, the vista, the light.

This book offers a working theoretical system, developed in my teamwork with my clients and supervisees, that bears the distinguishing marks of both Assagioli and Jung. Through introducing to clients the attitudes, approaches, and techniques from their respective systems in hundreds of cases, it has become clear that the systems are complementary. What has gradually emerged is a clinical approach that gives clients in a relatively short period of time a framework for living that is consistently practical and productive. Clients adopt the approach with enthusiasm because of the system's close fit to their life experience.

Subpersonality technique is basically a skill in practical living. The wide appeal of Jungian psychology today lies in its appreciation of the rich *personal* imagery of the unconscious.

Subpersonality work, little known outside of the school of psychosynthesis, is the extension of the personal unconscious imagery into its natural conscious functioning.

Beyond this, at the furthest reaches of higher development, lies the consolidation of the personality in a shaman or religious leader. Ken Wilber describes in his writings this dramatic growth process. Wilber believes that at each higher level the pieces of the earlier levels are negated so that further development can take place, but at the same time these pieces are preserved and integrated into the psyche, "not annulled but fulfilled."[6] In other words, spiritual development does not homogenize the psyche; subpersonalities continue to develop but are changed in form and function. Charismatic, world-changing figures such as Jesus, Mohammed, and Buddha had distinct personalities and unique perspectives that resulted from an *integration* of their subpersonalities. If high individual development homogenized the psyche, the teachings and behaviors of these three leaders would have been very much the same.

Along the same lines, the idea that unitary wholeness is the goal of healthy human experience has led to the treatment of multiple personality disorder (MPD) as if it involved abnormal splitting—the personality's formation of new entities to deal with new conflicts and situations. The major therapy goal for MPD continues to be complete fusion, to bring the multiple personalities into a single, "whole" personality. Integration, a coordination of the existing entities, is considered incomplete treatment. In actual practice, however, the goal of fusion has been known to eliminate psychic entities that must be reinstated because important personality functions have been lost.

Some theorists are beginning to assert that the dynamics of MPD illustrate normal mental function manifested in an abnormal pattern.[7] The significance for subpersonality theory in these newer studies is enormous. In the areas of neurophysiology, dramatic changes in physiological process have been observed and studied as multiples switch from one personality to another: brain wave patterns, changes in muscle tone, in blood flow, in dermatological reactions, allergies, and disease states.[8] The implication is that subpersonality structures involve not only mental organization of psychic energy into units of mind, but are directly correlated to the organization of the brain.

Finally, the notion of subpersonalities has a bearing on understanding the world scene. The characteristics of cultural groups were originally determined by the influence of the variety of subpersonalities in cultural leaders. Cultural groups could be regarded as the early subpersonalities of the world itself. The cultural groups of the world have in recent times been clustered together into practical economic and defense entities called nations. The nations are the present subpersonalities of the world. Like dominant social subpersonalities in the individual, the nations are concerned with efficient survival means that lead to the enhancement of the quality of life. The dynamics of war and peace and the process of development of security and well-being that are characteristic of subpersonalities in the individual are the same dynamics that occur in the international scene. The parallel study of the human psyche and international relations expands understanding of both the individual and the world. There are lessons on both sides.

2

DISCOVERING
SUBPERSONALITIES

ASSAGIOLI'S EARLY IDEAS

The idea of subpersonalities first appeared in Assagioli's precocious early writings.[1] In an essay of 1907, where his lifelong habit of approaching theory through both Western and Eastern psychological wisdom is introduced, he argued for a blend of Western and ancient Indian cultures as "the elements and the occasion for the work of unification of our 'individualities' " (or subpersonalities).[2] The origin of subpersonalities he attributed to the "tragic contrast between thought and feeling, between reason and faith, between conviction and adoration"; in other words, subpersonalities arise from the opposites in experience.[3] He further argued that all discordant aspects of the psyche, all the opposites, are to be accepted; there is no surrender of one or the other part of the psyche to stronger parts. Integration of the disparate parts has been accomplished when "all energies cooperate with the objective of reciprocally completing one another."[4] It is only a question of harmoniously bringing the elements or parts together to form a "beautiful and fruitful higher synthesis."[5] In this early writing not only does Assagioli feature the concept of subpersonalities as a central working premise, but also he explains the origin of subpersonalities in the natural experience of opposites. Also, at this early point, he advocated the goal of integration of the disparate personality elements. He wrote of these ideas before he had met Jung and before Jung had begun to formulate his own ideas on the subject.

Thus, in this visionary writing he introduces important principles of the psychosynthesis system which he would study and
elaborate over the next sixty years.

In a second early article (1909), which Assagioli referred to
late in life as containing even more of the seeds of the psychosynthesis system, he explored "power ideas" (*idee forze*, in Italian, or *idée fixe*, in the original French from Charcot and Janet; it
means a fixed, powerful idea), a concept directly preliminary to
his full understanding of subpersonalities. Power ideas he defined as "states of awareness which intimately fuse the intellectual and emotional elements."[6] The important characteristic of
power ideas was their self-contained energy that appeared in
external action.[7] They are the energetic power of thoughts and
ideas in relation to the other levels and aspects of a human
being.[8] Here again, he directed attention to specific psychological dynamics that have the qualities of subpersonalities: (1) subpersonalities are states of awareness; (2) subpersonalities contain
fused intellectual and emotional elements; (3) the energy of
subpersonalities is self-contained in powerful concentration; and
(4) subpersonality function can be observed in external action.
At a later time Assagioli adopted the term *subpersonality* for the
concepts he had originally designated as individualities and
power ideas.[9] His initial descriptive terms, however, highlight
significant characteristics of subpersonalities, namely, the individual uniqueness (individualities) and concentrated power of
these mental constellations (power ideas).

The discussion of subpersonalities in Assagioli's later full
exposition of psychosynthesis appears in the section about
methods for assessing the psyche. In this way he emphasizes the
importance of knowledge of subpersonalities as an entry point in
a systematic development process: understanding of subpersonalities is foundation work that precedes higher development. Of
subpersonalities Assagioli said, "Everyone has different selves
[subpersonalities]—it is normal."[10] "It is imperative for each
man and woman who wants to live consciously to be well aware
of (the) elements or components of their personality—not a

dim, passive awareness, but a deliberate assessment, valuation, understanding and control of them."[11] "One should become clearly aware of these sub-personalities because this evokes a measure of understanding of the meaning of psychosynthesis, and how it is possible to sythesize these sub-personalities into a larger organic whole without repressing any of the useful traits."[12] Assagioli advocated strengthening the conscious structures of the mind, the subpersonalities, before dealing with the unconscious. "There are real dangers in the premature irruption of unconscious forces in an unprepared and loosely knit personality."[13]

Psychotherapy or personal individual exploration permit deep examination of the dynamics of subpersonalities and create access to the direct management of inner states. "The organization of the sub-personalities is very revealing and sometimes surprising, baffling or even frightening—different and often quite antagonistic traits are displayed in the different roles [functions]. These differences of traits which are organized around a role justify, in our opinion, the use of the word 'sub-personality.' Ordinary people shift from one to the other without clear awareness and only a thin thread of memory connects them; but for all practical purposes they are different beings—they act differently, they show very different traits."[14] Assagioli advocated not only observation and analysis, but throughout his career he devised specific methods whereby psychic elements are mastered and changed. As he indicated, subpersonalities are the roles, the functions, established as habits, both positive and negative, that allow us to operate in the world. Subpersonalities are tools, and if any subpersonality becomes dominant, the wide scope of personality possibilities is limited and constricted.

It is often the realization of subpersonalities that brings about the first objective experience of the observing self, the personal center. "Revealing the different roles, traits, etc., emphasizes the reality of the observing self. . . . One realizes that the observing self is [not a subpersonality] but something or somebody different."[15] Assagioli pointed to the need for self-identification in

14

order to disidentify from dominant mental constellations, from dominant subpersonalities. "We are dominated by everything with which [we become] identified. We can dominate and control everything from which we disidentify ourselves."[16] Self-identification is "the inner experience of pure self-awareness, independent of any content or function of the ego in the sense of personality."[17] The disidentification process is a central concept and technique in psychosynthesis. From the objective psychic position of the observing I, the observing center of the psyche, subpersonalities are distinguished, explored, understood, modified, and controlled; they become a set of useful tools that are governed by the self, by centered consciousness. "The goal is a freed self, the I consciousness, who can play *consciously* various roles."[18]

"The experience of the point of self-awareness on the personality level (the self, or the center of consciousness) is the first step toward the experience of the Self, or, in existential terms, the essence of Being."[19] Assagioli was clearer than Jung in distinguishing the personal self, the personal center, from the transpersonal Self. "There is one Self—but there are very different and distinct levels of self-realization. Therefore between the self-identity of the ordinary or normal level of functioning and the full spiritual self-realization there are intermediate stages or levels, ever wider, clearer, fuller."[20] The awareness of the personal self, the I, the personal center, Assagioli understood as a projection into consciousness of the transpersonal Self.[21]

When Assagioli spoke in the seventies of the significance of the 1909 article, he pointed out that it was an early conceptualization of what is today humanistic psychology.[22] Like humanistic psychology his system of thought defined not only a psychological direction but also, most importantly, an educational, or psychagogical, direction. Psychagogy Assagioli defined, in harmony with Plato's use of the term, as "developing the inner fire within each of us"; thus, Assagioli throughout his career insisted on a broadening of the practical and active nature of psychology to become a learning process for all children and adults, aimed at the integral cultivation of the whole psyche.[23] Here he differed from Jung, who believed that in-depth development of the psyche is for an intellectual elite, and rather than direct education, development is best left to the spontaneity of the unconscious.[24] For Assagioli throughout his professional career, the educational function of psychology was of foremost importance. Unlike other psychiatric theorists who expressed themselves in esoteric and scholarly terms, Assagioli distilled his insights into simple, accessible language, more like aphorisms that are easily remembered than scientific jargon.

The course of work in psychosynthesis is basically a dialogue between conscious and unconscious thinking, much like Jungian analysis. Important unconscious images provide as they emerge a basis for conscious work. This differs from Jungian work in that, over a period of time, a dynamic plan evolves which is carefully implemented and tested through dialogue between conscious and unconscious images and action and experience in the world. As conflicts are resolved, the separate functions of thinking mesh, allowing the personality to operate from a monitoring and governing Center.

It is recognized that the major goal of psychosynthesis is always educational. Dispelling painful symptoms is only the first step. The therapist moves quickly into teaching individual personality structure and specific techniques, which the client learns to apply to his unique needs for his inner well-being and his effectiveness in the world, tools available for his lifetime.

The therapist in psychosynthesis is called the guide, in the sense that he has been over the inner terrain and knows the swamps, abysses, and cliffs, as well as the scenic wonders. He also knows how to get from here to there through the inner wilderness, where he has the skills to recognize the natural signs. In the guiding process, the guide makes the initial plan for a client, but as quickly as possible involves the client, teaching him to be his own guide. The guide knows he has been successful when his direction is no longer needed. The ultimate goal in the work is to access the inner guide, the Higher Self, the best therapist.

SOME BASIC TECHNIQUES OF PSYCHOSYNTHESIS

Let us briefly consider some of the primary psychosynthesis techniques developed by Assagioli and subsequent psychosynthesis practitioners.[25] First, *mapping* is the orientation of the client to his work through a general model of the personality. As work becomes more sophisticated, the unique qualities of the individual can be incorporated in personal maps. Initially, however, the model of the psyche which Assagioli devised on the basis of both Eastern and Western psychology is particularly useful. This model, which I shall describe later, is to be understood in the same way as the ball and stick model of the atom in physics; this figure is not what the personality looks like, but it is a representation of an understanding of how the psyche functions.

Probably the most useful and universally applicable technique in psychosynthesis is the *subpersonality technique*. This therapeutic approach allows an individual to magnify and dramatize the natural parts of his personality in order to clarify its structure and to observe the intricacies of its functioning. The real uniqueness of the individual is evident even in the first stages of subpersonality work. Once the subpersonalities are understood, the process of modification and transformation of the personality takes place primarily through *disidentification*. The first stage of disidentification is learning to move from Center, from the personal self or the I, to different parts of the personality with relative ease. Friction between subpersonalities leads to battles within the psyche as different parts vie for expression. In the disidentification process there is movement from antagonism to synergy with resulting reconciliation of opposites. The goal is to bring each subpersonality to its fullest development and highest potential.

As dominance of subpersonalities lessens, the individual is

freer to function from the I, personal self, or Center. In subpersonality work, this geographical, or "psychographical," position within the psyche is extremely important. It might be seen as the director's chair from where the subpersonalities are directed and managed, and it is from here that the will operates.

Because it is difficult for many people to move out of deeply entrenched patterns of behavior, Assagioli was very concerned about the development of the will. He did not understand will in the Victorian sense of having to force oneself to be virtuous. Rather, he saw will as a skill to be developed like any other skill. He saw it as closely associated with the personal self, the true act of will happening only from Center. Disharmonious forcing of the personality comes from subpersonalities. Ferrucci describes the psychosynthetic concept of will as the "capacity of an organism to function freely according to its own intrinsic nature rather than under the compulsion of external forces."[26] In this sense, the forced "will power" sometimes found in subpersonalities is seen as related to external forces, since subpersonalities are learned for social adaptation purposes. When willing happens from Center, there is a rise in the psychic voltage; the individual can move to greater freedom.

There is a tendency for many people to become enamored with the negative because of its long familiarity; even though the negative causes pain, nevertheless it is "home." When this attitude prevails, the learning of a positive life perspective is important in order to balance the psyche. There is an emphasis in psychosynthesis on the development of the positive within the psyche. One approach that is frequently used is the *ideal model technique*.[27] Using his imagination, the client constructs a model for his future development, the design of which comes from his own plan, from qualities of individuals he admires, or from great present or historical figures, or from all three. This model can be reconstructed many times as the individual's perspective on his own development changes. Focus can also be directed toward the development of specific qualities within the personality, such as peace and serenity. This is done with the use of symbols and mantras. There is also the practice of the recognition of beauty. With a dominant negative focus, there is little recognition that there is beauty everywhere; recognition of its presence has a healing effect.

The many techniques of psychosynthesis, drawn from a wide range of sources, are not considered important in and of themselves. In fact, it is a mistake to become involved in performing techniques to the extent that listening to the direction of the inner voice is lost. Then the work with the techniques becomes another form of busyness in which one focuses on the activity for its own sake rather than as a means to full development. The real value in exploring the techniques lies in a deep broadening of the individual psychological foundation for high development. The techniques are translated into everyday American understanding, but represent psychological, religious, educational, and commonsense practices of many cultures; at a deep level one experiences the wisdom of many peoples. The best use of techniques involves periodic selection of a technique upon which to focus attention. In listening to the inner Self, the intuition and the imagination are drawn into play, elaborating the technique and inventing variations in a lively way that taps the dynamic energy of the growth process.

The more advanced steps in psychosynthetic work are concerned with transpersonal growth: the development of the spiritual and the universal aspects of the personality. For many this development is a gradual process throughout the whole life. With others, sudden spurts of transpersonal development come as a surprise as the individuals begin to disidentify from subpersonalities that have governed and limited their lives. Transpersonal work is seen as change in consciousness level, however large or small, that results in a different world view, a different sense of one's place in the world or in the universe. As the personality becomes more and more integrated, there is openness to the perception of the flow of transpersonal energy, energy that originates in the higher aspects of our personalities and beyond us. In Assagioli's words: "The spiritual is the abundant

19

life [*la vita piu abbondante*]—actually the true, normal life, the attitude one should have in approaching the spiritual. It is like a little known land discovered to have great natural resources."[28] "Reaching full consciousness is not in the stratosphere, not vague, not effervescent, or something unfamiliar; it is life, intensity, variety, dynamism, ability to perceive more reality in the ordinary. The principal characteristics are (1) a perception of light, illumination, a light on problems and situations that reveals significance, (2) a sense of peace, of peace completely independent of external circumstances and internal state, (3) a sense of harmony and beauty, (4) a sense of joy, of rejoicing happiness, (5) a sense of power, power of the spirit, and (6) a sense of grandness, of vastness, of universality, of eternity."[29]

Eventually, the primary effort of psychosynthetic work becomes channeling energy from the Higher Self. The discipline becomes a process of fine tuning, of focusing small changes in the personality and in time priorities. This structure has been known in monastic life for thousands of years, but the challenge of the present age is to bring the subtleties of this approach to living into the secular world: business, family, social interactions, and so on. Such honing of the spirit seems dull to many in comparison to the life and death soap opera struggle of negative complexes. Thus, it often takes considerable time to quiet the personality in order to move into a genuine acceptance of this stage of work. Simple focus on the cutting the wood and carrying the water aspect of psychological life seems anachronistic in a television and media age where the most mundane aspects of our lives are glamourized. In this careful listening to the deep inner understanding, one often finds that the true expression of the values and direction of the individual life pattern do not follow expectations of one's social structure. Then the creativity and the ingenuity of the individual are tested in the quest to find choices for his life that follow this inner direction, and yet maintain his effective interaction and communication with others. The initial hard work that went into the integration of the personality is extremely important at this point. It is easier to

20

become a hermit and forsake the world than it is to be a member of society and live one's transpersonal vocation. Dag Hammarskjöld and Gandhi are examples in the twentieth century of this life style. As transpersonal work proceeds, there is increasing commitment to some form of service in the world. In all descriptions of the highest aspects of human development in Eastern and Western knowledge, there is movement out of the isolation of personal growth work into a concern for and participation in community, local, world, and universal. There is a sense of participation in patterns of evolution that go beyond the personal self, and in this participation a realization of the highest aspects of the Higher Self.

The importance of the development and integration of the personality cannot be overemphasized since it is the basis for individual impact on the world. But it must be kept in mind that the goal of this work is not egocentricity or self-adulation, but the building of a strong effective instrument for participation in the solution of the world's problems. "The effect of [transpersonal] experience is inspired action, the powerful impulse to act. Above all, the treasures discovered and won are expressed, effused, irradiated. Through collaboration with other men of good will, with those who have had similar experience, it is possible to dissipate the shadows of ignorance, preparing a new civilization in which men, happy and in harmony, will bring about the marvelous latent potential."[30]

JUNG'S CONTRIBUTION TO SUBPERSONALITY THEORY

Jung spent his whole professional life studying subpersonalities. Not only did he experience two subpersonalities in himself as a child and deal with numinous subpersonality figures as an adult, but in addition, virtually all the psychological processes he described are directly related to subpersonality function.

Jung's discussion of psychological types is a description of subpersonality types. He observed that four basic psychological functions—thinking, feeling, sensation, and intuition—give

21

rise to four psychological types. These are multiplied to eight by the way that energy is used: extraverted form, if energy is put out into the world, or introverted, if energy is absorbed. In working with the four functions, he saw the inherent balance between them, thinking opposite feeling, and intuition opposite sensation. He considered it normal to have one function dominant throughout the life, while its opposite function remains largely undeveloped and the other two functions are supportive to the dominant function.[31] Interestingly, this is the usual dynamic in the initial meeting with subpersonalities, but it is not necessarily permanent as exploration and modification occur.

Jung observed that there is in the psyche a strong drive for balance. This observation led him to view the ancient mandala figures that appear in all cultures as symbols of wholeness. The mandala is a simple visual pattern, the essential feature of which is symmetry. It is usually thought of as the "squared circle" in which the circle is divided into six, eight, or twelve parts, or it can be a circle within a square, or even concentric circles or concentric squares. Jung said that the mandala "can be called the archetype of wholeness."[32] Many, like the one here (see fig. 1), show a balanced figure of four points within a circle. In subpersonality terms the figure represents four equally developed subpersonalities around a point of balance, a center. In his discussion of the transcendent function, the possible transition from one attitude to another of higher quality, Jung indicates that the pull for balance between the parts of the psyche results in the definition of a center. In wholeness balance is established between consciousness and the unconscious.[33]

The structure of a subpersonality, specifically a negative subpersonality, is addressed in Jung's description of the complex. In his own words, a complex is "the image of a certain psychic [configuration] which is strongly accentuated emotionally and is . . . incompatible with the habitual attitude of consciousness. This image has a powerful inner coherence, it has its own wholeness and, in addition, a relatively high degree of autonomy, so that it is subject to the control of the conscious mind to only a

Figure 1. This mandala, by a Naskapi hunter of Labrador, represents "the Great Man," a symbol of the higher Self, the integrated psyche. From *Naskapi* by Frank G. Speck (Norman: University of Oklahoma Press, 1935), p. 43. New edition copyright © 1977 by the University of Oklahoma Press.

limited extent, and therefore behaves like an animated foreign body in the sphere of consciousness. The complex can usually be suppressed with an effort of will, but not argued out of existence, and at the first suitable opportunity it reappears in all its original strength."[34] Here, Jung describes vividly and in succinct detail an unruly subpersonality. In summary, the qualities characteristic of this particular type of subpersonality are that (1) it appears as an image; (2) it has an emotional tone out of harmony with the preferred conscious emotional stance; (3) it has inner coherence and wholeness; (4) it operates with a high degree of autonomy; (5) it feels like a "foreign body" in the mind, at least in initial contact; (6) it takes an effort of will to suppress it; (7) it cannot be dismissed or argued out of existence; and, (8) if suppressed, it returns in strength at the first opportunity.

Note that the concept of complex, however, cannot be directly equated with the concept of subpersonality. A complex is one type of subpersonality. Though Jung pointed out that complexes can be positive as well as negative, the general comments on complexes throughout Jungian literature in general regard them as negative. Jung himself said, "Complexes are something so unpleasant that nobody in his right senses can be persuaded

23

that the motive forces which maintain them could betoken anything good."[35] Subpersonalities, however, can be positive, neutral, or negative. In fact, there can be contained within one subpersonality qualities that are positive, neutral, and negative. Jung often identified positive subpersonalities as archetypes, as he did in the experience of the emergence of the significant subpersonalities in his own life.

In the study of archetypes and complexes Jung observed the omnipresent phenomenon of complementarity. Archetypes and complexes often appear in pairs that are opposite in quality, for instance, good and bad, light and dark, broad and narrow, and so on. Even when the second member of the pair of opposites is not consciously apparent, Jung assumed its existence in the unconscious as a motivating force. In individual development distinct pairs of opposites emerge into consciousness in dynamic equilibrium. Complementarity is an essential quality of the psyche: "the unconscious processes stand in a compensatory relation to the conscious mind. I expressly use the word 'compensatory' and not the word 'contrary' because conscious and unconscious are not necessarily in opposition to one another, but complement one another to form a totality. . . . The unconscious processes that compensate the conscious ego contain all those elements that are necessary for the self-regulation of the psyche as a whole."[36] Whether the complementarity of the conscious mind exists in unconscious elements, or the opposites stand in dynamic equilibrium together in consciousness, the fact remains that complementarity and its essential balance is inherent in psychological development.

Jung studied a number of different types of subpersonalities. The persona is the aggregate of behaviors habitually used in confronting and negotiating the social world. The shadow is the unrecognized aspect of the personality, either pushed into the unconscious as an unwanted element or newly emerging from the unconscious as a new facet of development. The anima and the animus are the contrasexual qualities within an individual—for a man, the feminine; for a woman, the masculine. Gaining

24

consciousness of these fundamental subpersonalities is one of the basic tasks of Jungian analysis. Most analysts observe that it is easiest to gain awareness of the persona. The next most accessible is the shadow, then the anima or the animus. Many analysands report an archetypal "royal marriage" dream—a dream in which the individual "marries," or harmonizes with, his or her anima or animus—marking a milestone in the development process. The balancing and equilibration of opposites in the psyche are considered important from the beginning of Jungian analysis, but the dream celebration of the symbolic marriage is marked as a significant portrait of balanced and integrated unconscious psychic energy, the ultimate goal of the psychological development process.

Jung's definitions of the terms *ego*, *self*, and *Self* were constantly changing in his writings as he sought an ever clearer understanding of the psyche.[37] For our purposes, attempting to encompass the way both Jung and Assagioli used these terms, appropriate definitions would be: (1) the ego is an aggregate of subpersonalities that confront and negotiate the world, (2) the self, or the personal self or Center is a point of objectivity, a center outside the subpersonalities, and (3) the Self, the Higher Self, or transpersonal Self is a deep guidance center and a totality of being. In *The Structure and Dynamics of the Psyche*, published in 1946, Jung presented the relationship between ego and the important concept of Self in a clear framework relevant to understanding subpersonalities, stating that the ego is a complex, or set, of subpersonalities. If the ego is assailed by material erupting from the unconscious, the ego's dominance is displaced, "not so much because it has been weakened in any way, as because certain considerations give it pause. That is, the ego cannot help discovering that the afflux of unconscious contents has vitalized the personality, enriched it and created a figure that somehow dwarfs the ego in scope and intensity. . . . [The ego] gradually subordinates itself to the stronger factor, namely to the new totality-figure I call the Self."[38] Here it is clear that Jung sees the ego as a subpersonality or set of subpersonalities subordinate to the Self. Jung saw the Self as both the totality of the psyche and as a center of the psyche, functionally, a "regulating center that brings about a constant extension and maturing of the personality."[39] In the Jungian framework, the system of subpersonalities, whether functionally persona, shadow, complex, or any other type of subpersonality, is subordinate to the higher Self, which Jung considered to be the governing archetype of the psyche.

A COMBINED THEORETICAL SYSTEM

The writings of Assagioli and Jung are complementary. Assagioli sought to speak to the practical understanding of problem solving, while Jung presents the deep inner mystery of the psyche. Combining the theoretical positions of these two men is rich; each theoretical position augments the other.

A combined system begins in the life predicament that brings the client through the therapist's doorway. Hardly anyone undertakes personal psychotherapy without the motivation of pain, though the number of those primarily seeking self-understanding is increasing. The freely told story of the client, a portrait of the present, contains all the details for the beginning work. With these initial words, the therapist begins to frame in his mind a conception of the uniqueness of the person before him and the growth pattern that, following Assagioli, projects in time far beyond the actual contact of the therapist and client. As the teamwork between the client and therapist becomes established and the client's knowledge base increases, the client takes more responsibility for the discernment of his growth pattern and learns that growth occurs both by conscious effort and by active cooperation with unconscious elements.

The personal history of the client is important because of its psychogenic nature. The therapist listens for the elements of the story that reveal the individual's developmental momentum and pursues that history, seeking to put into place some hypothetical causative factors that have produced the present painful predicament. Eventually all historical elements of importance will be dealt with, but only as they relate to the developmental process. At this point standard psychological techniques are evoked to reduce the anguish of the present situation. Psychotherapeutic education begins in the following sessions.

All clients wish to understand their own personalities. Thus, work with subpersonalities is begun with the dual purpose of diagnosis and instruction. As the therapist delineates the structure of the personality, the client is enlightened with a model of his own elusive mental functioning. In the first telling of the story of the predicament, the client revealed polarities in his thinking. These are now shown to the client for elaboration through exploring his life experience with these polarities. More often than not these polarities of thought are experienced as inner dialogue that is most loudly heard in decision making. A particular polarity of thought represents one way of approaching the world, one set of values, one life function, while another polarity of thought represents another way of approaching the world, another set of values, another life function. The polarities are sorted and three or four are initially identified. These polarities are subpersonalities, compartmentalizations of life functions that began early in the individual's development, which are directly connected to the dynamics of the life predicament presented.

The opposition between the subpersonalities is examined, stressing the normality and richness of opposites in the thought process. The usual experience of the opposition of the subpersonalities is the cacophony of mental war which is most blatant in stressful situations. Each polarity is examined objectively as to what it contributes positively and negatively to the client's life. Then the interaction of the opposed views is appraised. Through this process there is an initial delineation of the subpersonalities which not only is diagnostic in giving the therapist much information about the client's functioning, but is also equally beneficial to the client giving him real access to control of his response to the life predicament.

The recognition of subpersonalities creates a sense of mastery. At this point instruction is provided that indicates the framework for further mastery and control. In order for the client to understand the relationship of the subpersonalities to other parts of the psyche, Assagioli's model is didactically presented. The client is informed that he will begin his learning about all of these parts of the psyche in the psychotherapy process and be given the tools to continue lifelong learning on his own. The explanation begins with the first known parts, the subpersonalities; these are identifiable in the conscious thinking. For the most part they are within the field of consciousness, always accessible to conscious thinking as tools for operating on the environment. The field of consciousness is all one is aware of at any given time as well as those things that readily enter awareness with a simple switch of attention.

Sometimes the subpersonalities are partially or wholly submerged in the unconscious. A personality tool can be developed at an early age but then moved into inactivity for one reason or another. The subpersonality can remain inactive in the unconscious like a memory or it can be an unconscious motivating force. The preconscious (Middle Unconscious) is one of three arbitrary divisions of the unconscious into functional units. The function of the preconscious is that of storage, sorting, and categorizing. Elements easily accessible to consciousness, like your telephone number, are stored. Elements emerging from deeper unconscious levels pass through the processing of the preconscious. It seems logical that this functional area of the unconscious would be very involved in the shuffling and sorting process of creativity.

The subconscious (or Lower Unconscious) was the primary focus of Freud's work. He was interested in the chaotic elements of man's mind and in the instinctual process. Though he emphasized the negativity of this unconscious function, the subconscious is recognized as a pool of raw material which can be fashioned for productive ends by other parts of the psyche. Assagioli described it as the seat of basic psychological activities, including the regulation of body functions, basic drives, and primitive instincts, the raw material of dreams and elements of old complexes.

The superconscious (or Higher Unconscious) is the seat of man's higher development. Such positive assets as talents, high intelligence, even genius, and spirituality are functional potentials in the unconscious. Ferrucci sees the difference between the subconscious and superconscious in a time frame: the subconscious contains the elements of our past development, while the superconscious contains the potential for our future development. He notes that there is no moralistic distinction between these parts of the psyche; rather they are sequentially developmental.[40] The Higher Self, thought inherent in the psyche by both Jung and Assagioli from their study of Eastern and mystical psychological literature, is conceived of as a deeply unconscious, perennially present guidance center. The final unconscious aspect of this model is the collective unconscious, a psychological function Jung studied in great depth both psychologically and anthropologically. It is the template of universal symbolism; the inherent capacity in each human mind to symbolize in a similar fashion to other minds.

Theoretically, Assagioli thought that there can be movement of the entire field of consciousness. It can move toward the subconscious, or it can move toward the superconscious. This idea correlates with the principles of kundalini yoga, where the focus of an individual's life can move developmentally through the chakras, or entire energy centers of the body, the lower chakras being concerned with the fundamental functions of life, and the higher chakras being concerned with spiritual or transpersonal development.

Jung emphasized the idea of unfoldment of the individual through an unconscious process which is enhanced by conscious understanding. Assagioli, too, fully honored the unconscious process, but stressed the active participation in the growth process through conscious thinking. Planning, practice, and choice were emphasized by Assagioli, but also certainly indicated by

Jung as well. A working system contains emphasis on both the unconscious thought process and active conscious thought. From the first, a dialogue between conscious and unconscious elements produces rich, lively psychoactive material. This dialogue happens in a number of ways.

Images arising from the unconscious are studied for meaning. This conscious work creates a tension of importance around these images. As a result the images become elaborated, or new images arise in the conscious thinking, and more images emerge from the unconscious having a quality of responsiveness that furthers understanding. This dialogue pattern can have a short or long time line, it can be steady in form or sporadic, but whatever its form it acts as a healing agent.

The imagery process is focused first on the subpersonalities, to which are attached specific visual images that clients are encouraged to elaborate; in fact, those clients able to play most with the images derive the most benefit. Throughout the process the therapist/guide studies the speech of the client for the guality and presence of particular polarities that are the subpersonalities, thus always grounding the work of imagination in the client's actual experience. The client practices observing the guide's actions in order to learn to discriminate how each subpersonality acts as a tool in his environment. Names are initially chosen for the subpersonalities simply to act as easy reference, although the particular names chosen can have strong symbolic significance and often have developmental meaning. Sometimes names are changed because the development perceived in the personality part is different from what the name implies.

In this concretizing process the contrast and complementarity of the subpersonalities becomes ever more vivid. It is useful to visualize the inner dynamics using a simile like actors on a stage or a board of directors meeting. (As in diplomacy, the shape of the table visualized makes a difference.)

As soon as subpersonalities are sufficiently differentiated in the client's understanding, it is important to shift focus from the inner to the outer world. Life events illuminate the obvious, the subtle, and even the subliminal roles of subpersonalities. There is a reciprocal confrontation between the psyche and the world; dialogue with the unconscious and analysis of subpersonality participation in events precipitates change. Changed behavior is then selectively tried in the world and events answer as to its effectiveness. The new behavior, which can become an actual modification in a subpersonality, has effects on the equilibrium of the rest of the subpersonalities. A new balance between all the elements is required and actively sought. It is easy for the new developmental direction to be sabotaged by another subpersonality, another thought polarity which represents a differing set of values. Conscious choices are made as to what values to uphold and which to discard through negotiation with the polar opposites, the subpersonalities. At the height of psychological growth the world events become numinous and seem to directly mirror the inner process. Jung felt there was nothing haphazard about this process; he called it synchronicity. The inner work is always drawn out into the world with emphasis on finding meaningful involvement and effectiveness. Thus, the inner world and the outer world are brought into balance.

Another way in which the imagery dialogue between the unconscious and consciousness is enhanced is through the study of dreams. Dreams are considered a deeper form of thought that bypasses the limited modes of thought characteristic of the subpersonalities. Subpersonalities as they are originally developed are involved directly in survival and thus their modes of operation are necessarily severely focused in order to guarantee survival. Dreams broaden the thought scope by exploring perceptions and issues ignored by the subpersonalities in their survival function. Dreams can be read as messages directive of the work with subpersonalities. When the psychological work is hard or, conversely, if no conscious work is taking place, dreams can act as a comfort or a goad. The nightmare, behind its attention-getting guise, carries a growth message. Humorous dreams release tension and strain and foster perspective and balance. Evidence in the dream content of the beginning of new facets in the individual's development is of great importance. These facets may directly evolve into modification or whole new subpersonality shapes. Dreams often prognosticate growth; usually there is a time lag between these prophetic dreams, the evidence of a new facet in the subpersonality development, and its actual manifestation in the world.

Early in the work with subpersonalities the client is informed that each time he steps back to observe the subpersonalities, he is in a psychological space called Center. Centering is learned as a specific skill. It supposes a neutral mental space that is apart from the fixedness of the subpersonalities. It is initially an escape from the fractiousness of the subpersonalities. Over a period of time, however, its function as observer expands into director. Center directs by objective appraisal of the environment and selection of subpersonalities to deal most effectively with the world. Ideally, the individual stands poised in Center ready to act at any time with any of his resources. The introduction of the use of Center, a neutral mental space, into behavior results in an immediate change in social patterns. The objectivity and clarity of Center destroys artificiality in social situations.

Center is important in the development of subpersonalities. Moving back and forth between the subpersonalities and Center, using Center as an observation point, results in the skill to instantly recognize characteristic subpersonality behavior patterns. Recognition initiates modification. Appraisal is inevitably followed by choice for change. Jung described in detail the persona, the personality mask developed to meet the world safely. Subpersonality knowledge reveals the extreme limitations of the persona. Usually one or two subpersonalities perform the function of persona, while perhaps the rest of the personality is rarely seen in public. The objectivity of Center allows for a reformulation of the persona for a more effective use of a wider range of personality elements. The set structure of the unanalyzed persona makes the individual vulnerable to the repetition of entanglement in ineffective social patterns. From Center it is possible to see the extent to which one is entrapped in anachronistic subpersonality patterns that normally cause neurotic pain.

Center facilitates the integration of emerging unconscious material. From the objective observer standpoint of Center, dream material that reveals developmental direction can be related to subpersonality development. The relevant subpersonality to deal with specific dream information is chosen. Perhaps most important, Center's objectivity on the inner scene fosters the honing of the subpersonalities. Superfluous, inefficient patterns are dropped. The subpersonality becomes purer in shape and function. Indeed, in ideal form the subpersonalities become archetypal. The quality of the subpersonality remains unique to the individual but the shape becomes increasingly simple and universal. The final concept in this working system, already implied in the other concepts, is integration. From the first, integration, the balancing process of all the psychic elements, is undertaken. The initial observation of the subpersonalities reveals imbalance, and at that point commitment to balance begins. It is the important work of including equally the potential of all elements. This ideal, of course, is elusive, as well as being an ongoing project, but it becomes increasingly easy as psychological skills are established. This work is cyclical, in that sometimes balance is natural and at other times old patterns reemerge in response to circumstances that again demand a focus on intentional balancing.

Development of the subpersonalities is a feeling of reaching, reaching for one's highest potential. It is opening to the possibilities of resources in the superconscious. If conflictful elements of consciousness are eliminated, superconscious potential becomes available: greater intelligence, richer intuition, creativity, a spiritual context for one's world view. When the superconscious becomes active, the shift in subpersonalities may be swift and dramatic. There is a change to an overall higher level of consciousness. This is the emergence of the transpersonal. When the individual is no longer mired in the befuddlement of distorted psychic elements, clarity of universal connection appears.

If development is viewed like the structure of a building, the first work, foundation building, is the establishment of the subpersonalities. The foundation must be sound and whole before successive floors (greater overall perspicuity and higher levels of both inner and outer effectiveness) can be built upon it. If the psychological foundation is not whole, the experience of the higher levels can create imbalance, even craziness, rather than clarity.

The ultimate, most elusive, and mysterious element of the psyche is the Higher Self. In Center one has inklings of the Higher Self. In dreams an image of the Higher Self may appear. Both Jung and Assagioli hypothesized that the influence of this deep aspect of the person is pervasive, that it radiates into every aspect of the life. As conflictful elements disappear, that influence becomes more palpable. It is the absolute frontier of psychological development, and as such, is still shrouded in unknown. When the idea of the Higher Self is presented, it is not unfamiliar, for all people with even the beginnings of clarity recognize an organizing force in the life pattern. Every person who attempts to clear away the mental rubbish that characterizes our age and move into a wholeness with all of his resources is a pioneer in the study of the Higher Self.

3

ORDINARY GENIUS
Three Case Histories

Although subpersonalities are present in all of us, and can be discerned directly through observation of their behavior, subpersonalities are most vivid in the complex personalities of talented people; they are evident in their life histories as well as in their varied behavior and production. I have chosen to present three subpersonality portraits here that describe the uniqueness of three talented people.[1] These people are ordinary geniuses. They are geniuses in the sense that they are highly gifted people; within the confines of the circumstances of their lives, they are quietly, uniquely productive. They are ordinary in that they are like many people whose unique pattern of gifted living is only subtly evident. Lack of self-knowledge and mastery, together with lack of opportunity, keep their significance from celebration. With the slightest opportunity their psyches bloom like flowers, awesome to behold, and in my experience as a psychologist, I have had the privilege of working with many people like the three I present. Theoretically, if subpersonalities are developed, all people are richly talented.

These three case histories were chosen to be representative. They graphically display the process of work with subpersonalities over a period of time. The first case, Benjamin, demonstrates the course of short-term psychotherapy using psychosynthesis. This also is an example of the use of psychosynthesis as a followup to other psychotherapy programs. Benjamin's experience vividly illustrates the utilization of the natural mythopoetic function for healing. Helene, the second case, is a woman who, in the course of psychosynthesis work, emerged from twelve years of severe problems. The approach illustrates the search for and establishment of a strong, healthy psychological core through subpersonality work. The third person, Julia, is presented for her ordinary social adjustment. The strength of her psyche allowed not only the healing of childhood wounds through the psychosynthetic process, but acted as a springboard to her own higher development. Julia experienced an unfolding of her talent with an accompanying establishment of strong self-esteem. Both Helene and Julia experienced subpersonality transformation that brought about significant change in their lives. In addition, Julia's subpersonalities took on an archetypal purity that will probably be influential in her development for many years to come.

BENJAMIN

Benjamin seemed older than thirty years. His furrowed brow, hunched shoulders, and nervous glance that darted everywhere, but only rarely at me, the person with whom he was conversing, gave an impression of burden and age. He was average height, stocky in build, but more soft than muscular. Most striking, and what held my attention, was the steady flow of speech and laughter that beguiled and delighted.

He had stopped drinking seven months ago. At that time he had proclaimed himself an alcoholic and participated in a therapeutic program for a few months, his only other experience with psychotherapy; after that he considered himself strong enough to control the alcoholism himself. What was concerning him at the present time were fits of rage, blinding anger welling up in him out of proportion to situational irritants. As he talked he painted a portrait of a life situation that in itself was highly demanding. He spent sixteen-hour days, often without weekend reprieve, at a computer, ridden by the complete responsibility for the desktop publishing of service manuals for new products in a large company. His wife, a beautiful woman significantly older than himself, was driven by a perfectionistic daemon that felt obliged to monitor Benjamin's life as well as her own.

His pace of mental work was very fast; taking advantage of his sharpness, I introduced the concept of subpersonalities twenty minutes into the first session. For Benjamin this was beneficial as immediate psychological information; and it helped me as I formed my diagnosis. He readily identified three subpersonalities. The Wizard, spoken of first, was the site of the high rage. This polarity in his mind was a constellation of many experiences that began with survival needs. Benjamin's father baited and beat Benjamin and his brother, sister, and mother. In response the Wizard developed high intelligence, creativity, superb language skills, and deflecting humor and laughter. Initially, the subpersonality skills were used to redirect and control family dynamics at home, but quickly Benjamin learned that the positive qualities of these skills also won him refuge in other families.

The second subpersonality he identified was the Giant. Benjamin chose to describe the psychological quality of this part as "awkward, diffuse, and fuzzy." The Giant wished he had high intelligence. Though he saw the Giant as a huge man, the Giant wore diapers and had soft baby flesh. It felt like the Giant was the caretaker for the Wizard.

And finally, he identified a child part which he named Quicksilver. This part only appeared at times of high creative focus. He would say, "Ah, ah," in awe before the ideas arising. The intensity of Quicksilver could not be interrupted. Benjamin was aware that this part was more vague, more unconscious than the other two. The heavy, desperate dynamic of the Wizard and the Giant dominated his life, occasionally lightened by the delightful freedom of Quicksilver.

At the conclusion of the subpersonality work, in recognition of his illumination, Benjamin spontaneously remarked with laughter, "My castle is in disarray and needs much straightening." For him the mythopoetic function of the mind was powerful and completely natural.

My suggestion to him at the end of the hour were to focus his thought on Quicksilver when he found himself rageful, to think about "adopting" another father in image or actuality to help heal his childhood experience, and to see a physician to have his physical state checked and obtain guidance in diet.

From this first session to the point when Benjamin's energy for therapy plateaued—a significant piece of work having been completed—was four months, thirteen sessions. Every person has a different pattern of psychological work. Benjamin worked intensely and fast in every session, but cancelled and rescheduled frequently, for a break, for illness, for work, and for other activities. The next scheduled session his wife called to cancel, saying he was ill.

The second session was a marriage counseling session. The characteristics he described in his home life revealed the dominance of the wife. Focus was on practical strategy that introduced the surprising new concept of Benjamin taking leadership. Some mention was made of the Wizard's rage, but significantly, the main subpersonality found to be present in the home was the Giant. He had dreamed that he was trying to hide a sock. We laughed, looking at the poor Giant's position under the perfectionistic wife/mother's thumb. Leadership, as a new modus operandi, was identified without naming any subpersonality to undertake this function.

The presenting problem in the next session was his brother, a drug addict, in trouble with the police. From his experience in alcohol counseling, Benjamin had learned to speak of his mother as the perfect enabler, now separated from his father's problems and focused on his brother. I suggested we deepen the approach to this problem over what we had done the week before by beginning with a subpersonality appraisal of the situation. What Benjamin saw immediately was the deep enmeshment of the Wizard and the Giant in the family system. Quicksilver, however, was in a completely different space. As he stood in Quicksilver's shoes, he found objective wisdom and distance from the embroiling trouble. Quicksilver, who had only been available in creative work before, was suddenly more vivid and accessible.

A call came from Benjamin's wife; he was in danger of losing his job. Benjamin's story was that when his supervisor had yelled at him, he had walked off the job. The strain of publication deadlines and an impending move of the office was affecting everyone. The Wizard responded with rage. To that point Benjamin had been able to keep the Wizard's rage covered at work, keep it at home with his wife, and to himself in sleepless nights. We considered the appropriateness of the Wizard's response in light of the superhuman requirements of the job (when he later left, a computer graphics specialist and two assistants replaced him). The Giant was embarrassed by the Wizard's behavior. He was unable to contact Quicksilver. The strategy decided upon was to go back to work as though nothing had happened, at least to maintain the income for now.

I did not see Benjamin for two weeks because of his focus, controlled and steady, on rectifying the job situation. When I saw him, he had learned that, despite his effort, he had been fired. The Wizard said to run. Benjamin said that he had done that before. The discussion was about California with its opportunities for a new start and freedom from the pall of the job failure and his wife's censure. He felt his wife slipping away, her "bleats of pain" reminding him of his mistake. The Wizard, having had his say, his energy depleted, became silent. In the silence Benjamin began to talk about starting his own computer graphics business and his wife's encouragement to start writing.

Benjamin was depressed and in a lot of pain as he came into the next session, seeing his job end and his brother in jail. I said it sounded like slogging through a swamp. He said, a dark swamp. I asked who was his companion there? He said, a white steed. A white steed named Quicksilver.

A significant dream appeared in the next week. In the dream he is working hard to finish building a cubical object. His workshop is surrounded by high white columns. Suddenly he discovers that his work is back to only twenty-five percent completion. The symbolism of this simple dream is rich, the kind that can be carried with benefit for a lifetime. The cube Benjamin identified as representing himself, suddenly thwarted from achieving wholeness by the predicament of job loss. The columns, with their suggestion of classic beauty and antiquity, convey image of encompassing masculine strength. He announced plans not to seek another job for a month in order to assess his vocational direction. Much of this session was spent in education about the creative process.

He had left the job a few days earlier when he arrived primed to speak of general subpersonality dynamics, which were apparent in the quiet of these free days. If the Giant's work was questioned or not appreciated, he went crazy. Then the Wizard said to him: see, they're doing it to you again, they will always do it to you. The Wizard thought the Giant was useless. The Giant was intimidated by the Wizard.

Quicksilver, on the other hand, nurtured the Giant. The Giant was awed by Quicksilver; he would like to have been a big Quicksilver. It was also clear that the Wizard and Quicksilver were creative partners. The planned strategy was to hold round table discussions with these parts of himself for negotiation, for peacemaking, for diplomacy.

Center was introduced as rightful chair of the meetings. Center was defined as a psychological space apart from the subpersonalities, the calm psychological space suddenly available in emergency situations. Benjamin said he understood; he had had this experience. Then he said that it was like Dad. I did not understand what he meant. He said that these "brothers," his subpersonalities, needed a dad, an ideal dad. He said it was like Max von Sydow or Obi Wan Kenobi. I understood that he saw in these two figures models of integration and balance of the psyche, a facilitation of the establishment of Center within himself. Benjamin said they represented the kind of father he would want to be when he had children. He also said that Center was not in Center for him, but to the side. In front of him were social expectations; vision and understanding came in from the side.

The following week he took a break from the therapy process. When he arrived the next time, he said, "As I step back, the more of me comes forward." He reported that as a result of the table discussions, the turmoil between the subpersonalities was slower and quieter. The issue raised for the day was mendacity. The Wizard had early learned to spin tales that fascinated and delighted others, but at the same time covered any fallibility in Benjamin. His parents had both lied to cover the family problems. Benjamin found himself using this defense not only in the world but with his wife. Having chosen a woman who would help to establish structure in his life also left him shamed before her by his own inability to structure. After the Wizard spins yarns, it is the Giant who gets caught, suffers pain, and wants Benjamin to stop this defense. Quicksilver says, "Hey, you guys, this is not what should be."

Benjamin's wife wanted to return to school. He felt he had had many opportunities in these months for his own growth. Now it was his turn to support her while she studied. The idea of the challenge pleased him.

One session was spent on the pain of his relationship with his wife and not being able to find suitable work. His wife was under enormous pressure in her job, as he had been. She had developed a painful neuralgia that no treatment abated. He felt guilty that his days were relaxed and pleasant. Besides job hunting, he spent two hours each day working out. The strategy planned was to visualize his wife in the setting in which she was most relaxed, the beach, and to visualize the job opportunity he sought.

Another week passed with yet nothing appropriate in the job market. He was thinking of writing, as his wife had suggested. He told the story of his late adolescence. Leaving home at seventeen before completing high school, he joined the Air Force. During the next four years in the service, he completed high school, a two-year college, and had taken courses for a third year of college. He was also married and divorced. The Wizard told the story as he wanted to write it, full of unique, intriguing detail. A contract was made to spend three hours a day writing the story.

Writer's block occurred. Benjamin's response was to start running with the intention of entering a major race in a few weeks. He had been running several hours a day when I next saw him. His face and spirit were bright and clear. Running had never appealed to him before because he had no wind. Now he ran through the pain. He said, the Giant was no longer in diapers; he was still vulnerable, but it was the vulnerability of the hard-muscled adolescent.

He reported a dream. He was wandering across open land going to a city. He wanted to belong in this city, to say that he had grown up there. He knew, however, that no one would believe him; they would know he was lying. It was like a city out of a fairy tale, an old European city, in which he felt comfortable. It was Betsy's city.

I asked him who Betsy was. He said she was a girl he knew who was like his mirror image. We talked about the anima.

He also reported that on Mother's Day, in his family gathering, he had announced quietly without anger that if they could not be together without quarreling, he did not want to be with them. He did not want to play games anymore. Then he had left.

Several cancellations were followed by a session in which the energy for the work had tapered off. It was clear that after a large piece of work, his energy had gone to the inner integration phase. Sessions were planned farther apart. He had run the race in a respectable time. During his daily run he was planning his writing. Later in the day he typed out four pages single spaced of the story line he had developed as he ran. Two weeks ago he had taken a temporary job, which had reduced his running and writing time, but at the same time had opened a whole new world to him. He was working as a computer specialist in a university science laboratory. The Wizard and Quicksilver were amazed, wandering around the lab asking questions. Benjamin said that only a year ago he would have been intimidated by the intense intellectual focus of the scientists there. Now he was fascinated and wanted to learn about every research project. We talked about his good mind which he was freer to use now that some of the psychological baggage was unloaded.

The rage which had so disturbed Benjamin appears now only in one situation, when his wife treats him as incompetent, or questions whether he still might be a "juvenile delinquent," whether the new control in his life is genuine. One day he informed me that he had answered an advertisement for a job in Tucson, a job where all of his particular talents could be challenged. He was interviewed over the phone and hired within a week. For this job he not only had the skills, but the control of his personal life and tools for meeting any adversity.

HELENE

In a year's time Benjamin accomplished major psychological change that could be a basis for his further evolution. An alcohol recovery program and psychosynthesis provided the tools he needed. When I first saw Helene, on the other hand, she had been in therapy numbers of times over a period of twelve years. She had multiple problems. Her style in the therapy session was disarming, distant, vague, passive; it took several sessions to understand the problems. It was more than a year, spent mostly in crisis-type counseling, before Helene was able to be centered and gained significant momentum in making transformative shifts. The contrast of her personal appearance and physical demeanor from the first time I saw her to the present was striking. Except in the depths of crisis periods she dressed with simple, aesthetic taste, always attractive. At first I saw a wide and dreamy-eyed, vulnerable, thirty-year-old child, her energy so much in the top of her body, it seemed that if you touched her, she would topple. Her voice was sweet and weak, the sound trailing into despair. Some sessions she was depressed, hardly able to put sentences together; in other sessions she was manic, eyes glittering, her mind flying in so many directions she could not focus. Today, I see a solid young woman, with a clear intelligent gaze, soft spoken but with an air of authority. She gives a sense of grounded, even energetic, momentum without a trace of depression or mania.

The problems that emerged over the first six weeks were even more complicated. Psychiatric evaluation confirmed my diagnosis of cyclothymic disorder, cycles of depression alternating with elation; an antidepressant medication was initiated to establish enough stability for her to function in her daily life and to benefit from psychotherapy. This was the first time this diagnosis had been made. Since she was seventeen, she had suffered periodic depression, seeking therapeutic help in the low periods, and leaving therapy when she felt better. When depression returned, she thought herself a failure and turned to yet another therapist. In the first session she was panic-stricken because she felt the return of depression. She was to be married in a few weeks; her fiancé had never seen her depressed. They had both believed that the high of the in-love feelings they were experiencing would last a lifetime.

She also faced a deadline on her master's thesis. This was her second attempt to research and write a thesis. The first time her research idea was so celebrated that she had won a grant to support a study in Israel. She had been in Israel a month when the depression hit again, and she came home in failure. Helene was the only child of parents who were both high-powered professionals. It had always seemed natural to Helene that she would become a scholar. Her bright mind thrived on intellectual challenge; nothing gave her more sense of accomplishment than solving a puzzling relationship between ideas. The expectations from her parents were high, however, and her mother, with whom she closely identified, seemed to her a superwoman, difficult to emulate. She knew the pressure of parental expectations and her own expectations of herself as part of the depressive cycle. She lived always with a family commandment: you are what you produce. She was alarmed to find herself sometimes using alcohol to numb feelings. She had always suspected her father of being alcoholic. Helene's health deteriorated. She had recurrent minor illnesses. Continuing pain in her neck and shoulders was diagnosed as arthritis. Helene had been ill often as a child, and she remembered hospital stays that happened frequently at holidays. It was expected that she be the perfect child; early she learned to retreat into illness.

The marriage was in crisis from the start. Her husband had no interest in settling into married routine, but increasingly pushed Helene toward more romance and sexual excitement at the same time that she was fighting depression. While Helene needed order and simplicity in her life, particularly for her work, he took no household responsibility and lived a haphazard daily existence. She had a growing fear of him. Within eight months he had returned to his former girlfriend. He rejected marriage counseling or seeing a therapist on his own.

Helene's dreams at this time reflected the severity of her predicament. In one she was driving downhill into a flooded area; she immobilized the car in mud, and then sat on top of the car. In another she is screaming at a woman driving uphill on the wrong side of the road.

Ten months after she was married she took a new job which represented a practical application of her deepest interests. With the investment of herself in this job, she began to move away from the enmeshment of the marriage, out of crisis. After a pleasant anniversary dinner, her husband asked her for a divorce. Three days later he made the remark that if he did not treat her better he would lose her. We began to address directly his abuse of her. He then announced he was taking a job in another state. She affirmed her commitment to the divorce and they saw a counselor to end the marriage. After several months she began a new relationship with a man she had known for years, monitoring the relationship closely so that there be no love addiction on her part. In the summer she decided to explore the possibility that she had become an alcoholic and started attending Alcoholics Anonymous meetings. She had been off of medication for some time and her mood was even. And finally she had accepted the challenge of finishing her thesis, without fear, without pressure.

I reflected at this point, after two years of therapy, that she was healthy, living a daily life with steady energy and mood balance, she had changed her criteria and understanding of relationships, had moved away from the need for substance abuse to control her life, and was now focused on her own further development both in the use of her talents and in the integration of all aspects of her psyche.

The concept of subpersonalities was introduced in the first session. Like all the rest of her work the definition of subpersonalities was vague for many weeks. Tentatively, however, she began to appraise her own experience in subpersonality terms.

First, we looked at one part that condemned her for wanting to retreat from her life situation, and another part that wanted to lie under a mountain of covers. Later, she talked of an industrious part versus one that wanted to escape.

In appraising a confusing house-hunting situation, she identified a Pragmatist ("It's probably the best house you can get"), an Idealist ("You can make a good relationship anywhere"), a Pleaser ("If he likes it, I like it"), and an Assassin (having found several satisfactory houses, the Assassin insisted she look further, which only would add confusion).

In the third session she came with three drawings of subpersonality polarities of which she was aware. The Idealist she drew as an upward spiral. The Pleaser was loops around circles in all directions with no center. The Saboteur—she was not clear if the Saboteur was equivalent to the Assassin or a different subpersonality—was a coffin in a tornado.

A few details of subpersonality configuration emerged in the next several sessions because of the need to do ongoing direct crisis intervention. The Pleaser was a little girl, incessantly smiling inappropriately. At another point she said that the Pleaser fit into Japanese culture; she understood ultrapolite ritual. She admitted, however, that the degree of vigilance in the Pleaser was out of balance. It was the Pleaser who suffered the strain of needing to be a perfect child and in early years had escaped into the somatization of the strain, the childhood illness pattern. In opposition to the Pleaser, the Idealist panicked if there was a lull in her life. The only acceptable frame of living was high energy activity and output, and full capacity growth.

After more weeks of vague avoidance, I intervened, saying that it was imperative that we nail down the subpersonalities, see them vividly, so that we both as a team could work with them. Crisis alleviation was suspended in order to organize subpersonality information so that it could be used as a tool.

Four specific subpersonalities were clarified. Sandy was the Pragmatist, a long-haired, long-legged, normal girl.

The Pleaser Helene named Rosie. She visualized her as having round Rosie cheeks, and wearing a little girl dress with puffy sleeves and Maryjane shoes. Though the image was of a little girl, Helene said Rosie felt about twenty years old.

The Idealist was seen as a seven-foot-tall silver rocket. The metal body was seen as armored. The head was pointed. Of course, his name was Rocket. The Saboteur was Thorny, a black blob that lived in a swamp. At the sight of him, Helene became highly anxious; how could she deal with his terrible power? I instinctively pulled to the opposite emotional pole; I suggested he wore a rubber suit and she should look for a zipper.

In the dynamics of these subpersonalities, Thorny was in the middle. Rosie was next to him, in danger of being gobbled up. Rocket stood behind Thorny, fighting him and protecting Rosie. Sandy moved in all directions and was not bothered by the other three.

In subsequent weeks the only subpersonality evident was Thorny. Helene guessed, however, that there was another subpersonality which we had not identified. This one she named Sickle, the holder of the family rules. She was able to name twenty-three family commandments by which she lived. To the natural child Rosie these were inhibitive, abhorrent, but feared. We planned that she would look at a revision of the commandments. A few weeks later Rosie said that she was content with the family commandments as they were; this was her heritage, the family culture.

At this time I introduced the concept of Center. In the weeks that followed Center was only available to Helene in times of order and calm. Nonetheless, she observed that the work of trying to establish Center had displaced Thorny from his original central position.

Helene was astonished at one point to observe Rosie's compliance to her parents. Her mother criticized Helene's new husband, asserting her belief that Helene was far more intelligent than he. For two days after, Rosie criticized him, complying with the values of the mother, still trying to please mother. Not only Thorny's depression, but Rosie, too, was sabotaging the new marriage. At another time, Rosie, sensing that the husband needed some space, tried to please him by suggesting that he go hiking with some friends. When he had gone, Rosie felt abandoned and jealous, berating the husband on his return and deluging him with negative emotion. Helene regretted the rigidity she observed in the behavior patterns of Rosie and the other subpersonalities as well. Depressed and living in chaos, there seemed little she could do about it at the time. Nonetheless, the refinement of her understanding of the subpersonalities continued.

At the time she took the new job, she saw Thorny as deep under water, threatening to take over. Clearly, he was a seat of her emotional needs. Yet she observed him, realizing his power and threat, and in the very observation prevented his takeover. Unlike her experience in Israel, she started the new job, settled in, and was successful.

Suddenly, nine months after starting therapy, Rocket took a new form. She came into the session with a complete understanding of the transformation. His name was Iman, the I-man. He was a wizard in a long robe, with a white beard and a wrinkled face. She understood that Iman had always been part of her but had basically been shut off from her life when she was a year old.

I asked her at this time what was the fun-loving, humorous part of her that I often saw in her face. Despite the deeply depressed place she was in, a mischievous smile would often come into her eyes, reflecting the irony of her predicament. She saw an image of the Pillsbury dough boy, with a funny laughing face, whom we subsequently referred to as the Trickster.

A few months later she brought in a series of spontaneous drawings she had made. Helene had no training in art; she had been reluctant to draw for fear she might not draw well. The first early drawings she had made mechanically at my suggestion. The present drawings came from vital psychological process. The drawings were in sequence: 1) a snail approaching a bog; 2) Thorny in a bog with spikes of glass in his coat, which was covered with blood; 3) Thorny covered with small wounds ("He has no skin"), seemingly a figure of large eyes inside a coat; and 4) a spiral in the form of the Navajo life force symbol ("to send healing energy to Thorny"). All of these drawings were circular. As time went by, Helene began drawing mandalas. She saw the mandala drawings as healing from Center.

It took more than a year for Helene to ask whether Thorny was a saboteur of her relationships. She looked not only at her marriage but at friendship patterns as well. She identified his supersensitivity, which resulted in a desire for solitude. We discussed his woundedness, asking what would be the natural pattern of relationship for her if he were whole. Another discussion addressed the nature of the bog in which Thorny lived. With consternation the acknowledgement was made that swamp water is teaming with life.

As she was moving out of depression, separated from her husband and beginning to spend time with other male friends, a playful, flirtatious, sensual subpersonality became evident. Identified as Venus, Helene said that this part represented beauty and perfection. All her subpersonalities except the Trickster, even including Iman, were taken in by her. She objectively owned up to a love addiction to her husband and other former male companions. The strength that had developed in other parts of herself made it possible to be clear and determined in her choice about Venus's behavior. Venus was connected to the abuse of alcohol. Thorny chose alcohol to numb pain from stress and depression. Venus had begun to choose alcohol, on the other hand, to enhance sexual excitement. Work began to make different choices for Venus. Helene chose to stand in the position of Iman in her relationships with new male companions allowing the presence of Venus as background coloring rather than control. She found herself in the role of teacher to her steady companion, teaching him balance in the relationship from the bitter fruits of her own experience.

One periodic check of the current status of subpersonalities is to arbitrarily place them in a landscape. When Helene did this, Thorny, of course, was in the swamp. Hovering over the swamp was Venus. It was a long way to Iman, across open land into woods at a higher elevation. The Trickster was even beyond that across a boulder field. Rosie stood alone in the open fields. Sandy, who had disappeared from consciousness, was now identified as part of Iman. The Sickle, now a much smaller size, was on the other side of the swamp and had become rather indistinct and unimportant in the dynamics. It was concluded that Rosie could use the support and presence of Iman and the Trickster; this triad was to be practiced. Then Rosie could be free from anxiety, free to represent the peace and harmony that was natural to her.

A visualization found Iman at the top of a mountain as a representative of the Higher Self. He now wore a knee-length garment for ease in walking in the streets. His advice to her was to take one step at a time; there is no need for worry.

One year after the first mandala drawings of Thorny, Helene was moved to draw him again. He had grown green flagella on the outside of his body. There were three embryos inside him; one had a stem and leaf. With all the vibrant energy of the Trickster in her eyes, Helene said that he was a seed.

Throughout this work Helene reported many dreams. They moved steadily from themes of personal depression into rich expression of archetypal symbology. One dream was of a nurturing, kind old Oriental woman. The image was so numinous that Helene decided to adopt the old woman. She realized that there was in her subpersonality configuration no mother. The old woman would be mother and wisdom figure in her. At last an inner mother for Rosie. Recently experiencing much fear about the inevitable death of her aging parents, there was peace in the incorporation of the old Oriental woman into the dynamics of her subpersonalities. She named her Shao. As we talked about her desire to be a mother, to have her own children, to establish a family, she recalled another dream in which she met a man at a conference who was weeping for awe. He told her she would have a good relationship. There would be a sign when this relationship was to begin. Helene felt she was ready now.

JULIA

Julia was an ordinary person in society. She carried credentials of adjustment: married with two children, a housewife who, as her children became more independent, pursued a college education and developed a career. When she conversed, the topics were everyday concerns of women. There was nothing out of the ordinary in the way she moved or dressed except there was perhaps a bit more bright color. Yet, in her surroundings there were elements that contributed to and shaped the uniqueness that was naturally hers. Her husband was Japanese American. She lived in an ethnically mixed neighborhood, many of her friends being Hispanic and American Indian. Julia herself was blond and blue-eyed, mostly of Irish and French ancestry, although she did have a great-grandfather who was a full-blooded American Indian.

Julia sought psychotherapy because of her alarm at the emotional upheaval she was experiencing facing the increasing physical debilitation of her mother. Since Julia was four, her mother had been in a wheelchair, afflicted at that time by polio. Julia carried within her images of a childhood darkened by her mother's disability and depression, early responsibility for a younger sister, and fear of her own recurring illnesses. As an adult she once spontaneously drew a little girl surrounded by darkness who was painting a picture of a bright sun. It was in drawing and painting that she had healed herself as a child, and thus, despite neglect, she moved into the adult world as a normal person. It was no surprise that her chosen college major was art.

The first set of subpersonalities she identified described the middle-class woman she had become. Martha was a nurturing pioneer woman in charge of all household and parenting activity. Richard was the artist. Gayle, the comedian persona subpersonality, laughed and joked in a gentle, mellow manner, facilitating not only her own social life but creating a pleasant atmosphere for all around her. Finally, there was Elizabeth, a spiritual subpersonality, that was vague and shadowy at first identification and remained so until she was later replaced.

Within a week Julia realized she had omitted in the first identification process the extremely important and evident child part, Jeanie, that aspect of her that was wounded by her mother's affliction, and was now bewildered by its intensification. From this part came memories of the darkness of her childhood home, and her father's rage when he would return from one of his several jobs. This session focused on the needs of the child part Jeanie, released the present resentment toward her mother harbored there, and allowed other parts to function more efficiently in problem solving. Surprising to Julia, it was Richard who could confront the doctor about her mother's overmedication. Elizabeth arranged for a priest to say a mass for the sick. And Martha chose to use healing touch with her mother, massaging her shoulders, holding her hand.

When subpersonalities are delineated, sudden shifts often occur in the psyche. In her conscious thinking there arose in Julia's mind an image of the marriage of Martha and Richard. It was a simple realization of harmonization of energies springing from Julia's facile mythopoetic mental function, the gift of the artist.

It also came clear to Julia that in the stress of her mother's illness, she was living increasingly with Jeanie as persona, reaching out to others with complaint and dependence. One evening her husband fainted at a social gathering. The fear that over-whelmed her surprised her. Automatically turning to inner analysis, she found that Jeanie, as a bewildered child, saw her support gone. The scene seemed to move in slow motion, and she became aware of the other subpersonality reactions. Richard observed the man was working too hard and should see a doctor. Martha observed he did not eat dinner. Elizabeth advised Julia not to lean so hard, not to depend so much on her husband's presence.

Themes in her art work revealed a deep, unconscious healing process taking place. The wheels of her mother's wheelchair appeared repeatedly, even in abstract designs. The oppressive grief and pain of this symbol was evident in some pieces, while in others, the wheel became a universal symbol of synthesis associated with other positive symbols of development. A long series of prints explored the theme of womanhood. Her work became more simple, taking on the qualities of folk art as she thought in broader archetypal forms. At the same time she worried about her entrance into the competitive art world. She anxiously planned approaches to galleries, realizing the sales skill she needed to develop would be a teamwork of Richard and Gayle.

At this time she reported that she was happier than she had ever been in her life. She now knew who she was. She had no guilt for the choice of her direction to become an artist. The old question of whether she should become a secretary seemed ridic-ulous; of course, she was not a secretary.

Psychic changes occurred. Jeanie had a new blue dress. Where before Julia had seen her as a waif, she now was clean and healthy. She was aware of the beneficial presence of Jeanie in Christmas preparations with her own children. From Center a decision was made to no longer allow small obstacles to upset her; the feeling of frustration had always evoked loud complaint from Jeanie much to the discomfort of all around her. Julia realized that when Martha analyzed the world she saw it in a quite ordinary fashion, protective of Jeanie, and concerned with nestbuilding; as she spoke from Martha, she sounded like the universal women of the world. Richard, on the other hand, represented the transcendent, her artistic, individual vision.

At this time a series of events, positive and negative, occurred which brought about in the period of a few months a remarkable change in Julia's subpersonalities. It began with house remodeling that necessitated the destruction of the walls of Julia's studio, displacing her from her workplace not only literally but also in her psyche, where creativity shut down. Crises arose with her mother: she manipulated the well-meaning help of various relatives by sending them all on the same errand; and created a depressing, negative scene at Christmas festivities. Julia realized that when she stood in Jeanie's shoes, which was her habitual stance with her mother, she allowed her mother to talk to her in a way that she would never have tolerated from anyone else. An angry confrontation with her mother produced a softening and an apology. As Julia centered in her relationship with her mother, she realized that her mother's system for hooking her into the easily manipulated Jeanie was to praise her sister, putting Jeanie on the defensive. Christmas itself seemed surrealistic. The artist's eye saw the scene of the house torn up; in its midst, Julia sat holding a niece's new baby. Numinous images of death and rebirth were moving in Julia's psyche. Her dreams were turbulent and she was plagued with migraine headaches.

In the month that followed, her relationship with Star, an Indian friend she had had some years before, haunted her. Star had died, depressed by insuperable circumstances in her life. A painting emerged showing Julia walking in the light and Star in darkness. Her introverted drive to create at this time was tremendous. Several uncomfortable but minor physical problems brought back memories of painful childhood facts. Her mother's depression at the time of her birth was so intense that for many months Julia had been passed from one relative to another. She became acutely aware of children's suffering, small and great, around her. For the first time in years she prayed, she prayed for the well-being of children.

At the same time that she went through the throes of healing past wounding, she recognized the beauty and fulfillment of her present life. A New York critic visiting her art class said that when she painted from the child, she was good. Her dreams and her life with her family and friends were full of humor and affectionate warmth. In April the peace was destroyed by the news that she was to have a hysterectomy. Fear rose like a monster. The pain of childhood wounding and abandonment returned yet more intensely. As she thought about undergoing anesthesia, she realized the association of a phobia of having her face in water with overwhelming childhood depression. In the surgery she faced her worst fears of becoming the invalid that her mother had been.

As the date of the operation approached, a sudden change in the images of her subpersonalities occurred. The vague Elizabeth became Moon and Gray Wolf. Moon was the image of a young Indian woman and Gray Wolf, an old Indian man. And Richard took the form of Charlie, a Navajo craftsman. Jeanie felt enormous security with the quiet of the Indian images. She associated the appearance of the Indian subpersonalities to a healing of her own and Star's tragedies. Gayle regained her rightful place as persona.

The surgery went well and she healed quickly, but in the succeeding months of slow convalescence and metabolic adjustment, she experienced severe depression due to hormonal imbalance. Psychotherapy in the months of the depression were spent in directionless supportive work. When she emerged from the depression, the cycle of psychological work was completed. It had been completed in the unconscious. Much healing had occurred. The new set of subpersonalities, more vivid, more calm, more her genuine individual expression, had been expanded and firmly established as a portrait of her inner energy state. As Julia wrote, they were the "facets of myself that reveal myself (my Self)." Gray Wolf stood as sage, shaman, and advisor. Moon, known also as Mary, was the all-gentle, loving mother needed by Jeanie and Julia's own children. She was the provider of food, a deep spiritual center of rhythm and harmony. Charlie, an alcoholic Indian, was replaced by a stronger image, Horse; father, husband, artist, and craftsman, a hard worker, a warrior, strong independent, stubborn, and selfish. Another Indian figure had appeared: Wind, a wild woman, a shaman, a Muse, a warrioress. Gayle remained as persona, conductor of business, the mask of sophistication and protector of the inner embryonic, creative life. Jeanie was the beloved child, safe in this circle of strong, protective subpersonalities, the center of innocence, trust, and love. She was the natural child and the primitive artist.

In this amazing array of subpersonalities were the archetypes for Julia's present and future transformation. As Gayle conducted Julia's life, the other subpersonalities were in the immediate background as a resonance to business as usual. Now, in the studio, all of Julia's Indian subpersonalities contribute equally. Her artwork sells in several galleries. She is still active in the church and in her community, but she has also joined a group of Indian spiritual practitioners. Her very American family continues on; the daughters, now teenagers, think some of Mom's ideas are rather weird, but her husband is in harmony with the changes she has made.

ORDINARY GENIUS

Benjamin, Helene, and Julia are in the process of ongoing development today. Benjamin has moved out of the debilitating handicap of alcoholism to physical health and to owning and using his talent. Helene's life is now in equilibrium so that she can do the work she loves, and she has begun exploration of her own potential. Julia has used her personality as a springboard into her own artistic talent and spiritual growth, at the same time that she moves through a more thorough healing of childhood wounds. Each had a vivid, natural experience of his or her subpersonalities, each unique and a stunning portrait of individuality. These are ordinary geniuses, the jewels, the wealth of the world in every population, exquisite human art. They are not famous, but the unique configuration of psychic energy in each is cataly-tic, is ferment, to cultural development; they are the modern-day creators who say the unexpected that originates in the integrity of their understanding of themselves as centered indi-viduals who have many rich and valuable parts.

It has been my experience with gifted people that all under-stand the absolute necessity of the mental compartmentalization of their various capacities. It is seen in young gifted people: the eight-year-old who understood the part of himself who would conform to classroom rules and do the easy required work, and the other part that found it boring and would prefer to invent mischief; and the sixteen-year-old, now a Cambridge graduate student, who immediately named five parts of himself, all with different gifts. There is no discrimination on the basis of field; not only the artist in whom one would expect rich mythopoetic function, but the inventive theoretical physicist as well, experi-ence their minds as multiply partitioned and, thus, multiply talented. And perhaps most astonishing is the immediate self-esteem that appears in the undereducated or minority people who have lived in a shadow of believed inferiority, as they meet their own inner wealth.

It is granted that the cases here presented represent especially rich development of mythopoetic function. In these people, not sophisticated in psychological knowledge, there is a surprising parallel to Jung's own personal experience with his subpersonali-ties. Where the mythopoetic function is developed, the work is deep and rich. Where the mythopoetic function is not devel-oped, subpersonalities still are present, still represent an efficient compartmentalization of thought and behavior, though they do not have the fluid, facile movement of psychological energy evident in the easy imagery shifts of those with profound myth-opoetic function. For some, subpersonalities are matter-of-fact, rather than archetypal. The subpersonality framework then be-comes a framework of logic that supports strong personal under-standing and control. The uniqueness of the individual in the subpersonality configuration is still vivid.

Each case is presented chronologically. The overarching framework used in psychotherapy was psychosynthesis, but many other types of therapy were used in part as adjunct. The dynamic model combining Assagiolian and Jungian approaches presented in the last chapter is the basic model used, but the art of therapy is dependent on the therapist being responsive to the emerging healing pattern in the client. Varied approaches are essential. No matter the applied divergence of psychological method, the umbrella paradigm of psychosynthesis allows all to focus toward the individual's full development, truncating no part.

Subpersonalities can be an end in themselves, providing freedom from inner chaos and a means of organization and control. They also can be a beginning. Subpersonalities unlock the possibilities of higher development. They provide a foundation, and integrated base, that can be adjusted and reintegrated in the face of difficulty and imbalance to again provide the firm base for full development.

These three portraits are invitation to the reader to explore his own subpersonalities. In these three case studies I have tried to show the living experience of subpersonality work. Now it is important to see how these individual experiences fit into the theoretical model, and this we shall examine in the next chapter.

4

THE
CONTINUUM
OF DEVELOPMENT

There is a continuum of psychological development between the opposite poles of basic survival and the highest development. Subpersonality development runs the entire length of this continuum, providing continuity and stability as each new developmental level emerges. In this chapter the major ideas of the theory presented in this book will be drawn into a single model that describes this continuum of psychological development.

Initially, all life functions of all organisms are focused on survival. Most organisms retain this primary focus because the certainty of survival is never firmly established. The life history of a plant or animal consists of all time being devoted to the maintenance of life. The biological functions of oxygen intake and food production or gathering, followed by the oxidation of the food for energy and the release of wastes, is the perpetual cycle of all living things. In all its variations this cycle must function well before the organism has a surplus of energy to give to other life functions like establishment of safety and reproduction of the species. There are many points in biological cycles where slight variation in environmental factors results in the death of the organism. Unfortunately, during this period in history due to enormous changes in the earth because of ecological imbalance, many species are daily becoming extinct; the conditions for their life no longer exist.

Understanding of the psychology of human beings begins in

these facts. Generally, Western psychological understanding has not begun at the beginning; the survival of human beings as organisms on planet Earth is the beginning of all psychological function, the original birth trauma, and the first impetus to development. Expelled from the security and nurturance of the womb, the infant as a biological organism will necessarily for some time to come be focused on the establishment of her own survival. Unlike most other species, the human infant is totally dependent at birth and remains dependent for many years. Thus the predicament of the newly born human being is not only biological survival, but immediate social survival as well. Only a matter of weeks after birth, specific social response begins. The wider the range of this social response in interaction with adult caretakers, and the higher the quality of the care, the better the establishment of survival security.

EARLY DEVELOPMENT

If survival is to take place, processes of accommodation and assimilation have to happen. The infant must first *accommodate* to her environment; her lips must adapt to the nipple to feed—if a child does not feed, she dies.[1] Then the infant must *assimilate* what is needed from the environment for her own well-being; the milk sucked must be swallowed and digested, taken into the system to be transformed into muscles and bones and all other growing body parts.

The mind begins to develop in these processes. Each time the infant feeds, a neural tracing of that feeding is recorded and entered as data in the mental operating system that is one-pointed to survival. The data of all feedings are recorded in a mental cluster or schema. The process of accommodation in-cludes early social response. At first the infant's behavior is random, but soon she sorts out that the "big nuturant ones" around her make energy, sounds, and movements when she does certain things. Repeated over and over the child learns what responses bring the most energy from the caretakers, and the focus on survival leads to these responses being built into the schemas. When the child feeds, she performs the behaviors she has learned to ensure that she does not go hungry.

The schemas are discontinuous cognitive structures. For example, in the mind all information about feeding is isolated. But, as time passes and different experiences happen around feeding, other mental clusters begin to be used in conjunction with the feeding schema. Sometimes the child may be fed while the mother works, and the smile learned in the pleasure of feeding with the mother is turned toward another woman working nearby, who automatically delights in the baby's smile. Thus, the behavior of the feeding schema becomes connected with patterns of wider social learning, and with schemas of social participation. The clusters remain discrete and behaviors disappear when they are not needed. But the mental clusters continue to exist, reappearing again when they are needed. [2]

Many basic skills are developed in the early months. At first very fundamental processes are learned, such as looking, grasping, or placing, that become automatic. Then they are grouped according to actions needed to fulfill the life functions and, increasingly, the intertwined social functions. An instantaneous cue brings into action an elaborate series of behaviors that become increasingly automatic. It is important that many complex acts require little conscious control so that many behaviors become established habit. If this were not the case, development would stop with looking, grasping, and placing.

As the child grows she is increasingly aware of the boundaries between her own body and behaviors and those of others; thus the social self emerges. [3] Through the selective response of caretaking adults, the child learns to use only part of the vast array of mental data that is her personal experience. She attunes her behavior first to family culture, then to the wider community culture. This attunement is enhanced by the selectivity of cultural language patterns. Thus, within all children there is the potential for a far larger person than the culture supports. For every quality that emerges and is developed, there are other potential qualities, pieces of original experience of the infant as a unique being, that are relegated to the background of development, often to the depths of the unconscious.

As the certainty of biological survival becomes more firmly established, the one-pointed mind turns to cultural survival. Even though the patterns needed for continued well-being of the body are in place, one's life is still dependent for survival on the group with which one lives. Thus, the focus of development for the child becomes assimilation of cultural patterns. By living in harmony with those around her, she ensures her biological survival. The universal sacrifice for this necessary security is the predicament that we are denied the full potential for development of our individual gifts.

A differing perspective of the world occurs at each moment through such mundane detail as the placement of a child's crib in one corner of a room while a sibling's bed is in the other. Multiplied by millions of such details each individual has a unique experience of the world. This uniqueness is at best obscured, and at worst destroyed, by the enculturation process. Yet culture, the harmonious means for groups of people to live together, is essential to continued existence because of the demanding physical conditions of the planet. Thus, the early years of life are rightly spent in learning the means to cultural harmony at the expense of individual development. The early lessons create adults who automatically follow the patterns of their respective cultures, which is an absolute survival requirement. If individuality were fostered at expense of cultural learning, disharmony would prevail, and the whole group would be endangered because there would be no agreed way to meet emergencies, from small to great.

Benjamin, Julia, and Helene, whose case histories we examined in the previous chapter, each lived in environments that allowed them to fulfill all of the early steps of development. In a different environment they might not have lived to adulthood, or they might have lived but been seriously impaired. In all biological criteria, however, they have healthily survived, establishing physical and mental patterns that allow them now to work in the culture in which they live. Their sophisticated psychological dilemmas actually give evidence that survival development is in place, otherwise their focus would yet be on meeting basic survival needs.

SUBPERSONALITY DEVELOPMENT

Subpersonalities are a natural and normal product of development. As a child grows, the schemas become increasingly complex. New experience and repeated experience, with all its minute variations, brings into the mind immense quantities of information which must be sorted, organized, and stored. Biological functions are mastered, and life is maintained more and more automatically, leaving the child ever freer to join the group in which she is nurtured. As the survival thrust becomes increasingly social, the child is faced with different challenges in each cultural group in order to secure her position in the group. The template for the subpersonalities lies first in biology, and second in the cultural pattern.

The subpersonality is a particular kind of elaborate schema distinguished from other schemas by its social orientation and function. It develops its particular configuration in correlation with the unique personal history and experience of the child. The subpersonality is developed as a psychic tool for negotiating and mastering the child's cultural world and the expectations of that world. The core of each subpersonality is a necessary life function. Over the course of time shells of information and learned behavior are layered onto this core. If the problem solution developed by the early subpersonality does not work or later is no longer applicable to the life, the subpersonality will pass out of use. Those that are effective will be elaborated. When a child is repeatedly impacted with information from her environment about the content of a particular subpersonality core, the clustering of information around this core becomes exceedingly complex. Contained in the layers of the subpersonality is a developing self-image, an image of the world, and the feelings associated with these particular images.

As complexity of information and repetition of specific behaviors increase, the subpersonality becomes an important tool for the child in her negotiation of the world. An important subpersonality will carry "a) a consistent and ongoing set of response patterns to given stimuli, b) a significant confluent history, c) a range of emotions available (anger, sadness, joy, and so on); and d) a range of intensity of affect for each emotion (for example, anger ranging from neutrality to frustration and irritation to anger and rage)."[4] Other subpersonalities with less significant core content, and thus less import in the social situation, will develop some of these characteristics and not others. Assagioli explained that "each subpersonality which is developed enough to have a will, to be consistent, to think and to feel is a miniature personality, and has the same qualities of the general personality."[5]

Benjamin's Wizard is an important subpersonality. The core of this subpersonality is biological and social survival. Living in a family where the father's wrath was expressed in the form of beatings, early fear for safety gave impetus to experimentation with varieties of behavior to find a way of defusing the threatening situation. Development of specific social skills that clustered in this subpersonality, namely, keen intelligent analysis, wit, and showmanship, ensured survival. Even in the adult man the survival-oriented appeasing behavior of the Wizard (such as lowering the head, turning it to the side, and smiling, all the while talking nonstop relating an amusing anecdote) is the original behavior devised to thwart punishment, although now it serves to ingratiate him in society as a charming and entertaining man.

In similar fashion Helene developed Rosie. The core of Rosie is social survival. Helene experimented with various behaviors from babyhood to override the cool, distant, judgmental, and overprotective stance of her parents. Passive, weak, feminine behavior designed to please, accompanied with a wide-eyed, helpless baby stare, became the habitual ploy effective in winning affection in the family system. It was a learned role which as an adult Helene found she was still expected to play in the central family role as only child, and which generalized to become her major defense in the world.

In both the Wizard and Rosie there is a complete subpersonality development. There is an ongoing set of responses used in all social situations containing expectations. Both Benjamin and Helene have used these subpersonalities consistently from early childhood. Each contains a range of intensity of various emotions. The information that led Benjamin and Helene to specific experimental ploys to find an effective survival behavior pattern came directly from the family cultural system, two different subpersonalities emerging from two different family systems.

SUBPERSONALITIES IN THE TOTAL PERSONALITY

Personality is a set of subpersonalities. "A personality is a full congress of orators and pressure groups, of children, demagogues, Machiavellis, Caesars and Christ."[6] Since a personality is a mental system for negotiating the whole social world, each subpersonality performs a specific function complementary to the functions of the other subpersonalities.

Each subpersonality is unique since it is formed through the individual experience of the world. "Our varying models of the universe color our perception and influence our way of being. And for each of them we develop a corresponding self-image and set of body postures and gestures, feelings, behaviors, words, habits, and beliefs."[7] Thus, the personality, the *set* of subpersonalities, is also unique. "Represented are all passions, instincts, all vices, all virtues, all tendencies and aspirations, all faculties and endowments of mankind."[8] Although in each of us are found the same basic qualities, which will develop, interact, combine, and be harmonized following the same basic patterns, for each human being, the development and combinations of these qualities, and the order in which these combinations occur, happens according to a wonderfully individual process, a process that has unique requirements, unique timing, and unique outcome.[9] "Each mind evolves its own internal universe."[10] Cultural pressure, originating in the group function of survival, may produce ostensibly similar patterns in many members of the group—each culture produces certain subpersonality patterns characteristic of that culture. Nonetheless, the pattern of subpersonalities in the whole psyche of the individual is unique.

When Julia remarked that subpersonalities were "those facets of myself that reveal myself," she was reflecting the universal experience that knowledge of the subpersonalities reveals the pattern of the personality, the individual identity.

The ideal personality is a balanced set of subpersonalities in which each subpersonality is strong and its particular talents fully developed. Permanent balance of the subpersonalities is prohibited, first, by the waves of change in successive stages of inner growth, and second, by the impact of ever shifting environmental events. Each state of disequilibrium can foster, on the one hand, chaos and complaint, or, on the other hand, acceptance of the challenge to renew equilibrium, strengthen mastery, and fight the inner battles that build what is called character; whole effective subpersonalities are distilled in the fight, and such qualities as courage, endurance, flexibility, and other positive strong qualities become habitual. Thus it is fortunate that this ideal of balance is never finally achieved.

Subpersonalities develop over a long period of time. As we have seen, subpersonalities have their origins early in life, yet many reach full development and complexity only in middle, or even late, adulthood. By adulthood, in the subpersonalities most used, the layers built onto the core need or idea are thick and complex. The resulting complexity can be rich and rewarding or it can be stultifying and confusing. The talented display the multiple layers of the subpersonalities as creative fruition, while those battered and wounded by life are burdened and confused by the complexity of the multitiered subpersonalities.

Cultural requirements bring about a narrowing of the field

of consciousness in the growing child; the potential of who she might be is narrowed to ensure her group membership. Mental concentration is focused on those skills culturally deemed worthy, those that will enhance her value to the group. Thus some subpersonalities are featured, their growth fostered at the expense of others. One, two, or a few of these subpersonalities become the persona, the habitual stance in meeting the world. Others stand behind the persona immediately ready with the skills necessary for the daily round of events. Those subpersonalities that do not directly contribute to social adaptation are relegated to the unconscious, contributing to daily life little, if at all. In the unconscious some subpersonalities flourish and gain significant development and specificity of action.[11] In later life these subpersonalities become the basis for the developmental crises; the imbalance caused by their lack of expression, as opposed to the dominant expression of the rigid persona, creates the cutting edge of growth.

In the developmental years between six and twelve, when the basic knowledge of one's society is inculcated, the basic set of subpersonalities is also organized. Several subpersonalities become the featured behavioral agents. There is a point in the development of each subpersonality at which there is a "perfect" behavioral solution to the core problem. This achievement of internal equilibrium within a subpersonality creates strong triumphant energy, a fulfilling experience for the child. This basic solution, layered with all subsequent history, may serve the individual well for the whole of her life. There may be a point, however, occurring anytime from shortly after the initial triumph to any time in adulthood, where pain begins because the original solution has become anachronistic. The behavior, so carefully practiced, no longer fits. In some cases there seems to be no other solution, so the original behavior continues though it is no longer effective. In subpersonalities where a behavior was established years ago and has only lately come to light as anachronistic, the layers and layers of precedent and justification for the chosen behavior make change a major undertaking.

An anachronistic subpersonality can be a saboteur. The investment of the subpersonality in its initial purpose, that at one point served the individual well, can cause it to become militant to the extent of sabotage in its effort to maintain the original security that it represented. Little does that subpersonality recognize that its profound drive is out of place in the present life. Nonetheless, there are "no good or bad elements for our being, however negative they may seem to us at first. . . . Subpersonalities become harmful only when they control us. . . . What does it mean to be held a prisoner by a subpersonality? It means that it imposes its characteristic patterns on us to the exclusion of all others." [12] The saboteur subpersonality seeks to dominate conscious thinking and action or exerts subtle influence from an unconscious position that undermines conscious equilibrium.

Initially, subpersonalities are isolated from one another. They represent different poles of thought and function. For instance, introversion and extraversion are opposites in the use of energy, the first being inward conserving, and the second, outward dispersing. Yet these are essential poles of energy balance in all people and are built into different subpersonalities. In all sets of subpersonalities there are such fundamental polarities. The whole thrust of early childhood is to put everything into neat compartments, learning with pride the multidirectional pattern of culture; thus the conflicting opposites are kept apart, minimizing painful turmoil.

In the ideal personality all subpersonality tools are immediately available, not only on an individual basis, which is their initial way of operating, but also in various combinations. A given situation, however, may evoke response from more than one subpersonality, each of different function. Normally, subpersonalities will switch easily from one to another, depending on what subpersonality tools are needed, flowing gracefully as one thought follows the next, [13] a thin thread of memory connecting them. [14] Yet in that switch one can observe a new vocabulary and content of thought, slightly different body postures and movement, together with a new emotional stance experienced in the body.[15] Ideally, subpersonalities are teammates, working singly or in coordination as the situation requires. Like the tools of a carpenter's kit, each has its function, and its skills are honored in view of the goals to be attained; one would never use a saw to hammer, or a hammer to saw. Indeed, the highest acts of creativity and productivity necessitate the presence of balanced, developed subpersonalities operating as a single talent or as a team.

The major functional parts of Benjamin's personality are delineated in the three subpersonalities he initially named. A study of these three shows how he was able to bring about immediate change and establish a long-term growth direction. Benjamin's persona was the Wizard. Bright, clever, charming, disarming, the Wizard met and negotiated the world. Some aspects of the Wizard's behavior, however, were out of date and resulted in sabotage of Benjamin's life: first was the use of alcohol to relieve stress and numb himself; second was storytelling that became a habit of lying; and third was the rageful behavior learned from his father. The child part Quicksilver was largely unconscious, surfacing only at times when intense creative work was possible. The other part, the Giant, a big child in diapers, was the polar opposite of the Wizard: dumb versus smart, awkward versus skillful, clumsy versus smooth. Benjamin's skillful teamwork of Wizard, fine intellect, and Quicksilver, fast creativity, was celebratory, winning him much praise.

Helene presented in her appearance and her behavior a persona that was the result of a narrowed field of consciousness. The wide-eyed child subpersonality persona Rosie, terrorized by Sickle and the family's twenty-three commandments, tightly narrowed Helene's vision to issues of social survival. Her emotional vulnerability, Thorny, alternated expression with Rocket, her drive, ambition, and perfectionism. Thorny's choice of defense—retreat, depression, and, finally, increasing use of alcohol—were intended to preserve her from the manic qualities of Rocket, but they resulted in sabotage of Helene's personal life and work. Before the emergence of Shao and Iman, there was no teamwork between the subpersonalities; each functioned in alienated isolation from the others.

Julia's original persona was Jeanie, the needy, wounded child, and Martha, the perfectionistic housewife. They were both ineffectual and unsatisfying, a narrowing of consciousness creating more negative than positive response in others. The growth edges of Julia's personality were Elizabeth, her spiritual side, which was largely unconscious, and Richard, the artist, modeled on an art teacher rather than Julia's unique artistry, which was only beginning to be expressed. Gayle, the comic, was evident when the burdens of Jeanie and Martha allowed it. At this developmental stage the subpersonalities comprising Julia's personality were largely underdeveloped and lacking in unity.

THE TRANSFORMATION OF SUBPERSONALITIES

The transformation of subpersonalities is a process of change and polishing that can happen naturally or by design. In the natural process, waves of disequilibrium, whether of inner or outer origin, bring with them disruption of the status quo, which allows opportunity for reformation. The stable subpersonality, which is in harmony with individual development, holds firm, but like a stone smoothed by water, the subpersonality impacted by events is polished and honed.

In the development of subpersonalities there is always a problem that is inherent in the way that the mind develops as opposed to the process of socialization. A set of various subpersonalities that represent the individual's unique experience (the "true self") develops from birth. At the same time a set of subpersonalities develops simultaneously that is specifically cultivated for dealing with the social world (the "false self").[16] The transformative process for these two types of subpersonalities is different. In general, the true self subpersonalities are in need of development and strengthening. They have been largely displaced to the unconscious and must be brought to consciousness. The false self subpersonalities, on the other hand, are too dominant and powerful. Their roles need to be modified and reformulated in light of the development of the true self subpersonalities. In actuality these popular designations, true self and false self, do not give recognition to the fact that in appropriate form all subpersonalities have equal place among the personality tools. The denial of early personal qualities in favor of the development of social skills is a necessary but remediable predicament of normal development.

The subpersonality that was originally a poor survival solution and has always detracted from overall well being, or the subpersonality that has become anachronistic, will in the normal course of events be a source of disruption. It is an obstacle to satisfactory need fulfillment, and, more important, thwarts development—the individual is stuck in a mire of subpersonality garbage. The predicament is intensified when there is more than one offending subpersonality; the resulting internal war creates physical tension, high anxiety, and helpless depression. The normal outcome of the war is modification of the inadequate subpersonality, although sometimes the war needs to be repeated many times. At the end of the war, just as in war between nations, there is a redistribution of power and functional territory among the subpersonalities. This is a natural course of change, and the readjustment and polishing process is the basis for all higher development process.

Because of the pain of this process many people ask for assistance. There are many different helpful techniques available, but all techniques ultimately seek to energize the natural healing power of the mythopoetic function of the mind. The mythopoetic is the natural, fundamental language of the mind, a process laid down before the acquisition of a cultural language.[17] The "words" of this primordial language are symbolic pictures, some of which are numinous, that is, highly energized and psychoactive. The mythopoetic function is most familiar in dreams, but it is equally available in conscious thinking in the form of daydreams and rumination on events, which are remembered selectively, thus already moving away from the actual representation of reality and toward symbol. By deliberately choosing to shift mental images, energy changes are brought about first in the mind and then in the body. The energy changes are evidenced in the disappearance of pain and dysfunction from the mind and the body. This simple process is the basis for all effective psychotherapy, past and present.

There are five traditional stages in the change process for subpersonalities.[18] First, there is the initial *recognition* of a subpersonality. In this stage the characteristic pattern of behavior or form of each subpersonality is studied. A transformational shift of energy sometimes occurs in the first recognition of a subpersonality.

The second step is that of *acceptance and honor*. In the discernment of the particular shape of the subpersonality, the core archetype is identified. With this understanding all subpersonalities, even the malevolent saboteur, can be seen in the light of their fundamental essential function and thus become acceptable. "We can raise each subpersonality to its highest potential and thus discover that every psychological aspect has in itself the seed of its own transformation."[19] For many people the recognition process results in a sense of awe before the dramatic unique pattern of one's own personality, and the acknowledgment of the current actuality and the potential unfoldment in the personality that leads naturally to honoring all of the subpersonalities.

The final steps are those of *coordination*, *integration*, and *synthesis*, which happen in tandem. The old pattern of the subpersonality is de-formed, that is, pulled apart, so that reformation or transformation can take place.[20] The core archetype—a meaning, idea, or function—remains stable and is the basis for reformation in harmony with the individual wholeness. As subpersonalities are changed and polished, they function in closer harmony, accepting the "wisdom of equality."[21] At a new level of development even those subpersonalities that are clusters of antisocial behavior no longer fight but find alternative cooperative behaviors that are not antagonistic to the core functions of other subpersonalities and to the development of the person as a whole. For instance, the Wizard allowed Benjamin to accept the challenge of athletic running, rather than "running" away to California. Those subpersonalities whose original purpose was protective, but whose methods now no longer fit the life, are reformed into a new function, honoring the emergence of different security measures.[22] Those who dominate from undeveloped infantile positions like Rosie and Jeanie, give way to the wisdom and effective functioning of more highly developed subpersonalities, honoring their own right contribution as being rightly placed child qualities.

The archetypal core is not only the basis for practical function in the world, but it is also a psychoactive element in the psyche. Its recognition, conscious or unconscious, is the avenue to higher levels of development. The archetypal core is initially connected to the survival of the infant and thus has an extremely pragmatic function. But this core eventually becomes a psychoactive symbol of potential growth, part of the mythopoetic function, impelling movement, change, and healing.[23]

Coordination and integration happen in many ways, but all are contingent on dialogue between conscious and unconscious. In harmony with the creative process, the solution to the problem of reshaping a dysfunctional subpersonality is first a conscious collection of data, then a relaxed state in which the data are reshuffled in the unconscious, followed finally by a new form emerging from the unconscious and elaborated in conscious thinking. Active study is made of the erring subpersonality and the findings are then abandoned to the unconscious. New images of the subpersonality that emerge are then explored, elaborated, and tested. This process can recur a number of times before the transformation and integration of the subpersonality is complete.

As subpersonalities are systematically appraised, and new forms tested, the field of consciousness automatically broadens. More and more of the individual's functioning that had been relegated to the unconscious in honor of societal pressure, is brought to consciousness and held in equilibrium there. The persona, the rigid mask established for meeting the world, changes radically. At first it is made more flexible by adding new subpersonalities, but as confidence increases, "by peeling off each mask one by one, we move ever closer to discovering our underlying core—our true self."[24] Eventually there is freedom to act without a mask, no rigid persona but a flow of subpersonality expression that takes many forms. With this ability comes the realization that the individual behind the persona hides more from herself than from the world. Much of the pain that Julia experienced, for instance, was due to the fact that, governed by a socially conforming set of subpersonalities, a false self, she was so insulated from her true identity that she was handicapped in the development of her potential.

The inclusion and honor of all subpersonalities leads to self-esteem, personal power, flexibility in behavior, compassionate, broad interpersonal relationships, and, above all, a sense of wonder. "In every corner of my soul there is an altar to a different god."[25]

The waves of disequilibrium that hit Benjamin's life—alcoholism that was finally controlled, only to be followed by the loss of his job—sufficiently shook him so that a rapid transformative phase took place. His persona subpersonality Wizard, overtaxed and frustrated, was rageful. The name "Wizard" clearly conveys the archetypal function of intellect as master and defender of Benjamin's world. The original survival solutions established by Wizard were brilliant in the system of his childhood family, but Wizard was programmed to expect the world to recreate the family situation everywhere. Thus, the original useful wariness of Wizard was still functioning in Benjamin's adult world, even doing overtime, in situations where he was safe. This wariness sustained a physical and mental tension that was an exhausting waste of energy. To relieve the exhaustion, inappropriate behaviors were introduced which sabotaged Benjamin's life. Increased use of alcohol numbed his pain; story-telling took so many shortcuts that it became lying; rage, an introjection from his father, did not protect but rather alienated him in socially threatening situations. The mere recognition of Benjamin's subpersonalities, followed by basic analysis of their dynamics, began the transformation process. "Ah," he said, "now I understand." From that point, modification of the Wizard began. "Running away" became athletic running, a healing for both Wizard and Giant. Quicksilver, Benjamin's creativity, a part of his true self that had chosen to hide most of the time in the safety of the unconscious, became conscious, available for creative solutions to problems usually relegated to Wizard. Benjamin experienced an increased breadth of consciousness when Giant began to coordinate with Wizard. Then Quicksilver entered this more peaceful psychic arena, and finally, Betsy, the softer feminine side of Benjamin, began to emerge.

In Helene's family setting, the strong subpersonalities that represented her true self were displaced. Helene realized that Iman, her natural wisdom, another wizard archetype but distinctly her own, was lost when she was about one year old. Trickster, far too merry and mischievous for her serious family, lived mostly in the unconscious giving way to the conscious melodrama. The false self persona fostered by her family was Rosie, the subservient, obsequious child. Her wounded emotional subpersonality, Thorny, a weaker part of her true self, developed early in the unconscious, emerging in periods of illness. By adolescence, Rocket, a false self part, represented the ideal of family values, but was too high-powered for Helene's natural equilibrium. Then began the debilitating swings of manic and depressive moods between Rocket and Thorny.

The first major transformative step in this dysfunctional system was the return of Iman and the disappearance of Rocket. This change happened suddenly, engineered by the unconscious. In the presence of Iman, Trickster became more available. The internal war between Thorny and Rocket, driven by Sickle, stopped. Then began the slow transformation of Thorny, a peeling of masks. In a striking example of the mythopoetic healing process, Helene dreamt she was driving a car and came

75

across a child playing in the road. She identified the child as Thorny, her emotional vulnerability, now out of the thick protective suit. She stopped to take the child out of the road and teach her that the road was no safe place to play. Helene recognized that her emotional subpersonality was now willing to take risks but had no survival knowledge. Shao, the wise subpersonality adopted from a dream image, was the companion feminine energy to Iman. This newly roused and developed maternal energy in Helene provided support and nurturance for her inner child parts, as well as providing the foundation for the family she now hoped to begin.

Julia's transformational process was different from that of Benjamin and Helene. There was no internal war raging between her subpersonalities. Except for the wounded Jeanie, the initial recognition of her subpersonalities was characterized by blandness, particularly in the vague spiritual part Elizabeth. Disruptive external events—her mother's increasing debility, renovation of her house, a hysterectomy, and no doubt her art training as well—shook loose the stable equilibrium she had established in her conventional life. The fear roused by the impending surgery brought about a resurrection of the childhood anxiety that she would become an invalid like her mother. A sudden radical shift in psychic energy resulted in a brilliant mythopoetic healing. In ordinary psychotherapeutic context the emergence of numinous Indian subpersonalities in a blond, blue-eyed American woman would have been considered maladaptive, even bizarre to the extent of a psychotic break. From every point of view, however, the survival solution was masterful. Since Julia did have an Indian great-grandfather, the Indian subpersonalities were a claiming of legitimate family heritage. Moon and Gray Wolf emerged as a spiritual dyad that replaced Elizabeth. Soon, however, Moon also served as a remodeling of the subpersonality Martha, a persona subpersonality that embodied the stereotypically American housewife, anxiety-ridden and compulsive in compliance with early adaptive family false self training. In contrast, Moon and Gray Wolf established a deep inner calm. The agitation of Martha prevented the healing of Jeanie; the multiplied peaceful psychic energy of Moon and Gray Wolf, on the other hand, fostered it. The debilitating agitation of Martha transformed into a new subpersonality, Wind, clear life force energy. The colorful Gayle, overshadowed by Martha's efficient busyness and Jeanie's neediness, became the main persona, radiating charming, good-natured, feminine humor. Gayle is a well-adapted American culture subpersonality. In addition, the Indian subpersonalities opened to Julia a new artistic content and style congruent with her life expression. She was originally drawn to live in an Hispanic and Indian neighborhood, no doubt because of deep unconscious developmental pull. Now, however, due to the clarifying shifts within her, she could identify more closely with these people; her emphasis on the best of their spiritual tradition has been for them and for her a cultural affirmation.

THE NEUTRAL OPEN SPACE OF CENTER

Center is a psychological space apart from the subpersonalities. It is often, but not always, experienced psychologically and physically as being at the center of the organism. Perception of Center is that it is an open, calm, quiet psychological space focused on the immediate. In comparison to the partisan quality of subpersonalities, Center is psychologically neutral. It acts as the mechanism for the focus of attention in the psyche, like a hand that moves a spotlight or adjusts a tuning system.

In psychological literature of the East and the West, Center has been known by various names.[26] Designations like *the personal self, the self,* or *the I* denote the experience of Center as a personal essence. Assagioli noted the absolute importance of self-identification, that is, moving out of subpersonality constriction into the openness of self.[27] Neither term, I nor self, however, points to the separateness of this psychological entity from the subpersonalities. Center has also been called the *observer*, reflecting the experience of Center as distanced and impartial in relation to subpersonality dynamics. Designations of *no-self* or *void* reflect different but complementary emphasis of other ways of experiencing Center. *No-self* simply refers to the fact that Center is outside the usual self, the subpersonalities. *Void* refers to the experience of Center as empty. Center is often elusive and difficult to identify precisely because in comparison to other psychological elements, it is experienced as empty.

Center is the psychological position of the newborn. As development is presently understood it is possible that subpersonalities begin formation before birth. But fundamentally, the baby is psychologically centered, gathering and sorting the data about the world that form the basis for the subpersonalities. As the child develops, psychological focus shifts from Center to the developmental mastery tasks of the subpersonalities. In many cases by the time the individual reaches maturity, awareness of Center is lost through complete identification with the subpersonalities. At some point in maturity Center must be reclaimed for development to proceed.

It is common for people to experience Center naturally in several ways. The stilling of the thought flow, the patter of the subpersonalities, allows an experience of Center. Herein lies the appeal of formal meditation. Center is often experienced in natural settings apart from society; there is an automatic silencing of the subpersonalities when confronted by the awesome natural world. Another situation where Center is dominant is during an emergency; information is rapidly absorbed and action initiated, bypassing the inefficiency of the subpersonalities. Specific techniques can also be used to reintroduce awareness of the normal psychological state of Center.[28] When reconnection to natural Center is difficult, this psychological awareness, so important to the process of integration of the subpersonalities, can be established through the creation of an external center, a model who acts as a center, perhaps a psychotherapist, or an image of a numinous personage, a hero from history or present-day.[29] This psychoactive image of Center is sometimes called a guru. When the individual has developed an active awareness and use of her own natural psychological Center, the external center is no longer needed.

Ideally, individuals initiate all life function from Center, which is immediate, focused on the present, and uncluttered by past history and future anticipation. From Center the world is perceived accurately. The healthy psyche is "managed" by a well-developed Center, and it is from Center, the director's chair, so to speak, that the appropriate subpersonality to act in a situation is selected. The transformed subpersonalities are the well-polished tools that bring about effective action.

There are a number of stages in the adult rediscovery of Center. In the first stage, Center may be completely unrecognized. Well-developed dominant subpersonalities have completely eclipsed the original Center. These subpersonalities manage and direct the psyche in place of Center, always with less than optimal results. The orientation of these subpersonalities to specific, limited survival goals means that their management of the psyche is biased and incomplete, and discrimination against nondominant subpersonalities is inevitable. Thus, the full functioning skills of the individual are truncated in honor of a few survival goals.

The next stage of the adult development of Center is, then, its recognition. This step is a basic reclaiming of the mental space of infancy; where it was excluded through education and individual skill mastery, it is now reinstated as an essential working part of the psyche. Its state of calm observation, quiet objectivity, total intrepidity, immense absorption of accurate data, and wide consciousness are the same for the adult as they were for the infant. The natural reaction of the individual upon rediscovery of Center is "Ah, salvation at last," meaning that she feels that she has been rescued from the tyranny of the subpersonalities. It is the simple psychological experience of the salvation sought by every religion. In this recognition process the psychological focus, the life enthusiasm, is shifted to Center. The war between the subpersonalities miraculously stops, if only momentarily, and the individual steps into silence and peace.

The third step is the return of the war of the subpersonalities.

High enthusiasm cannot be sustained indefinitely. As enthusiasm for Center begins to wane, it becomes all too apparent that the understanding and skills of Center are as yet weak. The dominant subpersonalities reassert their authority, their long-practiced, strong skills. Commonly the strong subpersonalities initially distrust Center, seeing that state as a vague utopia not at all connected with what is needed for "real" living, in other words, survival. Consciousness narrows. There is pain and depression, a feeling of helplessness as the war seems stronger than ever. Center is again eclipsed.

In the next stage the individual reaffirms that the war is exhausting and unproductive and that Center, though glimpsed briefly, is ideally what she wants for her life. A commitment to the practice of Center returns, varying in intensity from vacillation to consistent strength. Like relearning a forgotten skill, the practice is undertaken in many forms. Because of the quality of Center, this relearning is not an exciting process; it is much like practicing scales in learning to play a musical instrument. Many people prefer the soap opera of the subpersonalities. Many are reluctant to engage the skills of Center because they experience initially a loss of identity,[30] which is actually the first step in the reformation of the subpersonalities into a more refined working order.

The fifth and last step is the actual development of the skills of Center. The open quality of Center must be practiced until the location of Center can be identified in the psyche, and "stepping" to Center from the subpersonalities can be accomplished at will. The firmly established Center is then available for the development of skills within the functioning psyche. The "executive," Center, has an office and now must begin to mesh with the workings of the organization. If Center was abandoned at the infant stage, though it holds the fullness of the individual, it had no practice in the actual workings of a biological and social organism in the world.

Center's first involvement is advisory. From Center can come wide discriminating vision. Initially, Center observes, and then from this perspective, makes suggestions to the subpersonalities. Over time, though the subpersonalities may still fight for power, they come to recognize the breadth of Center's contribution and what might be called a functional respect grows. Center's advisory capacity is highly facilitating to the transformation of the subpersonalities.

Finally, Center takes on management duties. As with all good managers, at times Center is directive, speaking from a wide vision, but much of the time it is merely facilitating and coordinating the whole action that is initiated and emerging from the subpersonalities. "From the Center, we can get into this subpersonality or that, we can regulate them, correct them, care for them. The knack to be learned is flexibility, so as not to be dominated by our subpersonalities, not to suffocate their expression and ignore their needs—in other words, to have a sense of compassionate, playful mastery."[31] In summary of the final developmental stages of Center, Assagioli says, "In order to strengthen and make stable the pure self-awareness of the observer, it is necessary to have periods of *inner* silence, gradually longer, to make what is called *the void* in the field of consciousness. Then one discovers another important function of the self: that it is not merely an observer, but it can also be active in *modifying* the personality. That is, it can direct and regulate the various functions of the psyche. It can be a will-er."[32] Commenting on the return of the subpersonality to pure archetypal form, the psychologist Marie Fay described an image: "I saw a circle and the subpersonalities as pie shaped, getting less diffuse and more 'pure' as they near the Center, or, perhaps more accurately, as the person follows them to Center. They then become like arrows to the Center. The experience of a negative subpersonality is different; when it moves toward Center, it takes on density, a resistance and hiding, which becomes more intense as it closes on Center. At some point, like an alchemist's fire, the intense heat breaks apart the density and there is numinosity in the purity of archetypal form revealed."[33]

Center is the executive branch of the psyche; it is never a subpersonality. As it focuses on the present, it coordinates the vast resources of the individual. Subpersonalities contain the personal history and are oriented toward future survival; elaborate safety rules based on history and future expectation emerge from the subpersonalities. Subpersonalities are formula oriented; each has learned a specific way to ensure safety. Since it is not preoccupied with survival, which has been taken care of by the development of subpersonalities, there is no fear in Center. Instead it can formulate the grand developmental plan that honors the transformation and balancing of all subpersonalities to their highest potential.

If we take a building as an analogy for development, then Center is the elevator with many levels. It is initially experienced and understood at the immediate level of functioning of the subpersonalities. Its deepest or highest level is the Higher Self, which is theoretically a planning center in the deepest or highest unconscious. At this level Center and Self are one. Between this level and the subpersonality level there are many experiential levels of Center.[34] Theoretically, Center can be interpreted as a projection of the Self into the conscious mundane life. On the various floors of the building, which represent specific levels of development, all the components of the subpersonalities can be recognized, studied, altered, and transformed, like changing the interior decorating of an actual building. This process is referred to as *translation*, while movement to another floor, another level of development, is actual *transformation* of the whole personality, or even the whole psyche, at ever higher levels.[35] If the subpersonalities move to another floor via Center, the elevator, they are on a different level of development. Center, through its facilitation of the transformational process of the subpersonalities, prepares to leap to a higher level of function.[36] As subpersonalities move from one floor to another, they move closer to the Self, the inner programming template that in the building analogy is the penthouse.

The initial work with subpersonalities aims at freeing the psyche from the focus of survival tasks. As the subpersonalities are deeply understood there is the natural realization of the enormous expenditure of time and energy on survival that is unnecessary and fruitless. The goal then is to relegate survival tasks to habit, to automated process.

There are several results of this work. First of all, in the deep exploration, hidden subpersonality pieces are brought to consciousness, which results in a broadening of the field of consciousness. Second, there is freeing of energy bound in the repression of hidden subpersonalities. Third, there emerges an awareness of the possibilities of the development of the superconscious. And fourth, there is momentum toward superconscious development with parallel development of subpersonalities. Psychological movement happens in the field of consciousness and in the unconscious; it becomes wider, deeper, and higher. It opens to the reality of the universe.

INTEGRATION: THE DEVELOPMENT OF GENIUS

The integration process is the heart of performance. Integration can be brought about by a structured personality analysis, followed by a plan of development of skill based on understanding. Or it can be a process in which the performer follows a master, who has followed a master, who has followed a master; in this case the process whereby one comes to mastery is mysterious and not altogether describable. Nonetheless, always, the essential ingredients of integration are drawing the individual to Center, eliminating the distracting noise of conflicted subpersonality voices, and balancing skilled resources. A look at the mastery of any performer in any field reveals that those who stand out have burned away the dross of subpersonality complexes that interfere with their maximum achievement of potential. If you think of an admired performer, however, you will see that the words "maximum achievement of potential" have a particular personal color, a unique expression, that is inextricably bound to the unique human personality. At no time is she a machine. Her personal self, using the shape of her subpersonality

83

tools, is the very vehicle through which she succeeds, whether she specifically identifies what is happening on a conscious level or not.

In history there are many examples of lives where the pattern of living resulted in the maximization of total potential, that is, in integration and wholeness. Consider first an example from Japanese culture. Miyamoto Musashi was born to a noble family in 1584. As a boy he was large for his age and always boisterous. His childhood talent lay in the area of pugilistic skill; by the age of sixteen he left home to undertake the warrior pilgrimage. He single-mindedly focused his attention on the samurai discipline of kendo, the art of swordsmanship, to seek enlightenment. His success was so great in the contests with other samurai that he was considered invincible by the age of twenty-eight. At this point, he stopped using real swords, substituting training swords of wood, because he was acknowledged a master and no longer needed to kill in order to prove his strength and skill. Nonetheless, he continued to maintain a rigorously disciplined life, pursuing absolute perfection in all undertakings. When he was in his fifties, he became known as a consummate graphic artist, his paintings and calligraphy being now among Japan's treasures. He was also a sculptor, founding a school of metal-work that continues today. In addition, he wrote poems and songs. It was during this period that he felt that at last he completely understood samurai strategy. He said, "When you have attained the way of strategy, there will be not one thing that you cannot understand."[37] *A Book of Five Rings*, a guide to strategy that he wrote two weeks before he died, is studied now in Japan and the United States, not by samurai, but by keen business strategists.

A similar story of personal development is recorded in Western history. Leonardo da Vinci was born in Italy in 1452. Because he showed early talent in drafting, his father apprenticed him at the age of seventeen to Verrocchio, a well-established artist in Florence. By the time Leonardo was twenty, he was acknowledged as a master of painting. After the painstaking training of his apprenticeship, Leonardo entered the service of Duke Ludovico in Milan, where he had a variety of duties: court portraits, production of pageants, playing the lyre and singing, designing and manufacturing machines of war, and even production of a central heating system for the palace. It was at this time that Leonardo began keeping notebooks of his wide-ranging interests. He approached both science and art in the same thorough manner. He continually stretched his resources to become expert in every field that interested him. His paintings are still celebrated throughout the world, and his inventions, created hundreds of years before their time, are studied today. He designed bridges, highways, a printing press, weapons, and scientific instruments. He designed the first skin-diving equipment and the diving bell, both viable designs today. He discovered the principle of air-conditioning. His is the first known sketch of a parachute. He was first to understand what fossils were. He designed an automobile and two types of aircraft. He made accurate anatomical drawings and was the first to question some of Galen's medical explanations. No one in history achieved so much in so many different fields.

In Western history, Leonardo da Vinci is called a genius, but the psychological life path of genius has not yet been deeply explored. If we consider the lives of the two geniuses, Musashi and Leonardo, heroes of their respective cultures, we find elements in common. First, there was boyhood talent. Then there was unstinting discipline and lifelong pursuit of mastery. And finally, there was a blossoming of knowledge and skill far beyond the initial limited area of discipline undertaken in youth. We have no reports in either case that in their youth they showed talent in more than a single area. Rather, the focus in both lives was on discipline with a single focus that required arduous work. In later life, however, both experienced burgeoning superior creativity in many areas; it seemed they could master any area of knowledge or skill.

Musashi and Leonardo stand out in history for discovering

in themselves multiple talents and skills after they had pursued one discipline for many years. The degree of excellence they achieved in many fields is seen as remarkable and forever admirable. Such development is a potential, however, for all of us. We admire it deeply because it touches a yearning in us for such wholeness. In the archetypes of the subpersonalities of all people, a configuration of potential exists. Indeed, we see in Musashi and Leonardo the rich development of shadow subpersonalities. Clearly, there is potential for talent in every subpersonality, each different from the others. In this case, "talent" means the potential for the development of skill. If the development of each subpersonality is viewed in terms of growth of performance potential, rather than in terms of merely eliminating complexes and conflicts to make life more comfortable, a sudden wealth appears in the arduous task of self-development.

Musashi's form of self-development, the way of the sword, was keenly influenced by the path of enlightenment known as Zen. The characteristics of the disciplines influenced by Zen training in the Japanese culture, whether it be swordsmanship, archery, flower arranging, or any of the other arts, are all the same. Around 1950, Eugen Herrigel wrote *Zen in the Art of Archery*, a slim book quoted in all the current literature on performance psychology. He was a German philosophy professor who studied archery with a Zen master for six years in Japan. He worked arduously during this period, blindly following the direction of the archery master, and facing seemingly insurmountable walls of frustration. He continually experienced the "desolate feeling of attempting the impossible."[38] His experience is illuminating. Day after day, he accepted the discipline of the practice sessions. On his way to the practice studio, he focused his full attention on archery, holding the idea in mind that archery was the most important and real aspect of his life. In the practice session, he concentrated exclusively on his breathing and experienced "impermeable layers of silence"[39] through which no distraction penetrated. Learning not to grieve over bad shots, nor to rejoice over good, he attained freedom from the buffetings of pain and pleasure.[40] Single-minded devotion to the ceremonial purpose of archery was necessary to establish the right presence of mind. In the right presence of mind he experienced the mind and spirit as being everywhere at once because of lack of attachment to anything, in essence like the image of water filling a pond that is ready to flow off at any moment; and also as a primordial state of mind, the symbol of which, the circle, is not experienced as "empty of meaning for him who stands within it."[41] In this practice, shooting becomes "not shooting"; art becomes artless; and the archer becomes an unmoved Center.[42] In this practiced psychic state, there is a loosening and equability of all powers, a collectedness and presence of mind that places the archer on the brink of new possibilities.

Herrigel undertook the discipline of Center. The focus for the beginner and for the master is the flow of the breath. Emptying the mind is supremely important so that the mind is not attached to anything, and thus can move in any direction instantaneously. Zen scholars point out that Zen practice is the rediscovery of the everyday mind and ordinary life; absolute simplicity like the clear mind of a child is the prerequisite for the greatest mastery. They describe what we refer to here as centering. Centering is the openness to move in any direction with one's resources; centering is the way to transcend one's bound life experience; and centering is the simplicity we have at birth. Out of the practice of Center comes mastery of technique, whether it be archery, flower arranging, cycling, playing the piano, or understanding the genetics of corn.

SUBPERSONALITIES AND PERFORMANCE

Every subpersonality has a talent that can be developed. The source of such talent is the core of each subpersonality—the basic functional purpose that motivated the development of that particular personality facet. This functional purpose is always connected with some aspect of survival. Over the years elements of life history are layered on top of the subpersonality core. These layers are also generated by the pursuit of the basic functional purpose and the many behavioral experiments trying to fulfill the basic function. And finally, there is a formula of behaviors and beliefs that the subpersonality has arrived at as the final solution to achieve the fulfillment of the basic life function. Some subpersonalities thus carry considerable psychological baggage. In Center, on the other hand, one is free of the baggage and the formulas of all the subpersonalities. The subpersonalities do not disappear, but are now background, temporarily out of the spotlight. The mind state becomes again pristine like that of the young child. Potential is unlimited.

If there is a desire or a need to develop a talent, one makes a choice to accept that discipline. Starting from Center, an intense polishing process begins. The talent of one subpersonality is isolated, and a strategy is devised for development. In the case of music, art, or athletics, meticulous physical practice is undertaken to develop the requisite body skill. If it is a different talent, other skills must be mastered. The history and behavioral experiments that are part of the subpersonality baggage are examined to determine if they contribute to, or detract from talent development. The formula that the subpersonality carries as the ultimate solution, the ultimate behavior, is revised repeatedly in light of growing skills. As the skills develop, the understanding of the goal of mastery is revised over and over. Thus the formula must be different with each step in understanding. Standing in the shoes of a subpersonality is too close-range for this process. Being in Center is essential for objective negotiation for the change. Yet at the same time, passion for the development resides in Center; subpersonality passion will only lead to imbalance.

In the process of development of the talent of one subpersonality, the other subpersonalities must be examined to see how they contribute or distract and modified accordingly. As this process proceeds, there is a spiraling of consciousness level. The developing subpersonality is moving to ever higher levels, and in the process drags the others along. They are necessarily supportive of the talent development and integrated at ever new levels. Competence then in one area leads to new competence in other areas.

Genius then can be defined in one way in terms of a particular subpersonality developmental process. There is focus on one talent in one subpersonality. The discipline to develop that talent is undertaken and pursued relentlessly. Superior development of one talent, one subpersonality, occurs while all other subpersonalities remain at a more ordinary level of development. Mozart is a famous example of this type of development.

In a second type of genius, however, as one subpersonality rises to higher levels of development through thorough discipline, other subpersonalities develop unconsciously as well. There is then suddenly a blossoming of skill and knowledge beyond the original limited talent area, as other subpersonalities emerge. Learning in one subpersonality produces learning in other subpersonalities. Also, at the higher level of development, the developmental process of other subpersonalities is rapid, free from the usual conflicts that afflict subpersonalities at lower levels. Examples of this type of development are Leonardo and Musashi, and more recent figures like Dag Hammarskjöld, who was secretary general of the United Nations and a mystical poet, or Peter Ustinov, the well-known actor, who is also a historian and writer.

In the first type a subpersonality functions on the level of the superconscious, as an isolated pocket in the superconscious, while the rest of the personality remains at a less developed level. In the second instance, there is a movement of the general level of consciousness toward superconscious function.[43]

In both cases there is the governance of Center. Herrigel accepted the discipline of learning to shoot with bow and arrow. His training was an intense experience of Center to the point that all subpersonalities were lost from sight. The vehicle for this mental training was to stop inner chatter and focus on the breath. Thousands of hours of practice led to Herrigel's experience: from the unmoved Center, the total detachment at will from any subpersonality influence, and the experience of mind and spirit as everywhere, which is complete openness and flexibility. In this disciplined practice the subpersonalities are polished so that they perform as finely honed tools under the absolute direction of Center.

5

THE UNFOLDING
PSYCHE OF HUMANKIND

THE SPECTRUM OF CONSCIOUSNESS: EARLY LEVELS

In numerous writings, Ken Wilber has presented a profound summation and interpretation of ideas from Eastern and Western disciplines, developing a design for a cohesive description of human development. In addition to history, he clearly suggests the shape of future psychic development of the individual and of the human race. He refers to this course of human development as the spectrum of consciousness. The subpersonality approach to the psyche is in harmony with Wilber's comprehensive theory.

It is the contention of many traditions that we, the human race, are presently midway to the fullest development of consciousness. Viewed in these terms, the focus of this book is precisely on this midway stage: how to recognize it, how to analyze it, how to disidentify from it, and how to transcend it. Wilber refers to this stage in human development as the *egoic*.[1]

The most important aspects of the egoic stage of development are precisely those of the subpersonality process. Presently, humankind's primary tool for operating in the world is thought, particularly of the nature of dialogue.[2] With the development of language, control of the environment has shifted to inner mental manipulation: before acting, the individual tests in his thinking whether his action will work to his benefit. In some situations one course of action is effective; in other situations he finds other courses of action are necessary. Because he must develop a repertoire of ways of getting his needs met, he develops many ways of being in the world, many masks, many personae, many subpersonalities. The designation *egoic* could be thought of in the sense of attachment to the conscious personality, akin to the popular meaning of the word *ego*.

Jung's description of the shadow process is important at the egoic level. The individual finds that some of the ways he has of dealing with the environment are effective, but socially unacceptable, and thus are pushed into the unconscious, becoming shadow to the dominant persona. Originally, elements of the personality that become shadow are developmentally potential personae, but punishment, or threat of punishment, by social agents results in these natural personae being repressed to become shadow parts speaking in the background of the conscious persona.

Wilber discusses individual development in the context of human history, and suggests, as have other historians of consciousness, that the development of the species is paralleled in that of the individual. Presently, the species has reached a level of development where the most common psychological process and expression is egoic. There are, however, three preceding stages to this present level of development, all well documented in archeological and anthropological data. No population at any historical time is homogeneous; though the most typical psychological functioning may presently be egoic, there are always individuals representing other developmental stages both lower and higher.

The characteristics of the three developmental stages preceding the egoic are not unfamiliar. Wilber calls these stages the uroboric, the typhonic, and membership. [3] The names of the first two refer to symbols from ancient mythology that had for early peoples archetypal meaning comprehensive of the life experience. The *uroboric* is symbolized by the uroboros, an image of a snake biting its tail, thus forming a circle. This symbol, better than any words, represents earliest man's embeddedness in nature, a timeless, spaceless lack of separation or distinction between the individual and the whole. Rather than mental, as in the egoic, the approach to life is instinctual and the focus of function is alimentary.

The *typhonic* represents an advance over the functioning of the uroboric. The Typhon, half man and half serpent, symbolizes the beginning of the emergence of mind, yet is a being still much a part of nature. This is mind differentiated from body. The typhonic stage of functioning is dominated by instinctual urges and the pleasure principle. This is Freud's primary process, the id. Body and object are not differentiated, which creates magical rapport between the individual and the object in the world that he wishes to operate upon. Telepathic hunting magic, which is akin to the telepathy experienced by the young child, is an actual psychological effect because of the lack of differentiation between mind and body. In early man there was awakening to awareness of mortality and to his vulnerability and the possibility of pain. Magical thinking was believed to be the best tool for self-preservation. From this stage through the egoic stage, there is need to actively reduce anxiety in the face of threats to survival. Each stage of development deals in a characteristic way with the predicament of vulnerability inherent in being a creature on this planet.

In the *membership* stage the anxiety was lessened historically through the development of farming. Vulnerability does not seem so great if you plant, harvest, and have storehouses full of grain. Connected with this newly invented planning for safety on a yearly basis was the development of language, which represented the true emergence of mental and conceptual function. Mental skills were necessary for transcending the present and planning for future well-being. The cooperation between groups of people for the accomplishment of their long-range goals necessitated delay of impulse and sublimation of emotional-sexual energies that had been characteristic of the preceding typhonic stage. The young child goes through a comparable mental developmental stage between the ages of about two and four when the child begins to understand time sequence, delay, and anticipation, and begins to cooperate with others in the meeting of his own needs.

Wilber points out that it would be impossible to leap from the magical thinking of the typhonic to the logic of the egoic; the intermediary step between magic and logic is the mythic thinking of the membership stage. Myth is combined magic and logic. The great mythologies were created in the historic membership period of human development. Likewise, fine children's literature, even that written today, is mythic; it combines magic and logic.

According to Wilber's theoretical framework, distilled from many sources and also in harmony with the experiential psychosynthesis subpersonality framework, there is in development no abandonment of earlier levels. "All the earlier fragments and lesser levels, all the prior stages, are taken up and preserved in the succeeding higher stages. Each higher stage *negates*, or goes beyond, but also *preserves*, or integrates, all prior stages, so that they are 'not annulled but fulfilled.' "[4]

Cursory inspection of subpersonalities of various individuals reveals that many of them could not be seen as egoic in their function. The cluster of subpersonalities described by an individual characteristically presents many functions other than those associated with the egoic level of development. In fact, in the healthy personality, all the early developmental stages (uroboric, typhonic, and membership) are represented.

Wilber considers several psychological principles important in the relationship between the developmental layers within the individual.[5] On any given level one can build, expand, or move elements of the level around; he calls this process *translation*. He cites the analogy with the floor of a building; you can move the furnishings around in any way that you like. Knowing your subpersonalities, experimenting with new forms and expression of each, in his analogy, is like interior decorating of the psyche.

The process of moving from level to level is *transformation*. In Wilber's analogy, transformation is moving from one floor to another floor, each floor representing a different developmental level, a different way of functioning. Movement takes place through three steps: differentiation, transcendence, and operation.[6] *Differentiation* is similar to the psychosynthesis concept of disidentification—stepping back from the personality, describing it, and thus objectifying it—the point being that a part of the personality is only a part at a particular level and is not the whole of the person. The second step, *transcendence*, is a natural consequence of the first process. Stepping back and objectively seeing the different aspects of the personality produces a natural opening to new possibilities, a natural fluidity because of easy boundary crossing between the usually isolated elements, and a receptivity to understanding of higher levels. Subpersonalities begin to move to new levels of functioning, but it is never a uniform process. The subpersonalities most involved in the individual's stable functioning in his world maintain this stability, while other subpersonalities begin experimentation with new concepts and activities of a higher level. There are many variations of this basic process.

The third step in this transformation process, *operation*, refers to the fact that once a level of functioning has been transcended, then it can be acted upon. When a person is identified with a subpersonality, he only sees through the eyes of that subpersonality, claiming as his self the values and actions of this part of him. When he disidentifies from that part, steps back, and is able to appraise the relative merits of this part's actions and values, he transcends this part's limited functioning and then is able to operate on it; in other words, he can pick and choose what he would have this part express in his life, exactly what tool this part is in the whole of him. If we are talking in Wilber's framework, a whole person would be one not only acknowledging all the pieces of himself, all the levels of development within him, but also the very ragged process of transformation itself, the growing tips in all the branches of the being, reaching out into ever new uncharted territory.

DEVELOPMENTAL LEVELS OF THE FUTURE

Wilber's description of past developmental levels is clear and convincing; his suggestion of things to come, gleaned from many sources, is equally clear, amounting to a veritable treasure map which gives sense of direction and the basic territorial features of future development. Not many have consistently experienced these higher stages. Thus, like a treasure map, we have described for us only a few rough features of the terrain and a few signposts. At this point in time we are all explorers and treasure seekers; it will be in the future that the road and the treasure are fully described.

The first higher stage described by Wilber is the *centauric*, the last evolution of the egoic.[7] At this level the work of integration is accomplished. In the centauric stage, "not only does an individual normally master his various personae, he tends to differentiate from them, disidentify with them, transcend them. He thus tends to *integrate* all his possible personae into a *mature ego*— and then he starts to differentiate or disidentify with the ego altogether, so as to discover, via transformation, an even higher order unity than the altogether egoic-self."[8] The conception of the personality system as the configuration of subpersonalities is part of a centauric understanding. In the centauric there is growing appreciation for the symbolic process in general, whether those symbols are found in subpersonality images, dreams, synchronistic events, or other pattern awareness.

The *subtle* level of development is the first transpersonal level.[9] The transpersonal levels are all characterized by a disidentification with the personality as it is known in the egoic, moving into an increasing unity of the psyche with the broader patterns of the universe. The subtle has two levels: the *low-subtle*, also referred to as the psychic, and the *high-subtle*. In the *low-subtle*, psychic experience is often available though not specifically sought. The low-subtle thinking operates on the results of formal egoic thinking (if a, then b) by establishing networks of relationships between egoic thought patterns, which is characteristic of subpersonality work. It is a higher order synthesizing between egoic thought patterns, a capacity which "apprehends a mass network of ideas, how they influence each other, and what their relationships are." [10] Wilber refers to this process as vision-logic. At a highly developed state, the low-subtle level experiences deep insight or even noetic or numinous illumination. All three case histories presented in chapter six illustrate some aspects of low-subtle process.

Those who operate on the *high-subtle* level are often referred to as saints. Though they may function in quite ordinary ways for most of their lives, they also may experience highly numinous images and symbolic visions of which saints in all religions have written. Some visions are spiritual guides, angelic beings, or *ishtadevas*, who are, in essence, personal deity forms. Jung would have interpreted this experience as evidence in the life of the Higher Self. Sometimes characteristic of these visions also are subtle sounds and audible illuminations. More important than specific content of the visions is the characteristic rapt absorption in numinous images. It is "not a *loss* of consciousness but *intensification* of consciousness through higher-order development, evolution, transcendence and *identification*." [11] This identification process is similar to the psychological growth process seen in the young child, but unlike the young child who focuses intently on adult figures, the subtle level adult focuses intently on god figures, the highest form of qualities, archetypes. "We are consciously meeting and becoming (via higher identification) ourselves in our archetypal and eternal nature." [12] This level is the "seat of the actual archetypes." [13] As subpersonalities evolve, they become more and more archetypal: simple, clear, and powerful expression of a set of qualities. The numinous power of the *ishtadeva* image, the guide image, or the angelic being image, draws the saint into his own development, his own archetypal expression. In the process of identification what is really happening is the emergence of Self in its highest form, but at the same time, in this same process, it is immersion into the Godhead, into the Universal.

Those involved in the *causal* level are referred to as sages. The realization of God happens within the person. The Self is clarified to the point of being a projection of God into the world (*lower causal*). [14]

In both Jung's and Assagioli's work the Higher Self is considered to be connected to the universal, to God. Finally, there is complete transcendence and release into formless consciousness, where there is no Self, no God, no subject, no thingness apart from consciousness (higher causal). Psychologically, this means that there is now realization that the seeming separateness of living on the planet had obscured the individual union with the Divine. The sage no longer contemplates divinity; he becomes divinity, a bit of God in the world. He becomes radically egoless, free of a separate self sense. Yet, "this state appears perfectly, radically, paradoxically *ordinary*, as in the famous Zen saying, 'How marvelous, how transcendental this! I draw water, I carry fuel.' "[15]

We have available to us only a few descriptive terms and a few characteristics, and so the transpersonal levels of development are only points on a treasure map. Within our experience and current understanding and knowledge, however, there are specific elements which help to paint a more complete picture of the terrain ahead. Since much attention has already been paid to the centauric in the description of subpersonality integration in this text, we shall move now to consideration of transpersonal levels.

BRINGING THE SUBTLE DOWN TO EARTH

Wilber's definition of the subtle level of growth is primarily gleaned from writings of obscure (to Westerners) religious adepts. Since the focus of this study is the process of living in the world in a complete way, it would be far more pertinent to explore the experience of the subtle in people who have lived more observable lives. The choice of individuals presented here is quite random; there are many more admired heroes of all the world cultures who could be studied in this way. Note that the subtle has great variety, that it too like all other developmental levels is expressed very much in terms of the unique configuration of the individual. These few models whose stories and ideas are presented briefly here are invitation to the reader to find his own models for the subtle among those he admires.

Both of the subtle levels will be considered interchangeably since it would be artificial to rigidly categorize the fluid process of the transpersonal levels. Besides, we do not have very much knowledge about these levels of development; thus any sort of pronouncement would be premature.

Definition of the subtle gives the appellation of "saint" to those involved in subtle experience. This is an unfortunate word in our culture; connotations of "saintly" are negative, implying a dedication to the divine that excludes the world. Sometimes recognition of some special goodness will win the description of "saintly," but embedded in this admiration is apprehension and mystery, as though certainly no "normal" person could manifest this behavior. The saints of the Christian church are not held in reverence in our general culture, but are seen primarily as people living odd lives in the Middle Ages—at best disciplined, at worst crazy. In fact, from their stories, the selection of these people as worthy of canonization gives more indication of the values of the human institution of the Church than it does information on the developmental process of the subtle.

St. Margaret of Scotland, however, lived a whole life. She is the only saint canonized by Rome who lived all of her life in family. She was queen of Scotland, married to King Malcolm III, who succeeded the reign of Macbeth. Born in the English royal line of succession, her family was forced to live in exile in Hungary because of turmoil in England. From very young, she was trained by Benedictines to live an ordered life of work and prayer. As she approached adulthood, she knew herself called to a religious life, but it was decided for her around 1065 by powerful royal alliances that she would marry Malcolm, then king of Scotland. Since Margaret was far better educated and cultured than her husband, he honored her and gave her power in many national issues. When Margaret died near the age of fifty, she had much to her credit. She was known as a contemplative, having kept her original intent to live the life of an austere religious, accomplishing this largely through rising long before dawn to perform her religious practice. She is credited with the reformation and firm establishment of the Church of Scotland. Through her diplomatic skills, peace was established between the warring Scottish clans. She brought culture and dignity to the court of Scotland. Endlessly, she worked for the improvement of the standard of living for the Scottish people. Margaret was loved for her limitless compassion for the needy; in the first hour of each day she personally ministered to the poor who came to her. She bore and raised with devotion eight children, three of whom were kings of Scotland, the youngest reigning twenty-nine peaceful years.

An extraordinary array of personality qualities was needed to live this life. Details of her personal experience are lost in the obscurity of time and legend, but the bare bones of her story paint a portrait of rounded individual growth and achievement. It can be inferred from her accomplishment that she functioned psychologically in the subtle. The breadth of her achievement indicates first a wide development of personal qualities; her impact on the nation implies rich integration of these qualities. The scope of vision logic is apparent in the long-lasting effect of her innovation; a marked change occurred in Scottish society, the influence of which persists today. One guesses her ability to be absorbed in the divine, to be nourished by her spiritual practice, by the fact that she did not waver in faithful religious practice though the distractions of her mundane life were enormous. It has been said of her that "no more beautiful character has been recorded in history."[16]

Nine centuries later a leader appeared on the international scene who could be compared with Margaret in many ways.

Dag Hammarskjöld, the second secretary general of the United Nations, had a combination of personal qualities that fostered a dedication to work and life goals similar to Margaret's. As she sought to establish peace among the warring clans of Scotland, he endeavored to establish peace among nations. Her personal devotion to spiritual discipline, which resulted in her fighting for the firm establishment of the Scottish church, is seen in the primacy of inner spiritual direction in Hammarskjöld's life and his insistence on the establishment of a spiritual heart for the United Nations, the chapel in the New York center. Both leaders worked extremely hard. Margaret's medieval practices of mortification of the flesh are mirrored in Hammarskjöld's penitent focus on his faults and the ever present allure of death. As she powerfully used her education and culture to serve God and the Scottish people, so Hammarskjöld was a combination of cold, powerful superior ability and humble self-surrender. It was recorded that Margaret did not laugh; Hammarskjöld readily smiled but he also did not laugh.

As an adult Hammarskjöld lived a strong blend of the influences of his father and mother. His father was provincial governor when Dag was a child, and the family lived in a sixteenth-century red castle. When he was nine Dag's father became prime minister of Sweden. Dag was exposed from an early age to the political discussions of his father and much older brothers who also became politicians and civil servants. Hammarskjöld's rise in his career was meteoric. Before he was thirty he was named undersecretary of the treasury and several years later, chairman of the governors of the Bank of Sweden. It was during this time that his habit of working all night began as he was forced to learn on his own what others learned through years of experience. His diplomatic skills were immediately evident. Remote and stiff, with only twinkling flashes of tenderness, his style was not that of the typical diplomat; through sheer integrity and force of rectitude he placed moral obligation on involved parties.[17] Gunnar Myrdal, the Swedish economist who won the 1974 Nobel Prize, observed that the young Hammarskjöld "could enthuse insignificant persons to achieve results beyond their ability."[18] In 1946, at the age of forty-one, he entered the foreign ministry as financial adviser and in 1948 became chief Swedish delegate to the OEEC, the Organization of European Economic Cooperation. In 1951 he was vice chairman of the Swedish delegation to the United Nations, in 1952 he was chairman, and in 1953, at less than fifty years of age, he was elected secretary general, the position he held until his death in 1961.

The secretary general sent "gift wrapped" from Sweden was complex: "he was a work demon of 'alarmingly swift perceptions,' whose moral rectitude exerted a quiet pressure on others simply because it existed; a person whose diplomatic skills were so subtle that they cancelled even the disadvantage of honesty; a man . . . characterized as 'courageous and good'; and who was politically a 'conservative-liberal-social-radical-internationalist.' "[19] Hammarskjöld himself had no question in his mind that he was the perfect secretary general. The qualities that suited him to the job illustrate a pattern of the subtle level of development. The main impetus of the work demon was a dedication beyond self, a dedication to universal principles. His alarmingly swift perception was the product of fine intelligence in an integrated mind. His moral rectitude arose in his decision to accept codes of behavior that would simplify life in favor of the enormous challenge of his goals as a civil servant. The sense of his presence that others, even animals, experienced was a product of his own self-discipline, which produced the powerful energy of integration and centeredness. The array of seemingly incompatible political stances he was able to take is an example of vision logic, the wisdom of the various subpersonalities forming a practical network. His vast courage arose from seeing himself as an instrument of God and a servant to unfolding universal patterns. His goodness was evidence of his reverence for life, which was his overriding political philosophy. He once said, "The sooner I become civilly served by automatons who have 'reverence for life,' the better I shall like it."[20] This short quotation illustrates the complexity of Hammarskjöld: his humor; his respect for his own abilities, in fact, a robust sense of superiority; his frustration at the lack of vision in others; but also his devotion to the planet and its inhabitants.

A natural simile for him because of his habit of finding relaxation in mountain treks and exploration of the plains of Lapland, was the comparison of his job of secretary general to mountain climbing. We harken back at this point to Assagioli likening high spiritual development to the ascent of a mountain. As Hammarskjöld arrived in New York to assume his post, he said to the press, "That much I know of this sport, that the qualities it requires are just those which I feel we all need today: perseverance and patience, a firm grip on realities, careful but imaginative planning, a clear awareness of dangers, but also of the fact that fate is what we make it and that the safest climber is he who never questions his ability to overcome the difficulties."[21] Here he speaks clearly, but often his statements were so layered that only those closest to him were able to follow the intricacies of his thought and gasped at the significance of his insights. His frustration in the slowness of others to understand led him to turn meetings into "galloping seminars" in hopes of teaching the basis for his vision. But he never stopped believing that "service of the United Nations . . . is profoundly meaningful—whether it bears immediate fruit or not. If it paves one more inch of the road ahead, one is more than rewarded by what is achieved. This is true, whatever setbacks may follow: if a mountain wall is once climbed, later failures do not undo the fact that it has been shown that it can be climbed."[22] And though he was a man who enjoyed his own abilities, he nonetheless had the vision to know that "private diplomacy is a means to an end. The avoidance of publicity is in the interest of the success of the operation . . . that is to say we sacrifice points. . . . I would accept the sacrifice because I think it is more essential in the long run for the sound development of international cooperation to achieve the *de facto* successes, even if they are unknown to the public, than to endanger a *de facto* success because of too great willingness to 'sell' the United Nations."[23]

Amid all of these subtle level qualities, there were others less developed. It appears to be a reality of subtle level development that not all aspects of the person develop equally and at the same rate. There may also be the actual necessity in the psyche of balance provided by different levels of development. Because of the input of high spiritual energy and illumination at the subtle end of the developmental continuum, there is need for grounding through subpersonalities still in contact with earlier survival-oriented functions. Hammarskjöld retained a "baby brother" subpersonality throughout his life, a playful lad who needed to belong, who submitted to the loving care of his mother and, subsequently, of other women. This part of him was evident in his mischievous joy in the political game. The child part is often a lightening balance of the heaviness of adult responsibility. His continuing juvenility, however, may also account in part for his not developing a sexual nature, although, like Gandhi in India and U Nu, a prime minister of Burma, he may have chosen celibacy in honor of his higher spiritual and work goals. Hammarskjöld remained maladroit in commonplace human situations, which infected others with his constraint. He was a bad mixer and he detested chitchat. Yet at times he could be delightfully humorous and warm, and he much enjoyed fun.

An adolescent subpersonality was fascinated in the Victorian style with the romance of death. However, it appears that this morbid interest, apparently never life threatening, acted as balance in his life. The extreme exhausting driving movement of his intellect and diplomatic talent were the opposite of the void, where instead of movement, there is rest. One pole demanded enormous output of energy; the other demanded no energy at all. One pole was extreme extroversion, unnatural to Hammarskjöld; the other, the opposite extreme of introversion.

Hammarskjöld was first called a saint in a scathing attack by Nikita Khrushchev in 1961 during the Congo crisis that led to Hammarskjöld's death. It was not until the publication of *Markings*, Hammarskjöld's private diary, after his death that the world realized how much the actions of this perfect bureaucrat were governed by his spiritual quest. The poems and meditational studies are the underpinnings of his brilliant political work. He has been called "cunning in the service of God."[24] His personal goal was humility, the balancing opposite of his superiority and complexity. He stood outside all formal faiths. In accord with Sufi belief he felt that perfect communion with divine love was quite enough religion. In his travels, however, he visited spiritual places, churches, temples and mosques, but refrained from participating in the institutions of religion. In *Markings* he makes the statement that is the underlying theme of his life: "Let the inner take precedence over the outer, the soul over the world, wherever this may lead you."[25] A plaque he left in the chapel of the UN, ordered shortly before he traveled to the Congo in 1961, reads: "This is a room devoted to peace and those who are giving their lives for peace."[26] He went to the Congo with the determined aim of negotiating peace, but there his plane crashed in the jungle. It was suspected that he was murdered by those who opposed him.

No one but grateful Britons would call Winston Churchill a saint. Churchill is a modern example of a bridge person; though much of his personality was egoic level or less developed, what set him apart from his compatriots was his intuitive vision, certainly vision logic, in the sense that his thought represented vast networking of immense knowledge, a manifestation of subtle level function. He foresaw and preached to the English Parliament and to the world the coming direction and impact of the Second World War. Then he undertook almost alone the visionary leadership of the British involvement in the war, having at the same time enormous influence on the leadership of the Allied forces. His writings about the events of the war and his *History of the English Speaking Peoples*, which is his statement of historical fact that shaped his own judgment, won the Nobel Prize for literature in 1955. Recognition was given to his command of the patterns of language. His use of the English language can still strike awe; it is the personality of Churchill you hear in his words, his unique perspective on the world.

The configuration of Margaret's personality is obscured by passage of time and lack of records; we are led to believe that her personality was fully developed, but at this point in time it cannot be known if she was truly remarkably whole or legend claimed her so. Understanding of Dag Hammarskjöld is also somewhat obscured by the privacy and silence of the life he led and the legends and misunderstandings that surrounded him. Winston Churchill's life experience and personality, on the other hand, have been written about at length; it is easy to have some appreciation for Churchill's real virtues and faults in this plenitude of words. Several subpersonalities evidence different developmental levels from the subtle. His nationalistic orientation was classically membership level development. His lifetime was a transition to an ever increasing world consciousness, thus his nationalistic crusade in his later years became anachronistic, an inappropriate focus for his genius. As England was losing its international impact, he clung tenaciously to the power of the British Empire. It was in fact not his clear-sighted, subtle-level skills in language and world understanding that often shaped the direction of his work, but a subpersonality deeply trained in British culture. In his old age it was this part that objected to the inevitable independence of India.

It is surprising to find in a world leader with such strong masculine power as Churchill the subpersonality of a dependent child. Always physically round and soft, he chose early to develop a strong pugnacious spirit, a bulldog subpersonality, establishing an image and actual manifestation of toughness. Yet, in personal settings he never lost a soft dependence, a demanding petulance. There is parallel here with the child part in Hammarskjöld.

Ragged development among great people is more often the rule than the exception. It is undoubtedly the point of pain created by conflicted underdeveloped parts of the personality that is partially the impetus to the rising of other parts to higher levels of development. More advanced development also requires the balance and grounding of less developed parts, as observed before in Hammarskjöld. In addition, it must be noted that if Churchill, and many other great people, had given the requisite time to their own full development, the world would have been poorer for their time-consuming choice. Each individual has the right to choose how to use his gifts. World leaders display all variations of unevenness of development. Few demonstrate subtle-level behavior. A very few, like U Thant and Dag Hammarskjöld, have led lives that appear to have a strong element of the subtle. It is significant that they have been international rather than national leaders.

SUBTLE PROCESS IN THE ARTIST

Perhaps we have the greatest awareness of subtle experience in its many variations in the work of poets, artists, and musicians. Their expression is commonly acknowledged as a manifestation of the spiritual. In their work there is the rich example of vision logic and absorption in the divine. Often, rather than being expressed in the context of any formal religion, their art is a personal expression of their struggle to remain within the bounds of human existence and yet open to the heights of spirituality. Almost at random one can open a poetry anthology and find the lively words of the subtle.

> Batter my heart, three person'd God; for you
> As yet knock, breathe, shine, and seek to mend;
> That I may rise, and stand, o'rthrow me, and bend
> Your force, to break, blow, burn and make me new.
>
> —*John Donne*[27]

> Little Fly,
> Thy summer's play
> My thoughtless hand
> Has brush'd away.

MULTIPLE MIND

Am not I
A fly like thee?
Or art not thou
A man like me?

—*William Blake*[28]

I caught this morning morning's minion, king-
dom of daylight's dauphin, dapple-dawn-drawn Falcon, in
his riding
Of the rolling level underneath him steady air, and striding
High there, how he rung upon the rein of a wimpling wing
In his ecstasy! then off, off forth on a swing
As a skate's heel sweeps smooth on a bow-bend: the hurl and
gliding
Rebuffed the big wind. My heart in hiding
Stirred for a bird,—the achieve of, the mastery of the thing!

—*Gerard Manley Hopkins*[29]

I taste a liquor never brewed—
From Tankards scooped in Pearl—

. . . .

Inebriate of Air—am I—
And Debauchee of Dew—

. . . .

When Butterflies—renounce their "drams"—
I shall but drink the more!

Till Seraphs swing their snowy Hats—
And Saints—to windows run—
To see the little Tippler
Leaning against the—Sun!

—*Emily Dickinson*[30]

At the first turning of the second stair
I turned and saw below

108

The same shape twisted on the bannister
. . . . .
At the second turning of the second stair
I left them twisting, turning below;
There were no more faces and the stair was dark,
. . . . .
At the first turning of the third stair
Was a slotted window bellied like the fig's fruit
And beyond the hawthorn blossom and a pasture scene
The broadbacked figure drest in blue and green
Enchanted the maytime with an antique flute.

—*T. S. Eliot*[31]

And from the work of a present-day prose poet, Annie Dillard:

> Something sees me, some enormous power brushes me with its
> clean wing, and I resound like a beaten bell. . . . Something
> pummels us, something barely sheathed. Power broods and
> lights. We're played on like a pipe; our breath is not our own.[32]

In each of these selections there is a stretched vision, the
willingness to be absorbed in a mystery beyond knowledge.
Even in speaking of the poetic process, the poet is drawn into the
subtle. Robert Frost described his thought process in a letter:

> The one thing I boast I can't be, is disillusioned. Anything I ever
> thought I still think . . . I take nothing back. I don't grow. My
> favorite theory is that we are given this speed swifter than any
> stream of light or water for the sole purpose of standing still like a
> water beetle in any stream of light, time or water off any shore we
> please.[33]

He speaks of his sense of the fixity of the sublime. It is always the
same truth. And yet in Frost's individual poetic expression is
illustrated the profound variety the subtle takes translated into
human form. How pale explanatory worlds stand beside the

extraordinary patterns of poets' vision logic and absorption in the divine.

Paging through poetry anthologies we find the gems of the subtle, but we also find much that is representative of other developmental levels, writing that focuses simply on the puzzle of life (egoic), on exploration of patterns of social network (membership), or on avid dissection of emotion (typhonic). When the subtle is tasted, it is an experience of being drawn out of oneself, a new plane free of the egoic and simpler levels, but never free of the unique human configuration of the expresser that is all developmental levels. Ben Shahn talks about Thomas Eakins's painting, saying, "Odd, that by departing utterly from himself, an artist could so reveal himself."[34] The shift of awareness is even more vivid in the visual arts than in literature. Here, not even the social connotations of words distract from the breadth and intensity of the subtle.

The paintings of Georgia O'Keeffe, for example, often illustrate subtle vision. Objecting heartily to critics' interpretation of her work, she described how personal her high vision was. In some of her statements about her work and process (which here are rather bald without her stunning paintings), there is a hint of the depth of this private process. When she spoke of her practice of roaming the natural world, particularly the New Mexico desert, she said, "I have picked flowers where I found them— have picked up sea shells and rocks and pieces of wood where there were sea shells and rocks and pieces of wood I liked. . . . When I found the beautiful white bones on the desert I picked them up and took them home too. . . . I have used these things to say what is to me the wideness and wonder of the world as I live in it. . . ."[35] She also wrote that her paintings "sometimes grow by pieces from what is around—hills, ram's head, hollyhock."[36] These are simple words that describe the complex process of contemplation on archetypes. "I long ago came to the conclusion that even if I could put accurately the thing I saw and enjoyed, it would not give the observer the kind of feeling it gave me. I had to create an equivalent for what I felt about what I was looking at—not copy it." [37] Here she expresses a mission to give the world some participation in her mystic absorption, in her particular vision logic about natural and manmade form. She said of her use of materials, "I had become fluent with them when I was so young that they were simply another language that I handled easily. But what to say with them? I had been taught to work like others. . . . I could see how each painting or drawing had been done according to one teacher or another, and I said to myself, 'I have things in my head that are not like what anyone has taught me—shapes and ideas so near to me—so natural to my way of being and thinking that it hasn't occurred to me to put them down. I decided to start anew—to strip away what I had been taught—to accept as true my own thinking." [38] Very early in her career, she decided to follow her own vision. But also in regard to this commitment to vision, she says, "I believe that to create one's own world in any of the arts takes courage," [39] which deals with the fact that expression of the individual vision of the subtle has not been welcome in society. Society, embedded in egoic thinking and survival modes, seeks the objective, the tangible, the sure, the safe.

In commenting about the struggle in art between the abstract and the objective, O'Keeffe said, "It is surprising to me how many people separate the objective from the abstract. Objective painting is not good painting unless it is good in the abstract sense. . . . The abstraction is often the most definite form for the intangible thing in myself that I can only clarify in paint." [40] She described her rationale for abstraction as a technique to express her unique encounter with sublimity, the ineffable. "I have painted portraits that to me are almost photographic. I remember hesitating to show the paintings, they looked so real to me. But they passed into the world as abstraction—no one seeing what they are." [41] Here is the passage from traditional human visual interpretation to another plane of understanding. Of multiple paintings of the same theme she says, "I went back (again) to the shingle and shell—large again—the shingle just a dark space that floated off the top of the painting, the shell just a simple white shape under it. They fascinated me so that I forgot what they were except that they were shapes together—singing shapes."[42] She echoes the profound absorption that Frost's words depicted of his own poetic process.

At Georgia O'Keeffe's death, it was critically observed that "no effort will be spared to convert her into a mere culture heroine. In the gap between her death and this banal transfiguration, one can at least look at her paintings."[43] We could translate these words into this present framework by saying that she will be canonized; she will be a mere saint. Instead of seeing her courageous expression of her lively vision as a model for one's own blossoming, she will be put on a pedestal and worshipped vaguely from afar.

A recent film depicted the aged sculptor Henry Moore rising early in the day to work unceasingly in a rigid schedule until dark, in deliberate, passionate, careful action, his concern being to explore fully as many of the emerging sculptural ideas as he could before he died. He was absorbed in the sublime. His reaction to the art of ancient sculptors revealed his vision. Where the spiritual is usually expressed through, in Jung's terms, intuition or thinking, Moore described it through sensation. "What I admire about this statue is its tension. If you run your hands down the legs or across the shoulder blades you can feel the tautness and hardness of the muscles. The . . . sculptor has squeezed tense physical energy into the whole piece."[44] "Look at the clenched fist and the braced legs. I like too the way the pleated kilt is used to emphasize the form of the body underneath."[45] "It has massive weightiness which you feel is indestructible and which is so true to the nature of stone, . . . It was almost a fetish with me that the making of a sculpture should be conditioned by the material used, that you shouldn't try to make stone represent an idea that could be more naturally done in wood or in clay."[46] "Carvings like this make a tremendous impression on me through their use of forms within a form. I realized what a sense of mystery could be achieved by having the inside partly hidden so that you have to move round the sculpture to understand it. I was also staggered by the craftsmanship needed to make these interior carvings."[47] "The mother-and-child theme in sculpture is a universal one. It poses for the sculptor the relationship of a large form to a small one, and the dependence of the small form on the larger."[48] Simple words, grounded in the material world of form, convey Moore's vision logic, which dictated his unique artistic style.

I had long appreciated Henry Moore's figure sculpture, but his abstractions, which I had seen only in pictures, eluded me. Several years ago I was in Geneva, trying vainly to experience the city thoroughly in two days. At one point, exhausted, I collapsed on a park bench, my senses overloaded, my mind satiated, distracted, scattered, and defensively closed. In front of me was an enormous sculpture, extending thirty feet to my left, filling the whole central portion of the small park. I recognized that it was a Moore. It struck me as I sat there as a massive, lumpish, and uninteresting three-part figure. I rose to walk around it, nonetheless, realizing my sated senses would probably perceive nothing. But as I walked the sculpture seemed to move. With each step the sensory input changed. I was surprised over and over by the changing forms, openings, and space; surprise turned to delight. I experienced an intimacy of space and matter. By the time I had circled the piece, I was in awe. Despite myself Moore had led me to his ineffable reach for the high.

The subtle experience of the composition of music is perhaps the most elusive to analyze in words. Looking at the personal lives of Brahms and Beethoven, one would not describe them as highly developed people. Yet in music composition both achieved subtle-level expression in their later years, perhaps even causal, especially Beethoven.[49]

Brahms was reticent about his work. In solicitous dialogue with his friend Joachim, a great violinist of the time, he described his experience of the subtle.

"Apropos of your flow of ideas," Joachim asked, "do you ever have, when composing, sensations such as those described by

Mozart in a letter to a friend? He wrote: 'The process with me is like a vivid dream.' "

"Yes I do," replied Brahms. "Mozart is right. When at my best it is a dreamlike state, and in that condition the ideas flow much more easily."

"Are you conscious when in this state?"

"Certainly, fully conscious, otherwise I would not be able to write the ideas down as they come. It is important to get them on paper immediately."

"Do you ever lose consciousness while in the mental condition?"

"Yes, sometimes I become so drowsy that I fall asleep, and then I lose the ideas."

"Can you do anything to induce this dreamlike state?"

"Yes, I early discovered that to obtain good results certain conditions had to be met. . . . I have to be absolutely alone and undisturbed. Without these two requisites I cannot even think of trying to compose."

"Are there any other requirements for entering this mysterious realm, aside from isolation and freedom from disturbance?"

"Yes, concentration to the point of complete absorption seems to be the key that unlocks the door to the soul realm, once I have the other requisites."

"Then you do not believe that composing is purely an intellectual process?"

"It is an intellectual process as far as the mechanics of composition are concerned. It requires patience and much hard work to acquire technical skill, but that has nothing to do with inspiration, which is a spiritual process."

"Who, in your opinion, was a perfect type of the creative genius?"

"Beethoven. He had lofty inspirations, and at the same time he was an indefatigable worker. We all have to work hard."[50]

Brahms's words describe the common experience of composers, the dreamlike absorption of the subtle state. But unlike the historical saints who were congratulated for achieving this state, Brahms goes on to describe yet another further condition for the artist, the mission of bringing the subtle insight into communicable terms through the very human process of hard work.

Like Churchill's, Brahms's personality development was ragged, some personality characteristics clear, others rough. The same was true of Beethoven; his fiery temper was legendary. But each had genius that drove him spiritually; it was all-important. During his productive years, Brahms was surrounded by supportive friendships and camaraderie, which provided considerable comfort in the way that he lived. Beethoven, on the other hand, due to his deafness, became increasingly isolated from other people. Beethoven's deafness was not simply silence but a constant buzzing in his head. That he continued to compose as deafness increased is remarkable; that his composition reached ever more advanced levels is heroic. His later compositions, the last string quartets specifically, are a completely different sound than his earlier works which bear the stamp of Beethoven's personality; in the later quartets there is causal-level composition, "music of the spheres." Beethoven said of his experience in these last compositions that "he reached so near the Godhead that he experienced music timelessly, all at once—the music he had power to write down was mere riff-raff compared to the music he intimately knew."51 Most of these compositions are not popular like his early works, actually not well understood by our egoic level culture. Beethoven's Ninth Symphony is considered to be subtle-level composition. This composition is often acclaimed as the greatest music ever written, but it is perhaps seen as such because of the fact that Western culture has not developed far enough yet to appreciate what Beethoven did after his ninth, and last, symphony. When Beethoven was composing the Ninth Symphony, the Missa Solemnis, and the last piano sonatas, he said, "Now I know how to compose." He recognized that at that point, the subtle level, he was at a new level of experience.

The developmental process unfolds; historical saints were given visions, but the artist unfolds into the subtle and causal experience. It is the might of the reach, the search for ever broadening vision that leads them into absorption in the sublime. This is the process, the path, that can be chosen; rather than waiting for a vision of God, the artist in any field takes the talent he has and works passionately. [52]

THE *ISHTADEVA*

In this final example of the subtle, we consider a practice of the saints of all religions, a means of choosing direct self-development, which in the Hindu tradition is known as the *ishtadeva* (a Sanskrit term usually translated as "chosen deity"). The *ishtadeva* is an image of the sublime that becomes absorbing to the point of identification; the energy of the figure is absorbed and becomes a transformative agent to the personality.

There was nothing about a client named Anne that would cause people to put her on a pedestal and call her a saint. She was fully involved in earthly life and not a pious person. The *ishtadeva* came upon her unexpectedly. In a dream or daydream she saw a hooded figure walking away from her into the desert. The robe the figure wore was vivid blue. At odd moments, usually at times of respite from the demands of her busy life, this figure came to her mind. It increased in numinosity; she eagerly anticipated this image and came to feel a love for this solitary figure. It was not a distraction to her work, since she found that she could acknowledge the figure in its brief appearances on one level in her mind and continue, at the same time, a systematic operation of her life through the action-oriented subpersonalities.

Suddenly one day, she saw the face of the figure. She cannot mark in time when this happened, or even say whether she was awake or dreaming, since the process seemed to operate apart from her mundane experience. It was the face of a woman, calm and quiet, with remarkable clear eyes full of light. From then on the image of the wandering figure became memory, and her preoccupation was with the face. When Anne thought about this inner experience, and that her life was not at all disrupted by this peculiar attraction, she theorized that she was experiencing the Higher Self. In a class studying Jung's writings about alchemy, she had learned about the phenomenon of inner guides that can be images of the Higher Self. In this context the process seemed to her natural and she trusted it. For some months the image of the woman's face remained her frequent companion. One day she looked in the mirror and saw the face of the woman. After that, the image of the face in her mind lost its numinosity and became memory.

A transformative image came out of Anne's unconscious at the same time that she remained in balance with all the other aspects of her life. It operated on her and changed her energy to the point that it changed her appearance. An *ishtadeva* can be chosen by the conscious mind as well. Saint Teresa of Ávila chose to live with the figure of Jesus before her, to which practice she attributed her transformation and vision.

SAGE IN THE WORLD

Wilber gives the name *causal* to the final level of development, the fully integrated state of mind. Jung contended that if one were to reach the Higher Self—in other words, all aspects of the psyche integrated with the Higher Self, a final synthesis—this would be the end of the individual's life. The psychosynthesis framework, on the other hand, considers high integration of the causal to be a level of development of living human beings. Certainly, Eastern religious disciplines have recorded that there have been some who have reached and lived this stage. They are called sages.

In causal integration everything becomes simple. During the centauric the inner psychic pattern spreads into complexity like that of the mandalas of Eastern art, integration carrying the enormous richness of every part of the psyche. In the causal every element is still there but it is tightened to the point that all of the psyche has become a single cohesive pattern; perhaps it is that every element is present in every other element, as in a holograph. As in an imploding star, the energy becomes intense and singular.

The portraits of Eastern sages consistently reveal a striking, even blazing, individuality.[53] Eastern artists depicted adepts at all levels up to that of the sage as heavily absorbed in the symbolic content of their spiritual work; at the level of the sage, however, all symbols disappear and it is the incredible uniqueness of the human being that shines out of the art. This is the manner in which the artists have chosen to depict God in man. There is no longer the stretching toward the spiritual; now the spiritual has been incorporated into the human being. "The soul no longer communes with that oneness or worships that oneness—it *becomes* that oneness."[54]

In causal transformation, the final synthesis, there is the most complete wholeness. The wholeness is so vital that it impacts the world. Historically acknowledged sages (for example, Buddha, Krishna, Lao-tzu, Jesus) have been significant because of their personal impact on culture. Their words and their lives, which embodied their thoughts, impacted the world not through power, which is the usual means of changing world institutions, but through unique wholeness. These human beings became archetypal; the clear structure of their uniqueness strongly affected whole cultures to the point that their images and spirits became part of the collective unconsciousness.

The most familiar image of the sage is of one who lives cloistered or in hermitage, experiencing absolute peace and openness with the universe. The monastic tradition hopes to foster spiritual development to the point of causal development. When Saint Teresa of Ávila spoke of "strength given by obedience [lessening] the difficulty of things that seem impossible," she was describing the blessing of the release of psychological energy provided by monastic rule, energy that is freed for confronting huge spiritual tasks. Religious habit establishes a set direction for action, whereas ordinary life scatters psychic force by consuming much energy in decision making. It is in this spirit that many in the present day who do not choose monastic commitment for individual development, do choose a clear rule of simplicity for their lives.

For the sage the monastic setting allows an end to inner wrestling. Dialogues between subpersonalities no longer have any relevance since the personality parts have been long since balanced and integrated. The life is more like an expression of art, the bringing together of seemingly disparate pieces into a balanced whole.

But what of the sage in the world? If the sage walks out of the monastery, he is no longer protected to simply exist in universal oneness. He carries his wholeness and acts from it; but his life is very different from that of the cloistered sage. Jesus, who left an Essene community to preach in the world, is an example of a sage living in a society antagonistic to him. The Jewish culture in which he worked espoused a dualistic theology. It was held that man and God are and always will be separate; the subtle was seen as the highest possible development for man. Thus, Jesus' statement, "I and the Father are One," was seen as blasphemy, and he was ultimately crucified. The early church was split on the identity of Jesus. One group, the Gnostics, understood that Jesus was teaching the full development of the person. In the Gnostic gospels are recorded teachings of Jesus that are similar to Eastern religious principles of the causal and are in harmony with Jesus' early training with the Essenes. He preached that self-knowledge is knowledge of God and that the Higher Self and the divine are identical. In these writings the emphasis is on illusion dispelled by enlightenment, rather than on sin and repentance, and Jesus saw himself as a spiritual guide rather than Lord.[55]

The Christian church accepted the dualistic theology of the Jewish culture. To retain Jesus as the great figure of the church, Jesus was promoted to deity, and his humanity was considered merely miraculous. The early church documents about Jesus were purged of elements that could lead to confusion about this dualistic position.[56] In the gospel of Mark, the earliest writing,

119

Jesus can still be seen as a sage, but in the later gospels he becomes only God.[57]

The sage is a person at one with himself and the universe, perfect human and perfect God. In the world, however, he is not free to be at peace. He must oppose with his oneness the splintered world. I quote at length here the writer Nikos Kazantzakis's poetic description of the predicament of the sage in the world. This formulation of a person's relationship to God were words Kazantzakis composed for himself as a meditational study.

1. The ultimate most holy form of theory is action.

2. Not to look on passively while the spark leaps from generation to generation, but to leap and to burn with it!

3. Action is the widest gate of deliverance . . . it does not "find"—it creates its way, hewing right and left through resistances of logic and matter. . . .

6. Our profound human duty is not to interpret or to cast light on the rhythm of God's march, but to adjust, as much as we can, the rhythm of our small fleeting life to his. . . .

17. Within the gigantic circle of divinity we are in duty bound to separate and perceive the small, burning arc of our epoch.

18. On this barely perceptible flaming curve, feeling the onrush of the entire circle profoundly and mystically, we travel in harmony with the Universe, we gain impetus and dash into battle.

19. Thus, by consciously following the onrush of the Universe, our ephemeral action does not die with us.

20. It does not become lost in a mystical and passive contemplation of the entire circle; it does not scorn holy, humble, and daily necessity.

21. Within its narrow and blood-drenched ditch it stoops and labors steadfastly, conquering easily both space and time within a small point of space and time—for this point follows the divine onrush of the entire circle.[58]

THE TRANSFORMATIVE INFLUENCE

And, finally, we are left with a mystery. Why do we grow beyond survival needs? Why do we seem to have a developmental course? Why does there seem to be an evolutionary pull?

> Blowing through heaven and earth, and in our hearts and in the heart of every living thing, is a gigantic breath—a great cry. . . . Plantlife wished to continue its motionless sleep next to stagnant waters, but the Cry leaped up within it and violently shook its roots: "Away, let go of the earth, walk!" Had the tree been able to think and judge, it would have cried, "I don't want to. What are you urging me to do! You are demanding the impossible." But the Cry, without pity, kept shaking its roots and shouting, "Away, let go of the earth, walk!"
>
> It shouted this way for thousands of eons; and lo! as a result of desire and struggle, life escaped the motionless tree and was liberated.
>
> Animals appeared—worms—making themselves at home in water and mud. "We're just fine," they said. "We have peace and security; we're not budging!"
>
> But the terrible Cry hammered itself pitilessly into their loins. "Leave the mud, stand up, give birth to your betters!"
>
> "We don't want to! We can't!"
>
> "You can't but I can. Stand up!"
>
> And lo! after thousands of eons, man emerged, trembling on his still unsolid legs.
>
> The human being is a centaur; his equine hoofs are planted in the ground, but his body from breast to head is worked on and tormented by the merciless Cry. He has been fighting, again for thousands of eons, to draw himself out of his human scabbard. Man calls in despair, "Where can I go? I have reached the pinnacle, beyond is the abyss." And the Cry answers, "I am beyond. Stand up!" All things are centaurs. If this were not the case, the world would rot into inertness and sterility. [59]

As one opens to evolution, there grows a passionate response that draws remorselessly into the struggle of birthing the Self. In Eastern thought it is conceived that all is spun out from an original source. It is the idea that all lower levels of existence were originally born from the highest level, and contain enfolded within them the potential to return to the highest state of existence. This process is called *involution*. In Eastern literature it is described in detail poetically, spiritually, and psychologically. Over and over in the biological process it appears. The matter of an egg does not dissipate but in development forms ever more complex patterns. In the sprouting of a seed or the growth of a child the involutionary process is illustrated. The concept of biological evolution presumes a random emergence of whole patterns; involution, on the other hand, suggests a predisposition of universal patterns into which an organism is drawn.

Another clue in this mystery is the Higher Self. Both Jung and Assagioli were interested in the pull of a higher patterning force in the individual. Jung postulated the Higher Self on the basis of dreams, seeing a process of complementation, where conscious thinking and acting are balanced and pulled by the unconscious. Assagioli postulated movement of the conscious center to ever higher levels of functioning, finally reaching the Higher Self. Their ideas originated both in their studies of Eastern and Western mystical literature and in their observations of the inner and outer developmental process of the people with whom they worked. Their conclusion was that the Higher Self provides information for change. The Higher Self, as a personal information center, is not only part of the individual but also touches the universal through archetypes and unity of individual psychic energy with wider energy forms. The archetypal pattern of the Higher Self can be likened to the genetic code in the cell. "Unconscious complementation . . . implies an inherent direction or goal. Complementation . . . for something missing or exaggerated presupposes a totality configuration or wholeness pattern, . . . an organizing superordinated center, an archetypal urge toward psychic totality."[60]

The change force (the Self) is involved in dialogue with consciousness by word, symbol, or action. The dialogue is experienced in dreams and life events. Its directive influence is sometimes accepted, at other times thwarted by the individual. The response the individual gives to the transformative information is of two kinds—Eros and Thanatos.[61] Eros is the embrace of life, a passionate desire and attempt to espouse all that is the fullest expression of the richness of the universal. In this spirit, the directive information is answered with desire for union, for making the transformative expressive in the life.

Thanatos, on the other hand, is resistance to any invasion of the boundaries of the individual; the fear of death is the fear of personal disintegration. When one is gripped by such fear, the only answer to the invitation of the Self can be resistance, negation, and attack. In this case, the goal of preservation of individual personal integrity creates a panic that underlies every decision, and the life is filled with the misery of misdirected action.

The analogy of a symphony orchestra to psychic process is enlightening. If the strings and the woodwinds and the other instruments resist the musical score and play whatever they like, the result is cacaphony. This is equivalent to the independent pursuits of subpersonalities claiming an autonomy that is destructive to the totality of the individual. If, on the other hand, the parts of the orchestra faithfully render the score, harmony is created and beautiful music is produced. The orchestral units follow the direction of the conductor; just so, the subpersonalities in harmony follow Center. The subpersonalities may speak and act individually, as the voices of the orchestra play different parts, but under the direction of Center (the conductor) their expression is harmonized.

The musical score is created by the composer. In analogy with the psyche, the Higher Self is the composer. The composer does not work in isolation; he has all the music of the ages, the music of nature, the music of the spheres as his inspiration. Likewise, the Higher Self is not isolated; all the patterns of the universe, the archetypes of the collective unconscious, feed the building of transformative patterns.

There is another interesting aspect of this analogy. When a

composer hears his work played by musicians, he is affected by it. He may say, "Yes, that is what I intended and it gives me further ideas." Or he may say, "No, they play it correctly but that is not the right sound. I shall change the orchestration to achieve the right sound." Similarly, the transformative plan of the Higher Self is not set in stone, but evolves on the basis of individual creative expression and the impact of shifting archetypes. The vision of the composer is whole but he grows over time and his scope becomes wider. Likewise, the Higher Self always contains a pattern of totality but as the individual expresses this pattern, in the uniqueness of the spontaneous subpersonalities, the Higher Self too grows in richness.

The connection of the Higher Self to universal patterns becomes evident as one grows. Personal growth is not insular; in fact, the connection to all other entities is the real burden of life, the real obligation.

We are one. From the blind worm in the depths of the ocean to the endless arena of the Galaxy, only one person struggles and is imperiled: You. And within your small and earthen breast only one thing struggles and is imperiled: the Universe.[62]

6

FAMILY AS
A COMMUNITY OF
SUBPERSONALITIES

The family is the keeper of culture. Every family teaches its babies to survive, thrive, and believe according to specific cultural tenets. By the age of three or four many aspects of informal culture based on the biological needs of the organism are in place. The years six to twelve, which Piaget described at length, are the years in which most of the formal structure of culture is learned. Nonetheless, it is well known to every person who works in Western schools, designated by Western culture to be the primary teaching agent, how much the child is embedded in the influence of family teaching during these years.

The sole occupation of the baby is learning how to be in the world. Her senses scan the environment, making recordings—visual, audial, tactile, and so on—that are stored deep in the developing brain. In the prelanguage years the child establishes the basis for her functioning as a human being for the rest of her life. Her family provides her teachers and models. As the only source of information, parents, siblings, and anyone else around are seen as omniscient teachers of "truths." The early sensory recordings are imprinted in her nervous system so strongly that many people are surprised in adulthood by instances of their own odd behavior, behavior they would not now choose, that was programmed into their minds early in life. For instance, a newlywed finds herself acting not as she would like but in accord with early recordings of her parents' marriage.

The culture is thus sustained by the flow of two psychological mechanisms, projection and identification. From the adult caretaker are projected cultural patterns, both conscious and unconscious. The newborn generation, its nervous system open and plastic, identifies with and absorbs, even before birth, the ways of the family adults who live, for their own well-being, embedded in the culture.

The millions of messages from the family in childhood result in the foundations of the complex unique subpersonalities. Sometimes messages are clear and easily incorporated as skills for effective living. If a child hears, "Brush your teeth every day," this lesson becomes part of the subpersonality that is learning personal hygiene, which can be a peaceful, satisfying process. There is real power of accomplishment for the small child who knows she has learned to brush her teeth. But sometimes lessons like "Brush your teeth every day" are accompanied by contradictory or confusing messages. What if the child hears, "Brush your teeth every day," but observes that when her mother smiles, she often has food particles in her teeth? This fact presents another message which is in contradiction to the original lesson. Because of the immense drive to learn that is in every baby, all young children are brilliant at interpreting the obscure message in this smile, and they record it faithfully.

Consider some of the possibilities producing this contradiction in Mother. She may not brush her teeth because she is lazy. One subpersonality thinks it is too much trouble to brush your teeth every day, while at the same time a caring mother subpersonality conscientiously teaches her child to take care of herself. Or she may be simply disorganized; the disorganized part says, "Oh, I forgot to brush my teeth yesterday." Another possibility is that she places her family's needs before her own: "If I get everything done for the family, I'll take care of myself." Considering still another possibility, this mother may be struggling with being a modern woman, pursuing a career at the same time she is raising a family: "I wear so many hats that, realistically, I don't have time to wear the self-care hat very much."

These distinct messages teach very different approaches to life. If the child observes that her mother believes for herself that it is too much trouble to brush her teeth and do other acts for her own self-care, the child learns as a "truth" that laziness, at least in self-care, is acceptable. If the resulting subpersonality gains dominance, we have a slob or, carried further, even a dropout in life. If she gets a message that disorganization is a valid way of life, she may develop a subpersonality that drives other people mad because she does not follow through on commitment. As an adult, a long-practiced subpersonality turns her body away, saying "I forgot." If, on the other hand, Mother habitually puts others' needs before her own, the child might absorb two different messages. Identifying with Mother, she could think, "Others are more important than I." If she focuses on her part in the relationship with Mother, she learns, "I am more important than others." These two lessons can be the basis for two subpersonalities of opposite nature; one or both can appear within the same person. Where Mother is setting out to conquer several worlds and of necessity has given self-care bottom priority, the child watching Mother's whirlwind learns "truths." She learns about hard work, resourcefulness, acceptance of challenge, and other positive things, but also learns that self-care is least important in life. She might develop a subpersonality that positively identifies strongly with Mother, and thus follows a brilliant career but she eventually dies of stress-related disease. On the other hand, the child may have experienced much pain in the situation, and she thus develops an opposing subpersonality that struggles with commitment to the work world. Or again, an individual may develop both types of subpersonalities that war within her.

Mother may never say both messages, the direct and the indirect, out loud to the child, or to the rest of the family for that matter. She may not notice there is any confusion. But the child, ever alert to what life is really about, understands the subliminal message and sees the basic position on which her mother's behavior is based enacted many times over in other ways, so that she firmly knows that she is learning two "truths": "Brush your teeth every day" and some other contradictory variation. Because these two "truths" do not result in the same kinds of behavior, they become part of two different subpersonalities. They are kept discrete and distinct from each other, and acted on in different circumstances. Because they are contradictory "truths," they can lead to conflict, even to inner war, at some point in the person's life. Fortunately, most of what we learn falls quietly into place in useful behavior patterns in the subpersonalities. Through the myriad experiences of childhood and adolescence, the original embryonic subpersonalities are enriched and elaborated so that we arrive in adulthood functioning well and with a minimum of conflicts.

If we know our subpersonalities, we have the tools available to work out the inevitable conflicts that do derive from the fact that our families are only human and cannot be completely consistent about everything. As adults we have the choice to reshape subpersonalities, discarding unwanted family elements: anachronistic behaviors, useless values, or predetermined life patterns. All of these elements may have served your family well years ago, but for you, the unique person that you are, living in this time, they are totally inappropriate. If you continue to carry these old pieces of family baggage, they become a burden, blocking huge amounts of energy that could be used for other things, and you rob yourself of the expression of your true gifts.

FAMILY AS THE PRIMARY COMMUNITY

No one is alone. We are born into community. Even if we were to choose ultimately to live in hermitage, we are first trained by the community into which we are born, and thus we would take into hermitage with us the essence of the community of our youth. But, also in hermitage, we yet live in community, a community of other living things and even of nonliving things. There are astonishing statistics that indicate that all people on earth share the matter of this planet: our bodies recreate, recycle themselves within a matter of days, incorporating physical matter from plants and animals and other humans to rebuild and renew, and the discarded matter from our bodies becomes available to other living things. Perhaps most amazing is the scientific analysis that claims that we breathe air during our lifetimes that was at one time or another breathed by every other person on this earth.

The family is the first community, whether it be only mother and child or an elaborate extended kinship system. The child is born helpless and dependent, and remains so for years. It is during this period, as we considered in the last section, that the subpersonalities are developed. Some subpersonalities are directly learned from parental figures, some are adaptive response, but all are tools for meeting the needs of the developing child, allowing her to adapt to what her community requires of her and yet, ideally, to also be herself. Some families provide a better environment for this process than others. Nonetheless, it happens for all children in all families in some fashion.

The family and the individual are both whole units. The family is a social and economic unit within a larger community. The individual is a physical and psychological unit within a family and a larger community. Likewise, the family and the individuals in the family are composed of subunits, descriptive and functioning subdivisions of the whole. We have been examining in detail the subpersonalities of the individual. In the family there is a similar structural pattern; mother, father, and each child function within the family configuration like the subpersonalities within the individual. In fact, it is logical that the shape of the family and its functioning serve as a template for the development of the psyche in the young child.

Within the family, individuals play specific roles, similar to subpersonalities in the personality. Someone is chief protector, another is clown, still another is communicator or achiever, and so forth. There are many mixtures and varieties of roles within unique family constellations. In my work, I have not found any individual with a set of subpersonalities that duplicates the family system in which she was raised, but it is probable that some people do have such personality configurations. What is apparent, however, is that individuals incorporate some elements of the family system into their subpersonalities, while other subpersonalities develop in a direction that represents their uniqueness as separate persons.

One of the complexities of family interaction is that parental subpersonalities serve as models for the child's developing subpersonalities. The child's new subpersonalities develop to be different from the parents' because she has a different genetic configuration and because she has different life experience. Nonetheless, there is enough similarity between some aspects of the parent and the developing subpersonalities of the child that they sometimes seem almost to be twins. In the attempt at efficiency in communication within the family, the assumption is made that they are the same and this assumption leads to the smothering of the child's individuality.

All subpersonality patterns of the personality which we examined earlier are comparable to the flow of interaction that occurs between family members. In my own experience, although I could identify that the two subpersonalities I first recognized were distinctly parts of myself, I also realized that one, Dagmar, represented my version of elements learned from my mother and the other, Camille, was a unique shadow subpersonality only beginning to develop, which was different from the elements represented by my family. The dialogue between the two subpersonalities would not have taken place in my family, but it is like a family dialogue that could have taken place in some other family. It is a typical dialogue between subpersonalities that one hears in one's thought, and it is also a typical discussion that one would hear in families.

A family is a unit of unequals. [1] Children are born helpless and for many years are trained and directed by parents. Parents are actually bigger and stronger than children and thus centers of power in the family. In the first encounter with the "family" of subpersonalities within the individual, it is immediately apparent that some subpersonalities are bigger and stronger than others. Often it is a major piece of work in the development of the person to even out the power balance of the different parts of herself, allowing the weaker ones, the child subpersonalities, so to speak, to have powerful, "grown up" aspects, or to simply be as respected as an adult, though still a child.

It must also be recognized that in family dynamics what occurs does not always represent pure interaction between the family subunits. The members of the family do not necessarily respond with clear family role expression. The dynamics are greatly complicated by the fact that a family is a group of individuals who each have a set of subpersonalities. If each of the members of a family of four has four subpersonalities, the number of types of interaction that can go on between family members is enormous—permutations of interactions in a family of four between dyads, triads, and quartets of subpersonalities equals 544, to say nothing of those combinations where more than one subpersonality from each person is involved. What actually happens in most families is that the stronger subpersonalities of the individuals tend to dominate, thus never allowing expression within the family of less developed subpersonalities. This often is not so much an issue of discrimination as it is an issue of practicality; to give all of the permutations equal time would not be efficient in terms of family functioning since some subpersonalities do not have much to do with the healthy functioning of a family on a day-to-day basis. Yet, there is a great difference in families where expression of all subpersonality interactions are a potential and those where tacit or overt rules exist that prohibit full expression.

There are open and closed family systems.[2] In the open system, there is honest self-expression. Differences between family members are natural and expected. Open negotiations can occur to resolve difference through compromise, agreeing to disagree, or by taking turns. Each individual can say what she thinks and feels, and can negotiate for reality and personal growth without destroying herself or others in the system. In this type of family the child observing that her mother does not brush her teeth can ask about it. The open family operates like the well-functioning individual personality where subpersonalities are balanced, and expression and action flow smoothly.

The closed family system, on the other hand, is characterized by distorted communication patterns. All members must be cautious about what is said. Everyone is supposed to have the same opinions, feelings, and desires. Honest self-expression is impossible, being viewed as deviant, sick, or crazy. And since differences are treated as dangerous, one or more members of the family are "dead" to themselves in order to remain part of the system. In this type of family the child dare not ask about her mother's personal habits, much less imply there is any contradiction in what she is being taught about brushing teeth. We hear again in the description of the closed family the echo of the inner dynamics of personality. When there are walls within the psyche, subpersonality expression is stunted, just as some family members in the malfunctioning family system are "dead" to the expression of their real identities.

In both cases, the open family and the closed family are doing their best to be good families. Their systems of interaction are a result of their best attempts to deal with the paradoxical struggle for separateness and togetherness that faces all families.[3] For families, as well as in all human life, the equilibrium of opposites is an elusive goal. The seeming contradiction between individual needs and group functions produces tension and anxiety. The right to differentness of the individual must be balanced with a certain amount of sameness among members of the group that allows them to function together. The freedom of each person to do what she pleases confronts issues of the family's responsibility for protection and safety. Independence, especially that growing in children, must be balanced out with nurturing support. Even the best functioning family is pressured in stressful situations by the pull of equilibrating and finely tuning the normal, yet often opposing, goals of the individuals in the family.

The pressure of opposites can bring into dominance imbalances and unresolved issues within the personalities of the members of the family, especially the adults, which results even in the best of families in some transitory variation of the fears and imbalances of the closed family system. If the parents are growing people, they as individuals experience over and over within themselves movement from balance to imbalance and back again. Newly emerging development within them may be in contradiction to what has already been established as a functional system. Thus there is a tendency to live on two levels; since the new cannot be implemented until it is sufficiently developed, the old way remains in effect for the time being. This results in inevitable inconsistency in the adults which the children "read." In a closed family system, inconsistency brings about confusion and erroneous learning. In an open system, the children are encouraged to talk about what they find confusing, which can be greatly enlightening to the adults.

The healing of the closed system predicament occurs first through new patterns of communication between family members, patterns that are characteristic of the open family system. By the means of the new forms of communication, painful issues can be slowly brought into the open and negotiated in new ways. Feelings that have been inhibited and covered over, now demand expression and recognition. As the process proceeds, trust between family members grows, and new modes of interaction develop. This family unit healing process, which honors the place of all members in the family system, is the same healing process that the individual undergoes as she finds new forms of communication between her subpersonalities, negotiates their conflict resolution, and cultivates respect and honor between all parts of the system. The closed family system becomes open. The conflicted personality is harmonized.

In the goal of achieving openness in the family, the issues of privacy and deception need to be thought through. Personal growth needs privacy. For growth to take place at all, seeds must be planted and left in a dark, quiet place for a while; a new part of the personality must gain a little strength, growing in the shadow, before it is strong enough to be in the world. Thus openness in the family allows for privacy. The idea of deception only applies when secrets are kept at other people's expense, where the well-being of the family is affected.

LEVELS OF DEVELOPMENT IN THE FAMILY

The institution of the family dates back to the time of human beginnings. It has taken as many forms as can be imagined.[4] But always its first purpose has been survival. When it comes down to the basics, every family is a group of people banded together for dealing with the issues of survival. In poorer parts of the world, this purpose of the family is dominant. In Western affluent society, we must remind ourselves that, at the bottom line, families are for survival. Our usual pattern of establishing a home takes the form of finding a house or apartment, moving into it our numerous accumulated things for our style of living, calling the gas and electric companies to establish service, and shopping at the nearest supermarket. In another part of the world, the establishment of a home that provides for survival may entail building the dwelling, planting crops for food, and finding fuel for heating. The concern about survival is more focused and real in this case. Only when survival needs have been adequately addressed can other developmental steps be undertaken with any ease.

As humans are part of the animal kingdom on this planet, reproduction of the human species is a biological necessity. If a group of people fail to have children, as was true of the Shakers, they die out. The Shaker community built prosperous farms and in their spiritual practice explored higher levels of development, but they did not believe in sexual interaction between their community members. They had hoped to maintain their community size through the adoption of orphans, but on attaining adulthood many of these orphans left the community to establish their own families. The Shakers provided an excellent family setting where survival needs were more than adequately met. In many families all over the world survival needs are not met before children arrive. The children severely tax the existing resources of the family. There is little hope then of the family reaching for a higher level of development. A survival cycle develops that uses all available energy of the family members. Ideally, first, a home is established that provides warmth, food, and other necessities, with its continuance securely projected into the future, and then, when sexual reproduction is undertaken, children can be welcome.

Within such a secure environment, the baby who is esteemed, highly valued for her intrinsic worth, grows daily in her understanding of her impact, effectiveness, and power. Esteem at its best in families is in the atmosphere of honor given to all. In our society, with its pressure of social expectations and competition, esteem is elusive and is a problem for many people standing in judgment of either themselves or others. There may be legitimate complaint against others' behavior, but behavior and the total worth of a person are different things; behavior can be judged, even rejected, without rejecting the person. Each individual has intrinsic worth and when that worth is affirmed as a child grows, the child naturally believes in her effectiveness. Mistakes can be lightly accepted as part of the learning process, not painfully absorbed as itemized indicators of inadequacy. When the environment is deficient in esteem for a child or adult, the expression of power takes on a desperate nature. Powerful acts are forced on the world by one subpersonality compensating for another that, like the family environment, questions the person's intrinsic worth.

There certainly are loving families, but to love another person takes first valuing oneself. If esteem is an issue, it is difficult to love oneself; constant questioning about one's own self-worth leads to a defensive questioning of the worth of others. The amount of energy bound up in this incessant questioning leaves little for the free, clear expression of love for others. In the adults creating a home, there may be subpersonalities capable of deep affection, and this can be seen clearly as babies arrive. But as the child grows to the point where she is a learner and judged by their community, other subpersonalities in the adults, more insecure in their own standing in the community, may take the spotlight. Suddenly, the warm atmosphere of esteem and love in which the baby prospered can disappear as everyone in the family becomes troubled by esteem issues. This is a signal to adults that there is need for them to confront their own esteem and power subpersonalities. Another type of solution to problems of esteem lies in valuable lessons of expanding the family love; understanding and befriending more unfortunate people, the elderly, the ill, or even loving animals, can reawaken that clear sense of intrinsic value of all, and the love that readily accompanies it. Love at this level of development is *agape*, brother love, not *eros*, sexual love. The family is the ideal setting for learning this form of love. In its ideal, the child goes into the world loving and concerned for all of humankind, and for the whole of the planet.

Survival, reproduction, power and esteem, and love, are all part of the basic nurturance of the child. First, a style of life must be established that welcomes children into an environment that provides well-being. Then the intrinsic worth of the child is celebrated leading to her belief in her capacity to be an effective member of the community. The higher levels of development are more individual, and are more pronounced in adult development. Thus they often are not explicit in family life. Yet the foundation is laid in the family for the inner development that she requires. If the family is an open system where clear communication is modeled, encouraged, and welcomed, the possibilities for higher capacities are acknowledged. The greatest key to children developing a capacity for higher development lies in whether they live with parents who consider it part of their way of life to be always growing. Whether they ever speak of this inner work does not matter; in fact, it is probably better not spoken of because of its embryonic nature. Since children accurately "read" adults on many levels in their attempt to understand the truths about life, they do see the psychological position of their parent. Certainly study of the arts, sharing of ideas and knowledge, study of world cultures, or the simple practice of religion all encourage the child within the family to begin to explore her inner self and the outer universe, thus leading her to an adulthood ripe for wholeness.

FAMILY MYTH

In most families stories are told about various members of the family, often across several generations. They are told in amusement, in pride, or in a sense of family solidarity. Sometimes the stories are not told; the emotional avoidance of discussion about certain family members lead children to assume there is a story there but it is one of shame. These stories, both positive and negative, are the family myths.

The impact of these stories can be so great that they affect the subpersonality formation in a child. Earlier we considered how the images of the collective unconscious, the archetypes, the big symbols of our lives, have a strong, numinous effect on development. The family myths work in the same way. They are heard as family symbols, illustrations of the family's deepest values, and are thus seen as prescription of how to be or how not to be. A subpersonality that seems to have no basis in the present family structure sometimes can be traced back to a story about a family member of another generation or of the extended family. The stories carry mystery and intrigue and thus work on the psyche like visual symbols.

If the stories told in a family are examined, they often reveal distortions from the original facts.[5] An artist looks at a subject and shapes it into a work of art according to her own inner values and perspectives. The same happens with a family story; some facts are omitted, others are remembered differently than they really happened, all in accord with the life perception of the family members. It is often helpful to examine family myths

137

in this light in order to uncover shadow elements that elude consciousness of family members, to examine them openly to discover if they are serving as positive models and incentives for the development of all family members, or whether they are producing unwanted restrictions.

CLOSE-UP OF A SUCCESSFUL LAWYER

Although Pete was a successful lawyer, to his great discomfort he suffered from high anxiety and difficulty in being close to others. One subpersonality, Joe, a thirteen-year-old child part of his personality, walked into every unfamiliar situation tightening and tensing Pete's body, sometimes to the point of illness. Not only was it obvious to everyone around him that he was "uptight," but, to his consternation, this physical state slowed his speech and his mental acuity. He was robbed of the edge of power in his professional effectiveness.

Eight months before Pete's birth, his mother's brother, Uncle Pete, was killed in a plane crash. Pete was named for this uncle. He said he knew little about Uncle Pete because the family did not talk about him. One day, however, he had a highly distinct remembrance from early childhood of a distant family friend at an obscure occasion commenting about his Uncle Pete's recklessness. Out of all the experiences of his childhood, this incident oddly stood out. He realized that from an early age he had been collecting data on this mysterious uncle.

He began to investigate. He learned by broaching this forbidden topic and directly asking family members that Uncle Pete was a daredevil pilot in World War II who had lost his life flying under a bridge. As a result of his death, Pete's mother and father changed their plans to move to Arizona where they were going to start their own business. Pete's father took over the part of the family business that was to be Uncle Pete's responsibility when he returned from the military. Looking back on his parents' lives, Pete saw them as entrapped in the family, stopped in their initiative to establish their own life. Ironically,

Pete's uncle was seen as a hero in the hometown, where a park was named for him.

Knowing the family story, Pete understood that he had probably been trained from before birth to be the opposite of reckless, not daring anything, making sure everything was safe. Pete's dominant subpersonality, Joe, that was constantly wary, was a product of very early teaching. He had developed two other subpersonalities that operated in accord with this wary life-stance: the Worrier, who rehearsed every situation in advance in as many forms as he could imagine so that he would be prepared for anything; and the Executive, who excelled at intellectual mastery.

When Pete first examined his subpersonalities, he identified a part that he called the Hedonist. This subpersonality only appeared in the world as an outrageous flirt who also liked to watch pornographic films, all much to his wife's discomfort. As time passed, he found this part excited by the challenge of mastery of skiing, while pornography began to have less appeal. When he learned the story of Uncle Pete, he realized that this part of him, the Hedonist, was modeled on this family forebear. But the risking, adventurous side of his uncle was forbidden to him by family tradition, so the Hedonist acted in mildly antisocial ways, looking for that same excitement.

Now Pete saw that he had an opportunity to undo some of his family training. There were many possible ways to accomplish this goal. It really did not appeal to him to be a reckless daredevil, but the introduction of more excitement into his life was a refreshing open door. The habitual anxiety was learned at a preverbal time in his development and thus was not accessible to conscious thought. Pete found that this habitual anxiety was best dealt with from Center where there were no messages about wariness. When he found his body tensing, he immediately centered.

After some months, another surprising memory arose. His mother had yet a second relative like Uncle Pete—back a few generations was Buffalo Bill Cody. Laughing, Pete claimed he knew nothing about Buffalo Bill Cody, but at the same time realized the layers of family influence in his psyche.

FAMILY AS CULTURE

The many cultures of the world have developed from isolated groups of people searching for the best ways to live on this planet. They established means for consistently meeting survival needs, and, to quell anxiety, they chose the wisest answers they could find to questions about the unknown, such as explaining the power of the forces of nature, or understanding death. Whether it be the answer of a hunter-gatherer of ten thousand years ago or the best explanation of modern science, the cultural answers to these questions are primary shaping forces of the manner in which we live as part of the biological cycle of the earth.

A child is born into a culture. From birth she experiences a certain way of living that insures her survival and her acceptance into the society of her home. She is taught to be part of a culture; as the personality develops, the culture is built into its structure. The family is a small unit of society that teaches children the accepted cultural pattern. If a child is born in Borneo, her family will have different cultural practices from those of a family in England. No pattern is right or wrong in itself. It is the honest answer to problems of survival and living together that a group has found in its best provision for the needs of its people. True, some cultures live answers to these vital questions that are more humane, or practical, or more in accord with some other criterion, but in all cultures there are positive, unique features.

It is the job of the family to teach the child the culture. Communities continue because succeeding generations show the child how things are done in that community, so that the child grows up harmonizing in intent and action with the fundamental perspective of the culture. The child basically understands cultural patterns by the time she is four. This teaching is often so well done by families and by communities that there is a strong belief in the individual that indeed the culture in which she was raised is the only correct culture.

An interesting portrait of the world dilemma that this thorough teaching brings about is presented by Paul Scott in his four novels about the mesh of the British and Indian cultures in India at the time of the Second World War.[6] For instance, he describes the plight of two English girls born in India, who depart for England at a young age to be educated. They hate England and are eager to return to India. The culture they had been taught was a mixture of English and Indian, and they saw those family members who had not lived in India as impoverished and dull people, not at all aware of what they were missing. Another variation of this theme is seen in an Indian, transported by his father to England to be raised by English people from the age of two. When he has to return to India in his late teens, he has no Indian language or understanding of Indian culture and longs for the cool pristineness of England. Much to the consternation of both English and Indians, he behaves like an Englishman. The English girls had spent the crucial years of babyhood being influenced by both cultures and were deprived if both were not present. Within their personalities they were oriented to both cultural perspectives. The Indian boy, on the other hand, spent the most culturally impressionable years in England, and thus knew only one culture, English, which turned out to be alien to his later needs to harmonize with the segregated Anglo-Indian society in which he found himself.

A hundred years ago when transportation was largely horse and buggy, and many people lived all their lives in one small community, knowing only one culture was all that was necessary. But today, when you can telephone anywhere in the world in a few minutes and fly there in a matter of hours, to know only one culture is blindness to the world at your doorstep. The English girls born in India were indeed living a richer life than their English cousins in England. What is sad about the Indian boy is that his father, seeing all the power that the English had in

India, only valued English culture. In shielding him from Indian ways, he thought he was doing his child a favor, rather than actually handicapping him and preventing him from living a productive life.

It was a great surprise to me, raised in the American Midwest, to learn that people speaking different languages see the world in different ways. Years ago I attended an international exposition in which all exhibits were explained both in English and French. Even with a limited reading knowledge of French, I could still see that the French descriptions were entirely different from the English. Words with different bases, and thus different connotations, were combined in different sequences, so that the French presented different emphases and entirely different insights in their explanations of the exhibits. If I had known only English, I would have seen the exposition one way. But knowing a little French, I saw it two ways, and thereby had a richer experience.

Nowadays, then, there is a new job for the family. Not only is it important to teach a child to live in harmony with her home culture, but also to gain appreciation for other cultures and the adaptability and flexibility to live in harmony with other cultures. There is a widespread belief that if everyone in the world learned English and adopted Western ways, there would be a homogeneous world culture and that that would be the right way for the world to evolve. This is a very sad belief. We would lose all the wonderful flavors of the world cultures. Indeed, using an analogy from world cuisine, we would become meat-and-potatoes people, losing all the soufflés, curries, lo meins, and countless other culinary pleasures that we are too ignorant to even know exist. If a child is raised in a home that explores and values other cultures, she is at home in the world and does not think of other peoples as enemies.

Balancing the subpersonalities is making peace. In fact, the individual who wrestles with the peace between ethnic aspects of her subpersonalities, as well as dealing with the other seemingly irreconcilable differences, is working on the peace of the world. A group of hundreds and thousands of individuals committed to the same process provides the world with people who are capable of establishing world peace. As it is now, peoples of warring countries approach the negotiation tables not having made peace within themselves. Thus, the best that can be hoped for in the treaties created is a truce. The process of owning one's own inner United Nations, and learning to live harmoniously with all its parts, is a personal contribution to world peace.

7

CULTURE
The Grand Projection
of the Mind

The patterns of the psyche are projected onto the world. In the field of psychology, the mental mechanism of projection is usually seen in a negative light. This mechanism is responsible, however, for the greatest production of humankind, namely, civilization. The very patterns of the individual psyche, both conscious and unconscious, are projected onto the world cultures. This happens initially through one leader or a small group of leaders, and then as time passes, through the influence of more members of the group. First of all, a cultural group solves the problem of biological survival, then establishes patterns of social survival that often take on rich cultural color, and finally, just like the individual, the group grows into wider possibilities as all survival tasks become more automatic. The multifaceted early cultures, and later the national aggregates, are products of the projection of the mind. World development patterns are analogous to subpersonality development patterns. The macrocosmic patterns of the world are a mirror of the microcosmic psyche. In this chapter and the next we shall conclude our study of subpersonality patterns by examining how they project out onto the world, first into a particular culture and then into the world of nations.

Projection was described as a defense mechanism in psychoanalysis, in Jungian psychology, and also in psychosynthesis.

144

Projection is a process in which "the individual places outside himself and into another feelings or attributes which belong within, and comes to view the mental image thus produced as objective reality."[1] It was a concept first discussed by Freud in connection with paranoia, in which those thoughts within the individual associated with harm, secretiveness, blame, disloyalty, or any other negativity toward others are not seen as part of his own thinking but are believed to be part of the thinking and intent of others. In Jungian psychology an emphasis is laid on the projecting outward of negative shadow material. The negative shadow subpersonality causes unwanted inner conflict; the easy defense against inner conflict is to see that material elsewhere rather than to acknowledge its presence in one's own mind. Projection is a mischievous defense. Through its eyes what is seen as real may have nothing to do with actuality.

However, there is another understanding of projection which is extremely important. Outside the framework of the pathological, it is possible to appreciate that through this same mechanism, the mind has a wonderful capacity for using its own content for creation in the world. Early peoples functioned largely in an unconscious mind state. Unlike the present when most people have a conscious personality of many parts through which to process the world, early peoples projected onto the world unconscious imagery and knowledge and saw it not as products of their minds, but as the reality of the world. Facing fearful survival problems, they had to find solutions or perish. An unconscious image projected on the world was a start. What followed then was experiment, the use of the body to test the formulation, the conscious mind dialoguing with the projected unconscious image, and then the production of other unconscious images to further develop the survival solution. This is the work of the artist, but it was also the ingenious survival work of early man. The product of this mental process is what we call culture.

Many cultures have developed extraordinarily rich patterns of living; early in human history there were many small isolated groups of people answering the imperative survival questions through unique images and patterns arising from the individual unconscious. This is the everyday art of culture. It was not seen as art, however, but as the reality of the world because of the mental mechanism of projection. The unconscious image projected onto the world could not be owned as one's own thought, but as something miraculous that solves survival problems, and, of course, must be the real world itself.

The startling result of millennia of projection on the world is that the structure of culture is the same as the structure of the individual mind. The subpersonality structure, functional mental constellations developed for the maintenance of the individual on the planet, is the same structure that can be observed in every culture providing functional solutions to survival problems.

To get a better sense of the mutual mirroring of subpersonalities and cultural structure we will make use of a comprehensive model of culture devised by anthropologist Edward Hall.[2] (See page 152.) It was his purpose in developing a structural description of culture to find a meaningful framework for diplomats and others dealing with foreign cultures to use in understanding differences between peoples. He observed that many errors made in diplomatic service were caused by cultural blindness in the diplomat; the unconscious indoctrination of each person into his native culture makes it difficult for him to interpret and to mesh with other cultures. Hall experimented with the idea that culture could be taught like a language.

He began with the premise that since all humans are biological organisms, we have the same basic needs and biological functioning as all other inhabitants of this planet. Through the process of finding solutions to survival problems, each geographically isolated group has developed its own life-style. All the nuances of cultural creation become like a language within that group, understood by all members in great depth and subtlety, but a mysterious code to the outsider. If all survival problems were solved logically, cultures would be similar, with little mystery. However, because many solutions to survival problems came out of the unique mythopoetic projections of individuals' minds, there are many elements in each culture that are a "foreign language" to other cultures.

Hall describes ten developmental aspects of culture. These he refers to as primary message systems in the "language" of culture.

The first developmental aspect of culture is *interaction*, which is, at its most fundamental level, the irritability of protoplasm. This irritability has been the historical basis for the development of communication between organisms. Communication was initially simply bumping between one-celled animals. Ascending the phylogenetic order, however, interaction increasingly involved sound as well as complex body codes. In human beings language began primarily as body language that incorporated sound, but over many thousands of years it has become the complex and subtle language we know today with its elaborate structure and comprehensive meaning.

The second aspect of culture that Hall considers is *association*. Beginning first with simple unitary cells in association, living organisms over time have become increasingly complex with different life functions performed by groups of specialized cells. The social structure is a mirror of the living organism; each group of people develops a complex form of maintenance with subgroups that perform specific functions. The various aspects of governmental structure unique to each group speaks a "language" of that group's worldview to other peoples of the world.

Subsistence is the getting of sustenance. All forms of work that are related directly or indirectly to food-getting are a central activity of a culture. Where there is want, this activity is anxiety-ridden; where there is plenty, minimal requisite attention is focused on food production, with superfluous agricultural effort being diverted to other areas of cultural development. A cultural group develops characteristic food-handling patterns, which have color and individuality (for instance, types of food grown and eaten, methods of food preparation and service, and so on); ethnic cuisine as an expression of group character is probably the most popular and accessible aspect of intercultural experience.

When living organisms are satisfied as to food and environmental conditions, reproduction can take place. *Bisexuality* in people has resulted in differentiated sex roles that take various cultural forms. The communication patterns associated with sexuality and sex roles are complicated in all societies and fraught with many cultural idiosyncrasies.

Territoriality and *temporality* are two aspects of culture that concern the orientation of organisms. The establishment and continued possession of territory is an activity associated with the quality of the organism's life. If the quality of the organism's territory is not high enough, the organism cannot survive. The physical aspects of territory deeply affect the worldview of people. All human activities have an orientation toward specific geographical setting, quality of land, vegetation, and presence or absence of water. Personal space becomes an issue as the population of the world grows; the world view of people living close together is different from those who live with space. Protection of territory has been in all of history a major source of friction and the cause of wars, small and large. Throughout the animal kingdom, there are patterns of communication about territorial boundaries; the aggressive posturing of animals at a territorial boundary is the equivalent to human massing of troops at the border.

In regard to *temporality*, all planetary beings are subjected to cyclical and rhythmic patterns of time. Seasonal cycles and the birth-to-death cycle are numinous mythological and symbolic themes in every culture. Industrialized societies are dominated by sequential time structure; other groups may have different orientations to time, like the Hopi, whose language orients their thinking to consider all events, past, present, and future, as happening in the present.

Learning is important for all animals, but for humans it is of supreme importance. Most of human learning for all groups is focused on absorbing cultural patterns and knowledge. Modes of education and the particular emphases of various peoples differs as to what they see as paramount in educating the young. In all cultures there are deep beliefs about the body of knowledge to be inculcated in the thought and behavior of children. These passionate beliefs vary widely.

Play is closely linked to the process of learning. The essence of play is the discovery of meaning. All young animals engage in play, which is a rich source of their education about the world. Beyond its educative value, human beings have developed a sophisticated appreciation of play. Throughout the world there are many forms of play that are extraverted, colorful expressions of the nature of each culture. Most cultures value the less structured nature of play as a relaxation and counterbalance to the focused activities of work.

Defense, as an aspect of culture, is a broad category dealing with the well-being of the group. It is a basic need of all organisms to keep themselves safe. Many sophisticated and complicated forms of defense have been evolved by human beings. The most obvious presently, as well as historically, are all the machines of war, as well as the focus on law and its enforcement. The practice of medicine is a system of defense that originated in the need to heal injury and keep people safe from disease. Religion is another form of defense, which, in its simplest origins, was first practiced in hope of keeping the vagaries of the natural world from destroying man. The beliefs formed by a group to deal with the unknown and the mysteries in the areas of defense and maintenance of well-being have often been important solidarity factors in group identity.

The last of the basic aspects of culture is *exploitation*, which refers to optimum use of the environment to meet the needs of the organism. The goal of best use of the environment necessitates experimentation. On the basis of the results of experimentation, the organism develops a concept of acceptable life style. In this category is all the richness of man's invention.

These ten biological developmental aspects of culture, whether human culture or animal culture, interact with each other; none functions in isolation. Within a human culture, connections between each of these areas—belief systems, symbols, myths, and common heritage—develop and are shared by the people to act as a stabilizing influence on the community. A state of equilibrium in steady fulfillment of survival needs is created, without which the community dissolves.

When confronted with the task of learning a foreign culture, there are three different content areas that must be mastered in order to be included as a member. First, each culture has a body of knowledge and practice in any of the biological activity areas which can be taught to someone who does not live in the community. *Formal* behavior is the set of commonly accepted procedures: "This is the right way to do things here." It is a basic stabilizing belief and activity structure which is usually upheld with fervor. In some cultures, formal tradition plays an important role; even where formal tradition is not strong, there are nonetheless a set of standard practices that are connected with the harmony, stability, and safety of the community.

Technical activity patterns can also be easily learned by a foreigner. This body of knowledge is explicit, objective, and exact because it follows an agreed-upon set of procedural rules. Science, as we define it in our culture, is only one aspect of technical knowledge and activity. In fact, there are technical aspects to every life activity; it is in the technical formulations that the highest, clearest expression of consciousness of a culture is achieved.

Most elusive in understanding a culture are the *informal* behavior patterns. Most of these patterns have their origins in projection. Idiosyncratic patterns originating first in one mind are projected into the group, whether by shaman or priest, or humbler folk, like a mother. The practices, accepted as a survival truth, become established over time in large cultural groups. These patterns of interaction are learned from babyhood and early incorporated into everyday living patterns so that little conscious thought is necessary for their maintenance. They are governed by complicated rules that are largely unconscious and difficult to directly communicate. It is hard for children and new-comers to know when they have violated the rules; anxiety in a foreign culture is a result of unconsciously sensing that there are rules one does not understand. Learning happens primarily by watching models; rather than a teacher saying, "This is the right way," it is an indirect message of "You'll get the hang of it."

These three different modes of expressive behavior, like the ten life-activity areas, are constantly interfacing, interacting, and affecting change, in some societies slowly, in others more rapidly. Each of these behavioral modes is dynamic and infuses energy into the cultural system. The inevitable strains and frictions that can occur between the modes because of their differing behavioral approaches contribute to a pressure for change in the society. Yet at the same time they create a dynamic balance that maintains a stable equilibrium for the survival of the group.

CULTURE AS A PROJECTION OF A DOMINANT PERSONALITY

Hall's model of culture is a description of the macrocosm that is a product of the microcosm, the mind.[3] The dynamics of the individual personality, with its array of subpersonalities, is a portrait of a miniculture. Perhaps it is not any particular culture you can name in the world, but nonetheless, the subpersonality miniculture has the potential for a full-blown human culture, a direct mirror of the unique individual.

If a group of people conformed to the practices represented by one set of subpersonalities in one member of the group, a societal configuration would emerge that all would identify as a culture, having all the aspects described by Hall. No doubt other aspects of culture would also be present, which we sense in dealing with the varied peoples of the world but find impossible to formulate in Western terms because we necessarily operate through the limiting lenses of Western culture. The exotic color of cultures, those peculiar characteristics that endear and attract, or, contrarily, that infuriate, repel, and even cause wars, is due to the active archetypes—the cores—and the dense experiential layers

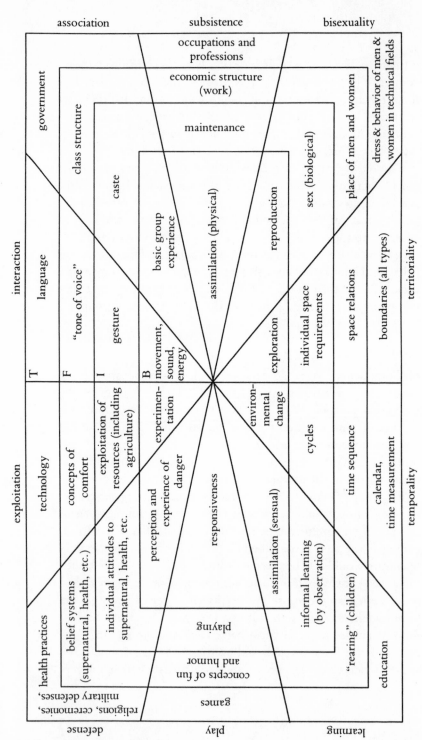

Figure 2. A model of culture, showing the biological basis (B) and its resulting informal (I), formal (F), and technical (T) aspects of human activity. Adapted from Edward T. Hall, *The Silent Language*, copyright © 1959, 1981 by Edward T. Hall. Reprinted by

of the subpersonalities. A consensus process happens in a group of people, whereby they agree on subpersonality patterns that are to be common interaction and behavior in the group. These come from the subpersonality archetypes; projected into the community, they create a "home" for all the people, a basis for all to belong.

It is probable from the history pieced together about early times that original cultural shapes did begin on the basis of modeling a single personality, namely the shaman's. In early society, the shaman, or the wise man, was the seer, who answered the survival questions from the depths of his own experience. The shamans were more evolved than others of their group, and thus served as models for their group's developmental process.[4] Indeed, the first developmental stages of many cultures could well have been a grand projection of one personality on the world. Over time, of course, many generations of shamans of that cultural group would contribute to molding the cultural shape.

To illuminate this point, let us as a simple experiment consider the subpersonality configurations of Benjamin, Helene, and Julia presented in chapter six, as hypothetical shamans of hypothetical cultures. Three striking, distinctly different portraits of possible cultures emerge.

A culture patterned on Benjamin's original personality would be heavily masculine because of the dominance of masculine subpersonalities. Since we know of Benjamin that the Wizard was the overriding subpersonality, so that its expression would be the dominant style, the culture would be extroverted to the point of theatricality, intellectual with an emphasis on cleverness, and also fantastical. The balanced, clear, creative qualities of Quicksilver, which were in the background in Benjamin's life, would be in the background in the culture as well, focused on the necessity for survival and expressed in great flashes only in the areas of exploration and learning. The coloring of the Giant—physical softness, largeness, and awkwardness—would appear in areas concerning physicality, such as issues of sustenance, sexuality, play, or even defense, but always with a focus on rules. Feminine expression would appear only in a weak form or not at all.

The culture suggested by Helene's original individual functioning is predominantly feminine, and because of the persona subpersonality Rosie, focused on polite sensitivity to others' expectations. Before the advent of Shao, a feminine wisdom figure, none of the personality parts were focused on technical living, which resulted in Helene's haphazard existence. In a culture this would manifest as dependence on magical practice for survival rather than practical problem solution. With Shao's influence, technicality would be characterized by feminine simplicity and practicality, except in the areas of learning and temporality, where there would be both masculine and feminine approaches because of Iman's presence, solid masculine linear scholarship. All basic biological functions, except sexuality, would be de-emphasized in a culture modeled on Helene's original personality.

If Julia, with her present set of subpersonalities, were a leader in an ancient human group, her cultural influence would have been in the direction of emphasis on peaceful harmony between people and with the earth. Because of the subpersonality Gayle, social interaction would have been characterized by laughter and light playfulness as well as caring and compassion. There would have been order, practicality, and emphasis on visual aesthetics.

In each hypothesized culture, beyond survival needs it would be purely idiosyncratic which activities would be emphasized and in what form. Each subpersonality would impact cultural formation in a unique way.

The individual patterns of subpersonalities in cultural groups, multiplied by thousands, even millions, has resulted in the ferment of national character, producing both positive and negative results on the national and international scene.

The subpersonalities of Americans are more widely diverse than any other nation on earth. Our history as a people coming together from all parts of the world has brought along developmental elements from practically all of the world's cultures. This amalgamation has produced a psychological stimulation that underpins the high level of technological invention and industry that has been attained. In almost all parts of the country, especially urban areas, one is constantly in contact with people newly arrived to the United States, or second- or third-generation Americans who still carry at least in some part of their thinking the influence of the culture of their forebears. The result is that in any lively interchange in all areas of American culture, the differing life perspectives are constantly abutting. The resolution of the inevitable resulting tension pushes individuals into a creative mindset; there must first be acknowledgement of the reality of the differing views followed by emergence of a new perspective, not identical to either original view, but more likely transcending them both. The establishment of a world-wide Western style culture, as some like to foresee, would annihilate a fundamental basis for creativity. Culturally diverse American society is an ongoing productive experiment with the implication for world reality that all cultures can contribute to the advancement of each other.

In the Soviet Union these same interchanges of cultural values and benefits has begun to happen in recent decades. Because of the size of the country, there are many cultural groups included within its borders. Since the revolution in 1917 the enormous illiteracy rate of the Russian people has been drastically reduced (99 percent are literate today compared with 20 percent in 1917) through establishment of universal education. The result is increasingly able business and professional people, trained by the standard Soviet educational system, but raised in a variety of cultures. They converge on the cities where they work together. Cultural identity is maintained by the fact that the Russian curriculum is taught in more than forty languages.

THE INDIVIDUAL'S CULTURAL HERITAGE

Up to now in this chapter we have been discussing the way in which a culture reflects individual subpersonality structure; now let us turn to the reverse process, namely the way cultural heritage contributes to the formation of subpersonality structures in an individual. These two processes are, of course, deeply intertwined and there is a constant movement back and forth between, on the one hand, the prevailing subpersonalities in individual members of a particular culture and, on the other hand, the characteristics of that culture.

In the process of subpersonality formation, the incorporation of cultural elements is inherent and inevitable. Subpersonalities are first tools for meeting individual survival and societal needs. This is a process of adaptation, which means that the child will learn, before he even has language, many subtle nuances of the family cultural attitudes and perspectives.

Since the child is vulnerable, it is particularly important for him to learn the parental attitudes and procedures to be used in times of threat and danger, small or large. On a nonverbal and early verbal level, the child incorporates basic responses to threatening circumstances and learns the basic ideologies that answer for his people the unanswerable questions. Even if the child in later life learns in another cultural setting a whole new set of answers to cultural questions by which he then learns to live, yet in some functional aspects, he carries remnants of the important early cultural formulae, for example, inexplicable superstitious behavior, or deep respect for the beauty of his culture of origin. These early-learned fundamentals of culture are difficult to erase, so deeply embedded are they in the psyche, as well as being difficult to teach to someone else. As has already been noted, they are learned more through modeling and emotional osmosis than any formal teaching.[5] "There is no way for human beings to forge a valid identity outside a particular historical situation."[6] "The development of personality and the acquisition of culture are one and the same process."[7]

My Apprenticeship by Maxim Gorky is one of three books he wrote about his childhood in Russia during the last years of the nineteenth century. Its imagery is enthralling—poetically lyrical and beautiful in some places, and stark and brutal in others—

painting a simple but vivid child's picture of Russian culture. One finds this culture also embedded in the heavily layered works of Tolstoy and Dostoyevsky. The clarity of Gorky's depiction was acknowledged by Tolstoy who said, "The man seems to be all eyes. . . . The wonderful thing is that he saw and noted down things other people were incapable of seeing or, if they saw were powerless to record."[8]

At the end of the book in a few succinct words, Gorky describes his own personality structure. In the midst of analyzing the effects of some of the harsh experiences of his childhood, he delineates two parts of his personality that he saw as products of the survival strategies he developed in response to the demands of the culture. "There were two persons living within me. One of them had experienced far too much that was filthy and nasty and had as a result become rather timid. This person who was crushed by his knowledge of the horror of everyday life had begun to look upon it distrustfully, suspiciously, with a helpless feeling of compassion for everyone—even for himself. This man dreamed of a quiet, solitary life with books and without people, of a monastery, of a life as a forest-warden, of living in a railway man's hut, of going to Persia or working as a night watchman on the outskirts of some town. There were fewer people in this kind of life and one was more remote from them. The other man had been baptized by the holy spirit that he had read about in books written by honest and wise men. Although he realized how terrible reality was, how insuperable its horrors were, although he felt that its strength was enough to tear his head off or trample his heart under its filthy boots, he still persisted in defending himself, and was always ready for a quarrel or a fight. This man transferred his love and compassion for people into deeds and like a hero from a French novel he would pull his sword from its scabbard and take a fighting stance."[9]

Here are two subpersonalities. The first is a battered child, flinching from expected pain, nursing inner wounds, and seeking escape because of his awareness of his deep vulnerability and that of others. The second is a heroic defender, a warrior, taking on the righteous cause of preventing suffering for himself and others. The wounded child and warrior protector subpersonalities are familiar. All the words of this quotation could have been written in any culture; it is an expression of a universal experience of subpersonality function.

The particular color that Gorky expresses here, however, is shaped by Russian culture, not American or Chinese. Only a Russian could have written this particular book. In reading this passage descriptive of Gorky's personality after reading the rest of the book, one understands his emotional focus to be one of deep suffering of the individual and heartfelt empathy for others' suffering; a sense of helplessness before the ever erupting circumstantial hardship of life, and a feeling of impotent rage, all of which is part of a historical Russian perspective. The "Russianness" of Gorky's writing and life perspective is acknowledged by the Soviet writer Paustovsky, who says of Gorky, "For me, Gorky *is* Russia and just as Russia without the Volga is unimaginable, so Russia without Maxim Gorky is equally unthinkable."[10]

In fact the warrior part of Gorky is a typical personality configuration referred to in Russian as the *ozornik*. The ozornik is one "who rebels against . . . outrages and whose feelings boil over in active hostility and pugnacity, with an accompanying desire to shock people out of their complacency and self-satisfaction—a nonacceptance of a dreary monotony, a meaningless life."[11] In all languages there are designations for particular patterns of behavior that are seen frequently in the culture that give people quick reference to common subpersonality manifestations. In English, for instance, there are personality designations such as "brat," "wallflower," or "bully," which do not describe a whole personality but usually only the behavior of a single subpersonality or a small group of subpersonalities.

The particular ethnic color of an individual's heritage can be manifested in the subpersonalities in a number of ways. First of all, ethnic group identification is often seen immediately by the individual as part of the original image of the subpersonality he observes. "Ralph is Italian," "She is a Jewish mother," or "He has a Chinese face." This immediate acknowledgment of ethnic identity recognizes a pattern of historical family attitudes, sometimes celebrated as part of the family richness, sometimes burdensome and limiting, reflecting an ancient defense pattern that is no longer useful. Often the simple ethnic label enables positive elements to be claimed that may not have been acknowledged consciously. It also allows the disowning of anachronistic pieces of belief and behavior that do not fit in the effective whole of the individual. There can be genuine surprise at the ethnic identification: "I had a Chinese great-grandfather, but I hardly ever think of him." In this case, there has been a subtle incorporation of attitude and value patterns that is recognized by the unconscious as Chinese. Many people in American society have lost sight of their original ethnic heritage, because the family aim of becoming thoroughly American has left the ancestral heritage obscured after several generations. For them the study of their family's original cultural practices, such as its language, customs, or history can provide deeply enriching and broadening material in the development of the individual.

It sometimes happens that an ethnic identification is made in a subpersonality in its first recognition that does not represent family heritage. Then the ethnic identification is important in its symbolic significance. Some qualities of the particular culture have meaning to the individual growth pattern. One woman, plagued by a demanding, recalcitrant child subpersonality, found a shadow personality part, a wise old African woman representing her inner wisdom. Study of African culture increased the depth of this subpersonality, making it alive and active as a part of her behavior, and giving her access to a means of displacing the unwelcome power of the child part.

CULTURE AND SUBPERSONALITIES

Subpersonalities defined in terms of function often are not seen as having any ethnic qualities other than American cultural influences. The career, the social, or the purely defensive subpersonalities may be essentially "American" because it is their job to skillfully negotiate society. Their expertise in accommodating the person to his world demands deep and subtle absorption of American patterns. If, however, a particular subpersonality is examined with respect to the level of comfort it might have in other cultures, a cultural orientation is often revealed. It may be that this very part expresses the reorientation to American society by the ancestral immigrant, producing action on a daily basis so completely in harmony with American patterns that the original ethnic perspective is masked.

Then, of course, there are subpersonalities which have no specific cultural orientation. There is no importance in these as to how the basic human needs are fulfilled as long as they are fulfilled. Often these parts are child parts, adaptable and malleable to an extreme. In this respect, they are primary change centers within the personality, indeed closer to Center than those subpersonalities that are highly enculturated. No matter which culture this subpersonality found itself in, there would be immediate orientation and rapid learning so that the individual would be quickly safe and at home. Associated with such adaptability is creative and inventive thought. In the artist and the inventor, this aspect of the personality is often a persona subpersonality.

Adaptable subpersonalities are different from functional subpersonalities, although both learn cultural patterns. The functional subpersonality is complexly layered with learning and acquired skills. There is in this type of personality aspect a cultural heritage underlying a structure that mimics the present cultural environment. If this subpersonality were to be thrust into a new culture, however, the strong structure of enculturation that has served it well in its home environment would prevent rapid adaptation. In fact, in such situations, the subpersonality would most likely create a defensive posture because of discomfort and confusion. In order to adapt, this specialized subpersonality must go through a painful process of tearing away layers of the old cultural rules and rebuilding a new system.

The adaptable subpersonality, on the other hand, is structurally more simple. Its fundamental needs and motivational attitudes remain simple and its investment in cultural patterns, though it may use them well, is limited. Thus, thrust into a new culture, this type of subpersonality aspect adapts quickly, using a style of open learning and acceptance that is characteristic of early childhood learning.

Those subpersonalities that directly represent archetypal energy whether in human form, like a king or a clown, or in nonhuman form, like a tree or a bear, often transcend cultural expression. These subpersonalities, unlike the adaptable kind just described, may not be very adaptable. There is in them a particular classic energy, expression, and style, that remains constant. If the individual were to move from culture to culture, the basic expression of the archetypal subpersonality would remain the same. It is a pure energy, a bare, basic expression, whether it fits in the culture or not.

It is important in the growth of the individual to honor the original impact of his ancestral culture on the shape of his personality. Many people in the United States have little knowledge of the cultures from which their ancestors came because there was such a drive by immigrants to become American. They tried to leave their cultural heritage behind in honor of the society they chose to join. As a result, their children have varying amounts of the family culture hidden away in their personalities. The teaching of the American family has largely been, Be American, Succeed American.

In my experience of my own subpersonalities, when I came to know a number of them, I was surprised to find a wide diversity of cultures represented in my personality, some elements of which have explainable antecedents while others are more mysterious. At one point, Dagmar, the lady executive, and Camille, the more idealistic poetic side, were joined by Sophie and Garnet. A little later I became aware of a tiger, a green hippopotamus, and a lady who lived in the Himalayas, but these were less important.

My first image of Sophie was of a heavy-set woman with tight, blond curls, a round, heavy face and small eyes, who was seated on an ancient Grecian-style chair, which I called a throne. I immediately knew that the woman was Polish. Puzzling over the elements of this rich image, I finally connected it with my Polish great-grandmother, but for the Grecian throne I had no ready explanation.

When I watched for the expression of Sophie in my life, I saw that Sophie was the "great doer." With dogged endurance, Sophie undertook far too much for anyone to do. Not only did she execute projects for all aspects of me, but she also accepted as her responsibility fulfilling everything expected by those around her. Her intelligence was dulled by confusion; she was not able to set priorities but simply worked blindly to the point of exhaustion. She was humble, self-effacing, shy, and felt guilty if she had not met everyone's expectations. She seemed ironic and contradictory next to Dagmar's intelligent, organized strength.

Here in Sophie, I recognized my grandmother and parts of my mother. The pattern of behavior has been carried on through four evident generations and probably countless generations of ancestry. I, as the fourth generation, still had a Polish peasant woman in my personality. I felt pride that Sophie could work hard and devotedly, and it delighted me to honor Sophie as I would my own grandmother. Where I had been habitually functioning under high stress, the observation of Sophie provided objectivity that immediately reduced stress. All the other parts now helped with organization and prioritizing, and they all celebrated the fine accomplishments of the "great doer."

The Greek throne still remains a mystery, but the way symbols work, it probably holds a key to Sophie's future development.

The cultural aspects of my other major subpersonalities represent a wide variety. Dagmar is a functional subpersonality, very American in character in that she has a strong sense of political savvy, competition, and ability to accomplish what she sets out to do. Underlying the strong American traits, I found my northern European family heritage. Dagmar really would only be comfortable with English, Germanic, and Scandinavian cultures. It surprised me to find so fine a distinction as Dagmar's sensitivity to French culture compared to her ease with the Swiss.

Garnet is a gypsy; she is nomadic and carries a diverse ethnic identification. It could be French or Egyptian, perhaps Spanish or Greek. She is one of a dark-haired, dark-skinned, dancing people. This personality part has a persistent archetypal energy that at the same time expresses a strong flavor of cultural cross-identification. The ethnic orientation of this subpersonality was not part of my family of origin at all.

Camille, on the other hand, is an adaptable one. Close to nature and carrying simple natural values, she is unburdened by cultural structure. Her orientation is artistic, thus she is fascinated by variety in any form, including cultural. In any social structure she adapts in a simple way and flourishes.

THE ASIAN HERITAGE IN AMERICA

For those with European cultural background, blending in, losing the ethnic characteristics of the "old country" has been relatively easy. After a few generations the family heritage was put aside, the new generations knowing little about the culture of their heritage, becoming thoroughly American. The cultural ideal of white Anglo-Saxon Protestant as the image of success can be learned.

For those whose skin and facial structure are different, assimilation has been another process. Consider the experiences of Cliff and Clara.

Cliff said, "Why am I an American, and I have a Japanese face?" Cliff was third-generation Japanese-American. He looked back on a childhood offering him most everything he needed in material support, and as an adult much richness in friendships and loving people around him. Yet, he found himself troubled by a child part that was weak and wounded. Looking for the origins of this mysterious troubled part, Cliff found two factors. He was born to his parents shortly after they had left the World War Two American relocation camps for Japanese Americans, which was for many a degrading experience. The other factor was being a Marine in Vietnam; like many combat veterans from that war, Cliff suffered shock from the experience. The image Cliff had of this child subpersonality within him was a little Japanese boy who had been brutally beaten and abandoned to die. He spent years trying to heal this part of himself, seeking help from others, seeking nurturance in relationships, and working desperately on his own. Part of this healing process was to affirm strength in other parts of himself. He again recognized the strength of the warrior he had met in himself in Vietnam. But this time, in the healing effort, he chose to develop in this part a skill and ritual that was Japanese. He studied aikido.

Over a period of years he became an adept practitioner of aikido, attaining the coveted black belt. The effect of the discipline and the centering process required began to affect his whole life. He translated his learning into conflict resolution technique, the peaceful warrior, which he taught others. His vision was so clear that his language became poetic. It was at this time that he determined that the child part should be allowed to peacefully die. In the child he had carried a negative cultural image. In his work in aikido, he was living the positive Japanese cultural image, adapting and developing it now within American culture. [12]

Clara's father came to the United States from China to attend graduate school just before the Communist revolution. When the political structure of China completely changed, he was unable to return. His wealthy family in China became destitute. In the United States he married a woman of German ancestry who came from a poor Midwestern American family. Clara's father established himself well in this country, and the family became wealthy. From the time Clara was small, all she could remember of her mother was her harshness. Her father was more nurturing; as she became older, she also saw in him the model of success. Thus, unconsciously she strongly identified with her Chinese heritage. She learned to speak fluent Chinese and worked for a time in Hong Kong.

When Clara identified her subpersonalities, she found first a bewildered, frightened six-year-old Chinese girl whom she named Chris. Next there came two overwhelming figures, Karen and Bertha. Karen was cold as an adding machine; she prescribed rigid rules for Clara's behavior to keep her safe. Bertha was a monstrous defender, dressed in a primeval warrior's leather outfit. Bertha followed the dictates of Karen. In the background was Maria, who was pretty, realistic, and could be either calm and quiet or merry. Maria knew the power of Karen and Bertha, but did not take it very seriously. Much relief was brought into Clara's life when Chris was befriended by Maria. Later there emerged a wise older woman part, who was associated with Clara's growth as a professional.

Clara saw at once that trouble in her personality was in the subpersonalities modeled after her mother's behavior, Bertha and Karen. She saw them as northern European in their cultural style. Though she felt she was presenting a fine expression of herself in her identification with her Chinese face and her rich Chinese heritage, the balancing of her personality, and, thus, the peace in her life lay in her accepting and integrating the German parts of her personality. Starting at a point of pure revulsion, which was actually her anger at her mother, Clara studied German culture, looking first for what she could feel positive about, and then could love. In this roundabout way she began to deal with the anger toward her mother that had been too painful to face, acknowledging finally the love that had been there all along.

Making peace within themselves for both Cliff and Clara meant dealing with their alien cultural heritage. Cliff was taught by our society to reject his Oriental heritage and own only his finely polished American ways. Clara, on the other hand, was taught by her mother's harshness to disown her German heritage, which is closer to mainstream American culture than Chinese, and to identify almost exclusively with Chinese culture, thus making Clara feel like a foreigner in her own country. The wholeness of their lives was dependent on their owning the true richness of their double cultural heritage.

IDEOLOGIES: GROUP MYTHS AND SYMBOLS

Like people, cultures are rife with conflict. The many dimensions of survival, both for an individual and for societal groups, inevitably lead to conflicting goals. One way to understand the management of conflict in cultures is to consider the development and function of ideologies. What is ideology? Most basically, ideology is the doctrine, myth, and symbols of a social group. [13]

Ideologies develop in cultures to fulfill several needs. First, many ideologies are connected with the development of power and strength needed for protection. Ideologies act to unify effort in developing protective mechanisms. The step beyond power for protection is power for advantage. Ideologies thus support and motivate all powerful action for protection and advantage.

Another factor in the development of ideologies is the strain created by conflictful elements within a society. The balance between such basic opposites as freedom and structure, stability and change, and efficiency and human needs, for instance, is difficult to achieve for both individuals and groups. Thus, beliefs develop which help to settle the questions of balance so that the group can function. For example, in communist countries, ideologies emphasize structure, while in democratic countries, the ideologies emphasize freedom. When the issue is settled philosophically, the countries can get on with peaceful mundane function. Because of the strain of opposite strivings within human needs, there is a chronic tendency toward the faulty integration of society, which is eased by the development of ideologies—beliefs, myths, and stories.

Many ideologies can be analyzed in terms of specific socio-psychological factors. One is catharsis, a displacing of a group frustration onto another group: for example, the Nazi ideology that the Jews had control of too much of the wealth of Germany. Many of the speeches of Churchill during the war contained phrases that activated deep ideological images and were aimed at rallying morale and group solidarity. Whether it be war or some other societal endeavor, the purpose of ideologies is always to create group identity and focus diverse individual resources in a particular direction. Another type of ideology is advocative; it aims to develop awareness of a problem area in society and bring about change. However, if the idea advocated is too far from societal awareness, it often has the effect of entrenching existing positions rather than bringing about change.

The ideologies of a people form a vast network of "interacting symbols, patterns of interworking meanings."[14] A map is created that reveals both the problems of a culture and the possibilities for change, the malleable aspect of a society through which growth and development can take place. In areas where a group is settled into an efficient functional mode, ideologies do not develop; if a way of dealing with an issue or a life need of a group has been established that works well and causes little friction, there is little reason to develop a doctrine, myth, or symbol about it. There may be ideological content that is part of the history and heritage of a group that relates to an issue, but when an issue is settled, the ideology is no longer a compelling factor in group awareness.

How does an ideology create an effect on a group of people? The answer to this question is illuminated by comparing ideologies with science. Both are focused on the delineation of problem areas where there is a lack of information, but they operate in different ways. The language used by each has entirely different qualities. In the case of science, the goal is to remain objective, disinterested, and dispassionate. Thus, the language is restrained and seeks, above all, clarity. The purpose of ideology, on the other hand, is to gain commitment, so the language tends to be ornate, suggestive, and filled with moral sentiment. Throughout history, ideologies have played a strong role whenever science was not able to ease people's anxieties by giving a reasoned solution to a problem. Since the ancient Greeks had no scientific explanation for the diurnal movement of the sun, they quelled anxiety about the sun's permanence with the belief that Apollo took charge of the chariot of the sun and faithfully drove it across the sky each day. Those issues that are settled by the reason and clarity of science become part of a people's peaceful aspects of living even though science may not yet have answered all questions. Through ornate, emotional, suggestive language and moral sentiment, ideologies gain commitment to "solutions" to problems that in fact do not have clear solutions.

Ideologies often contain metaphors, the power of which lies in the power of archetypes, this time on a societal level. Most metaphors present a visual image that shifts the thinking out of a logical framework into emotion, and large patterns of meaning connected to both animal and human heritage are accessed. The ideological metaphor often makes a false analogy. "War is hell" (American, WWII) and "War is the father of creation" (Japan, 1934) are very different beliefs. Each presents a visual image that transcends the literal meaning of the word *war*. Thus a larger mental framework emerges around the original concept. The visual images created have motivational power. In this case, the motivations would be for actions in opposite directions: "War is hell" leads away from war, while "War is the father of creation" leads toward engaging in war.

These two examples of ideologies from different cultures are a minute sample of ideological patterns of two different peoples. Behind each statement, however, there is not only the literal experience of war but the history and network of a whole people. The highly complicated total ideological framework of each group is largely consistent in itself, having strong elements in any one direction that are counterbalanced by elements that coordinate and correlate with elements in other directions.

IDEOLOGIES AND PERSONALITY

Ideologies develop and function in society in the same way that belief systems develop and function in subpersonalities. Like ideologies for the group, the belief systems of the subpersonalities have their origins in the attempt to accommodate to the realities of the world. The essence of a subpersonality is its belief about how to function in the world. Upon examination of an individual, those subpersonalities that are first evident are those associated with conflict. Likewise, the ideologies that draw attention are those that cause conflict within a group or between groups. As the conflict area is resolved in the case of both ideologies and subpersonalities, their images tend to fade in importance and other growth issues of the society or the individual take their place. Ideological fortresses of society are like the belief systems of protector subpersonalities; in areas of uncertainty, they try to establish certainty, safety, and stability.

A culture creates an imprint on the developing infant mind, which results in the development of subpersonality belief systems. The individual adult then, in turn, can impact culture as a result of the evolution of his individuality. The natural subpersonality belief system within him may be discrepant with his culture, but can have appealing form, or present a solution to a problem, and thus may impact the shape of culture. An example of this process is seen in the life of Einstein. His individual strength defied the early stigma of misdiagnosed retardation. Over a long period of time he tenaciously developed initially nebulous ideas until a concept of reality emerged that has impacted the whole civilized world.

A network of ideologies formed by a group of people is a map of their culture. Likewise, the belief systems of subpersonalities are a map of the dynamics of an individual. As ideologies are a matrix for change in society, the central beliefs in subpersonalities are also the matrix for the transformation of the individual. The subpersonalities form a consistent set of interacting functioning beliefs within the person, a set of interworking meanings like the set of ideologies of a culture. And, as with a given culture and its set of ideologies, even though a given personality with its array of subpersonalities may be conflicted and maladaptive, nonetheless, within both, an intricate set of checks and balances creates a complete unit, in one case a multifaceted culture, in the other a multifaceted personality.

The characteristic function of ideologies in a culture is also valid for the function of subpersonality belief systems in the person. In subpersonalities, as in ideological catharsis, there can be displacement of frustration on symbolic enemies in the form of projection. In subpersonalities, as in ideological morale building, there are always mental messages that concern internal morale and solidarity; in fact, when these are missing, the individual tends to fall into helplessness and depression. As do ideologies in culture, subpersonalities serve in the establishment of power for protection of the person. Similar to the mechanism in cultures, the protector aspects of subpersonalities may be seduced by the glamour and excitement of power play and the striving for superiority, which gives rise to the seeking of advantage over others.

The natural mythmaking ability of the human mind, the mythopoetic function, emerges in the creation of ideologies, attempting to penetrate issues that are rife with uncertainty and raise anxiety, and, in the process, reaching experience that goes beyond what verbal capacity can express. An example of this is the image of the bald eagle with its wings spread, which in American culture is a powerful image of freedom. In America's early years as a developing nation this symbol countered the fear of a repetition of European autocracy, and it now continues as a symbol of an ideal, not only for the United States, but in some respects also for the world. In a similar fashion, the subpersonality constellations quell anxieties by establishing belief systems couched in metaphoric images that present the deepest, richest potential of the individual, which is difficult to grasp in any other than metaphoric or mythic language. "There is part of me that is like an aspen tree." "There is a part of me that is a bear."

These people are not literally aspen trees or bears, but again, as in the case of ideologies, the discordant meaning results in transcendence, and the universal qualities of aspen trees and bears are understood as a potential in the development of the individual. The subpersonality moves into an archetypal expression that is bigger than the original conception of the conflicted subpersonalities. As many have fought actual wars under the figurative banner of the American eagle, the American dream, or the American way of life, so aspen trees and bears and other images have brought forth the courageous inner warrior who fights the wars of internal conflict to establish the peace of integration in the individual personality. And like the network of multileveled meanings of ideologies in a culture, so there is the network of the interaction of the meanings of all the symbolic content of the several subpersonalities of the individual, a vast panorama of potential.

THE ZUÑI: A DIFFERENT STORY

I would like to end this discussion of the mutual interaction of culture and personality with a short account of the Zuñi culture and its effect on anthropologists who visited it.[15] The Zuñi world is a very different one from the modern Western cultures we have been examining so far. The Zuñi culture has been an autocracy in which the interests of the individual are subordinated to the needs of the whole group. If an individual does not want to live by the rules, he is expected to leave the pueblo. No individual leader arbitrarily rules the group; rather, the group is ruled by a life philosophy.

Historically, the Zuñi have lived on desert land, and the reality of life there for an agricultural people is the need for water. So great is the focus on the beneficent properties of water for their life that the primary way of designating a positive aspect of anything in their society is to refer to it as "water-filled," for example, water-filled rooms or water ladders, meaning solid, useful ladders. Thus, their autocratic way of life evolved around practices developed to obtain water for their crops. Over a long period of time, an elaborate ceremonial procedure developed for invoking the forces of nature, the gods, to send rain. It is believed that if the procedure is not followed exactly, there would be no rain. The welfare of the whole group served by safe repetitious ritual always takes precedence over individual initiative. The focus of the events in the set calendar are on the elaborate rain rituals; the most important work of the priests is in the use of their personal power to bring rain. Their belief in perfect performance of the elaborate ritual is comparable to the Zen Buddhist practice of military and fine arts. The goal is to clarify and perfect the centered energy of the practitioner so that there is harmony with universal patterns. In this psychological state, the Zuñi priests believe that they can bring enough rainfall to ensure the survival of the people.

In 1530 when the Spanish in Mexico first heard about the Zuñi, the tribe was reported to have seven "mighty" cities. Through disease, conflict with the Spanish and other raiding Indian tribes, and later the American army, they were reduced to a population of seventeen hundred living in one village in 1879.

The exigency of the need for water, forcing these people to rally their powers to deal with nature, brought about a system of tribe-wide discipline in which each individual knew his important part in the harmonious functioning of the whole group. The original seven cities represented seven clans arranged in hierarchical order. The hierarchy established a rotating authority over tribal matters and a governmental form, effective to the point of a perpetual state of peace and crimelessness. Four of the seven clans represent the four directions, north, south, east, and west. Each of these groups is associated with a season of the year: north with winter, west with spring, south with summer, and east with autumn. The hierarchical authority shifts according to the season of the year, that clan being responsible for the ceremonial practices of that time of year. The fifth and sixth clans are the upper world and the lower world; they are involved in all the activities of the people. The seventh clan is considered central, the heart, the first and last. In hierarchy, it is considered to be first or last. There is also a traditional sequence of precedence that involves all individuals.

Within each clan, there are six groups, each named for a god, a totem. For instance, in the north clan there are crane people and evergreen oak people; in the west, there are bear, coyote, and spring herb people; in the south, tobacco and maize people. Individuals of each group believe themselves to be the "breath children" of their totem. Each clan has specific important activities to perform for the benefit of the whole tribe. There are also separate societies with elaborate auxiliary functions. As the structure of the society works, each member has a function and understands his contribution to the whole. The identity of each individual is confirmed by the many symbols of the direction of his clan, giving him a firm, rich sense of group inclusion.

The seventh clan, the central, all-containing, or mother clan, functions in a role of synthesis. In their concept of Earth, this clan is central in the Zuñi tribe, and the Zuñi are the center of the Earth. These are the Macaw people, having all colors of the tribe, containing all others and divisible into them. Historically, it was from the central clan that the others evolved when two ancient tribes banded together for their mutual benefit. They designed a septuarchy, but it was always the responsibility of the central clan to maintain the solidarity of the Zuñi people.

In 1879, the anthropologist, Frank Hamilton Cushing, traveled to New Mexico with an anthropological expedition from the Smithsonian Institution.[16] When the group arrived at the Zuñi pueblo on the Santa Fe River, Cushing felt he could not learn much about the people if he lived at the mission station. Impulsively he moved into an empty room he discovered on a visit to the pueblo. The Zuñi allowed him to stay because they felt that there might be some advantage in cultivating a relationship with him in their negotiations with the American army. The other members of the expedition moved on, disapproving Cushing's act and leaving him dependent on the Zuñi. He spent four-and-a-half years in the pueblo, his work supported by only one

Smithsonian official. He was eventually forced to leave by the American government because of his objection to the military seizure of Indian lands.

The Zuñi taught Cushing to live like an Indian, which was difficult for him because he was frail. After arduous training, he was admitted to the prestigious high order of the Priesthood of the Bow and became a leader of the tribe. He participated in all aspects of Zuñi life except marriage, studying with particular diligence the skills involved in crafts. His letters reveal the toll of hardship in the work but, at the same time, the personal triumph and expansion.

There are evident in Cushing's experience at least three parts of his personality: an astute, brilliant scientist; a physically weak subpersonality; and a hardy noble Indian. These parts of him appeared to be in conflict not only during his experience at the pueblo but during the course of his whole life. His professional side, even though he was only in his mid-twenties when he left the Zuñi, displayed enormous talent that all in the field looked to for an important contribution. His writings were empathic, clear, and beautiful, presenting to the anthropologists of the day a new way of working—participant observation. His professional work, however, was constantly interrupted by bouts of illness that left his work fragmentary and incomplete. His life was short; he died at the age of forty-three.

The third part of his personality one might think of as a shadow subpersonality. Years before Cushing went to New Mexico, he dreamt repeatedly about the land of the pueblos and of kachina figures. At the time, he had no awareness of the meaning of the dreams. He had never been in the southwest nor exposed to any information on kachinas. Looking at a museum photograph, he one day discovered his dream image of the kachina, identified as "Zuñi, New Mexico." He then was eager to accompany the Smithsonian expedition that set out for those lands. While living with the Zuñi, he became so much at one with their ways that they could love and respect him to the point of giving him honor as a leader and long remembering him after he left, wishing he could return. The Indian subpersonality, first appearing in his life when he searched for arrowheads for countless hours as a child, became well developed in the pueblo so that when he returned to Washington, his personal identity was strongly Indian; he customarily signed his letters not only with his anthropological title but with his Indian designation as well. When Cushing hosted the visit of Zuñis in the East, he was greeted by an Indian brother with an embrace and the prayer of greeting between two priests of the Bow who had long been separated. In front of the Zuñi, Cushing was embarrassed about his life in Washington, as if he were "a country boy fallen into decadent ways of the city and trying to look innocent before the parents who had found him there."[17] In contrast, the simple peace, order, and fairness of the Zuñi way of life commanded Cushing's deepest respect.

The main thrust of his work after his return was not to write a complete exhaustive scientific treatise on the culture of the Zuñi, much to the disappointment of the anthropological community, but to use his knowledge and influence to try to convince the American government that forcing the Zuñi into a Christian mode would destroy them. He searched for a way of integrating the Zuñi society into the inevitably expanding American society. In this endeavor, he honored both sides of his personality, meeting the demands of both the scientist and the Indian in him. The illness-prone subpersonality served as a buffer, an escape, from a world where two such different subpersonalities would often find the world quite punishing.

Ruth Benedict was another anthropologist who was deeply impressed by the Zuñi. Benedict is known primarily for her book *Patterns of Culture*, in which she explored several Native American cultures, including the Zuñi. In her preface to *Patterns of Culture*, Margaret Mead speaks of Benedict's personal struggle to find cultural identity. "*Patterns of Culture* is concerned with a problem that was central to Ruth Benedict's own life—the relationship between each human being, with a specific hereditary endowment and particular life history, and the culture in which he or she lived. In her own search for identity, she had persistently wondered whether she would have fitted better into another period or another culture than she fitted into contemporary America. She was particularly concerned with the extent to which one culture could find a place for extremes of behavior—in the mystic, the seer, the artist—which another culture branded as abnormal or worthless. . . . She herself was rather concerned with the question of how narrow definitions of normal behavior penalize or give preference to certain innate capacities, and of how the widening of cultural definitions might enrich our culture and lighten the load of rejection under which the cultural deviant now labors."[18]

Both Benedict and Cushing happened to be anthropologists—or rather, they chose to be anthropologists in order to explore their own personal adaptation. Their deep personal sensitivity, however, is not unusual. Many people have a sense of alienation or incompleteness in the culture in which they live. Most learn early, undoubtedly through the process of attunement with the representatives of their culture responsible for their upbringing, to repress the offending part, the true self, and conform for the pragmatic reason of belonging to their culture. This repression of individual subpersonalities, even if the individual is very much in tune with his culture, leads to the discomfort of psychic imbalance. Some learn to develop the divergent parts in a quiet way that avoids censure, but nonetheless, they live a truncated expression of the real richness of their persons.

Not only Cushing and Benedict but many others were attracted to a thorough study of the Zuñi. They were certainly not attracted because the Zuñi culture was one in which the individual could fully develop. The fascination with the Zuñi culture, not only scientific but popular as well, is caused by an instinctive recognition that the Zuñi structure is an external working model of the ideal inner psychic integration.

Within the Zuñi societal structure is found a macrocosm of the inner psychic structure: a center, surrounded by subunits, identified with symbols and functionally networked. In the Zuñi structure, there were no individuals that function for themselves irregardless of the welfare of the group; individuals harmonize their lives with the total social unit. The result is peaceful, cooperative living. Likewise, subpersonalities, networked to each other in a meaningful, functional way, result in a peaceful, well-focused, effective psychic balance. The Zuñi lived harmoniously under their system until they were exploited by the Spanish and warring Indian tribes.

If this ancient culture that began its evolution thousands of years ago is compared with the relatively infant American culture, it is important to look back to the original natural circumstances in which the cultures developed. The portion of the planet that the Zuñi inhabited was desert. The United States grew first in vast, unexploited, fertile lands. As skilled persons, industrially sophisticated, swelled the American population, it was a heady experience to forge ahead ever westward finding more and more untapped resources. The American culture developed from the start with superabundance just demanding hard work to bring it into ever greater productivity. In all other parts of the civilized world, cultural patterns and exhausted resources have limited the development of nations; the United States had no such fetters.

From the start, the direction of the American culture was, in Hall's terms, exploitation. The Americans have done an incredible job of using resources and developing a material base that has never before been possible in the world.

The Zuñi, on the other hand, an ancient people not exposed to the industrial revolution in Europe, had, through thousands of years, only a limited resource base. Their desert home forced them to focus their lives on methods of obtaining water. Hall calls this defense. Certainly, their intent was to keep themselves safe from the tyrannies of nature and provide for their survival. At the highest level, however, their civilization was based on spiritual discipline, an integration of all resources to the highest level of harmonious function.

In the total world scheme, one could regard these two cultures as subpersonalities of the world personality. In this framework, the American culture, as a part of the total world structure, emphasizes the cultural function of exploitation, using resources in inventive, efficient ways with the result of a historically increasingly higher standard of living. The Zuñi, on the other hand, an ancient culture now embedded in American society, in its purest form expresses spiritual discipline as a way of life. Of course, each culture is very complex. Every aspect of Hall's description of culture is functionally operating in both cultures in complex form intertwining and networking with every other function at many different levels. The historical biological bases for the development of these two cultures has determined that the dominant activities of each society are different. The different dominant activities create different world views. Different world views make interface between cultures difficult. It is the same for subpersonalities developing on the basis of specific situational factors; the result is one where the emphasized values and functions of the personality part conflict with the emphasized values and functions of other parts. Communication is difficult; networking of effort is difficult, until each recognizes the validity of the other's position as part of a functional whole.

8

THIS
SMALL PLANET

THE INDIVIDUAL WRIT LARGE

The psyche mirrors human institutions, and human institutions mirror the psyche. Echoing Plato's statement, "The state is the individual writ large," Assagioli said in his discussion of the integration of personality that the personality "presents interesting and suggestive analogies with that of the modern state, with the various groupings of the citizens into communities, social classes, professions and trades and the different grades of town, district, and state officials."[1] In this age, in the work of understanding the world and the individual psyche, Plato's metaphor succinctly draws attention to the profound relationship of macrocosm to microcosm. The structure of the modern state is familiar: a centralized governing body (king, dictator, council, legislature, etc.) oversees the well-being of land and people. In the many nations, there are various forms of governing bodies and rules by which they function. But in all governments, there are similar departments that take responsibility for the management of survival tasks and the development of comfortable living patterns for the population. In all modern states there is provision made for all basic life needs.

It is unusual to think of the structure of the psyche as being in microcosmic relationship to the familiar structure of the state. Nonetheless, the healthy personality has a governing body, Center, that oversees the well-being of the functioning aspects of the personality, the subpersonalities. The government developed by the Zuñi, who are a people close to their inner nature and the natural world around them, directly reflects psychological structure. Their inner dynamics of balanced psychological process is projected onto their societal organization: a central group surrounded by satellite groups with an elaborate system of interactions.

In a similar way, but not so deeply reflective of psychological depths as with the Zuñi, the dynamics of the modern state mimic the inner functioning of the individual. For instance, if there is not a strong governing body (inactive Center), a dominant faction (dominant subpersonality) imposes its wishes on the people (other subpersonalities). Since all interests are not represented, there is discontent and disharmony, which produces a state of lower productivity and lack of well-being. In fact, any possible dynamics of subpersonalities and Center has its analogy in the management of some country in the world.

It is reasonable to go a step further and look at the next logical hierarchical level. In the present period of history, the very small size of the planet Earth in relation to the size of the universe is being vividly brought to the attention of all nations. Astronauts have come back from outer space with photographs of the whole planet hanging in vast space. Even without leaving the Earth, the size of the planet in the mind's eye of all modern persons has been reduced by elaborate transportation and communication systems. Compare our experience of the speed of computers and rockets of today with the experience of stone-age people who possessed only rudimentary language and traveled on foot.

As a result, the concept of sovereignty of nations, which has been traditionally unassailable, is now called into question. The interests of nations, once isolated and independent, now overlap. For example, the quality of the air and of ocean water is of concern to all people of the planet. No nation has the right to act in its own interests, assert its own sovereignty, if danger to planetary resources important to the well-being of all nations is the result.

At the present time, the nations function largely autonomously. In the League of Nations, established after World War I, and now in the United Nations (UN), there have been the beginnings of a world governing body, a Center. There has been, however, limited international trust and respect for the UN. If it is in a nation's sovereign interests to abide by the UN's dictums, it will do so, but if the nation's interests are violated, though it be in the interest of well-being or justice for other nations, the UN declarations are often discounted and ignored.

The analogy of the individual psyche to culture and to the communities of a nation is straightforward. More challenging, and perhaps more interesting, is the analogy of the individual psyche to the world. The individual and the world are both in a state of dynamic growth, of evolution. Within both there are seemingly irresolvable conflicts. Most separate nations, like the separate subpersonalities, have achieved internal equilibrium and order.

Analysis of world patterns is useful in understanding individual dynamics more deeply. In such an examination, the individual achieves a sense of place in the world scheme. A deeper appreciation for and understanding of Center is attained when it is considered in analogy to the United Nations. To see the world in terms of the natural structure of the human psyche suggests that the psychic model of inner healing is applicable to our planetary woes.

INTERNATIONAL DYNAMICS

The nations are the subpersonalities of the planet Earth. Like subpersonalities, some are more similar to each other than others. Some are so different that misunderstanding and resulting conflict are inevitable, just as it happens with subpersonalities that experienced divergent development. Like subpersonalities, each nation has undergone a developmental process that has resulted in an ideological basis for its functioning. Over time each nation has answered fundamental cultural questions surrounding the adequate fulfillment of survival needs, and has established these answers as cultural values evolving the structure of the national life, including government and all other activities. Like dominant subpersonalities, dominant nations have a strong investment in the correctness of their respective sets of values, and a corresponding belief in the incorrectness of nations holding different values. It is possible to see this display of dominance on the part of some nations of the world at any time in history, the values in question shifting with different national groups.

Like dominant subpersonalities, dominant nations try to influence the behavior of other nations. The world press, the broadcasters of international dialogue, give the most space and time to coverage of the positions and actions of the dominant nations. Strong world leaders vie for influence, competing to convince the world audience of the correctness of their respective political and behavioral positions. In the mind of the individual, the dominant subpersonalities engage in the same rhetoric. Much time is consumed by the dominant parts creating verbiage in the thought patterns that overrides, influences, or simply drowns out the wants and needs of other subpersonalities in order to retain power for their respective dominant positions. A dominant subpersonality maintains that its way is best and its beliefs are truth. It considers other subpersonalities to hold inadequate behavioral positions, or if it suspects that there is value in their approaches, the dominant part will spend extra time and weight of authority to expound its position in order to retain its power.

Similar to shadow subpersonalities in the background of the individual psyche, nations that are nondominant because of their small size, impoverishment, or some other cause, are in the background of international dynamics. Their opinions and actions do not carry heavy weight in the world scene. These nations are numerous, and each reacts differently to the power of dominant nations. Some are resentful, jealous, and angry toward the power and affluence of the strong nations. They may act to undermine the strength of dominant nations through activities like sabotage or forming an alliance with one dominant nation in opposition to another. Other nondominant nations may act toward dominant nations in a subservient fashion; they curry favor with those who hold power or act in a self-effacing or even a self-debasing manner with stronger nations. Yet, other nondominant nations are content with their world positions, even valuing their noninvolvement in the frays of international power politics. Their focus is on the development of high-quality living conditions, differently defined by each culture, seeking a small sanctuary of peace in an embroiled international scene.

Like the nondominant nations, the shadow subpersonalities in the individual can be saboteurs, undeveloped self-debasing parts, or wise elements in a turbulent personality. Their activities are background to the chatter and powerful action of the dominant subpersonalities. If they cause trouble, they are noticed. The self-effacing parts are seen by the dominant subpersonalities as useless or as servants to their power causes. The wise shadow subpersonalities in the turbulent personality are largely ignored; the dominant subpersonalities consider them to be boring and naive.

DOMINANT NATIONS

No one would contest that two recent dominant nations, dominant subpersonalities of the world, have been the United States and the Soviet Union.[2] They have been called the superpowers, the designation arising in the until recently ongoing rivalry in building military might. Another dominant nation, Japan, has been outside the military arena since World War II, but has had a position of economic dominance. These three nations differ significantly in fundamental characteristics. Japan has only half the population of the United States and the Soviet Union, which have populations roughly equivalent. Yet Japan has successfully rivaled both superpowers economically. Recently, the economic position of the Soviet Union has become so dire that it has been referred to as a Third World nation. In land mass, the countries are drastically different. Japan is dwarfed by both the former Soviet Union and the United States, the former being sixty times larger and the latter twenty-five times larger than Japan.

Historically, all three of these dominant nations came to world prominence recently. Prior to World War II none of them were seen as controlling influences on the world scene. In comparison to other nations experienced in world power, the United States and Soviet Union have been "young" and unsure about the use of power. Recently, they have dramatically moved out of a period of antagonistic rivalry, the Cold War, which has waxed and waned since the end of World War II. Specific ideologies in the countries, namely, anticommunism in the U.S. and anticapitalism in the USSR, fed the antagonism. At the time of World War II, the United States and the Soviet Union were allies, and the hated enemy was Japan. Over the brief intervening forty years, Japan, devastatingly defeated by the Allies in the war, specifically by the United States, rebuilt its society to great strength and became a staunch ally of the United States. During the war no ideologies were harsh enough to describe the "Japs"; caricatures depicting the Japanese as evil were displayed everywhere. In recent times, in the American economic community, there has been largely respect and admiration for the Japanese, though laced with jealousy over their phenomenal economic success; nonetheless, the hated image of the "Jap" has been all but forgotten by the general United States populace. In the last half of the 1980s, there has been an erosion of the negative image of the Russians, which was once an emotionally dominant ideology in the United States. Invective and inflammatory language so recently directed toward the Soviet Union has now disappeared.

The dynamics between nations are the same as those between dominant subpersonalities: harsh rivalries based in antagonistic ideologies, values, and belief systems are also the rule in the dynamics between dominant subpersonalities within the individual. Likewise, the development of nations parallels that of subpersonalities. Specific provocation by environmental and/or historical factors brings about development of characteristic response patterns to survival problems, that is, the culture of the nation or the specific functional subpersonality in the individual.

At a fundamental level there are many environmental factors affecting these three dominant nations that create different life experiences, which in turn promote divergent answers to survival questions. An inspection of a map of the world discloses strongly contrasting experiences in the essential human activity of food production. The United States has large tracts of arable land clustered along the fortieth parallel, ideal farm land. Southern parts of the country provide variety to the northern-grown food staples.

In contrast, the Soviet Union, with the largest land mass of any nation in the world, has limited arable land because most of the land lies north of the fiftieth parallel. The major cities of Moscow and Leningrad are as far north as Juneau and Anchorage, Alaska, yet do not have the amelioration of climate provided this far northern state by warm ocean currents. Winters in the USSR are long and severe. Cold weather crops like cabbage and beets are the most successful. Limited crop variety affects the Russian diet. Long winters and limited diet are factors affecting human temperament; if survival is hard-won, temperaments are more serious than in circumstances where nature provides abundantly.

Japan, a series of small islands, has little land mass in comparison to the two large countries. Lying between thirty and forty-five degrees latitude, the nation has good conditions for food production, thus the land is heavily cultivated. Not enough food, however, can be produced for the population, so that Japan has always depended heavily for much of its food upon the sea. A predominance of seafood in the diet produces a different physical balance.

In the three nations the patterns of food production and food consumption are different, and it is to be expected that the physical constitutions of the peoples would be different. Indeed, it has been noted, for example, that third- and fourth-generation

Japanese Americans who have been living on the meat and varied fruit and vegetable American diet are taller than average Japanese.

Given environmental factors are the initial spur to the specific survival choices of a national group and so the diverging cultural patterns are clear from the start. The same is true for the individual; the environmental factors at birth and during the early years create a mental set that affects development of subpersonalities and lasts the lifetime of the individual. As years pass development of the individual subpersonalities is affected by the events of personal history. Likewise, a nation's history further delineates the characteristics that set it apart from other nations. Events create ideology, beliefs, bases for direction of action.

All three of these powerful nations retained outmoded forms of society as late as the nineteenth century. Unlike Europe where feudalism faded away in the twelfth and thirteenth centuries, both Japan and the Soviet Union remained feudalistic until the 1860s. The United States at this time, too, was struggling in one part of the country with slavery, another form of feudalism, its influence permeating the whole population in the passionate Civil War. The serfs of Russia were finally freed in 1861. It was not until the revolution of 1917, however, that living conditions began to change significantly for the common Russian man. In Japan, the Meiji Restoration of 1868 returned power to the emperor from the feudal war lords. This revolution resulted in a sudden drastic shift from an isolated feudal society to a modern Western state, including the creation of a parliament and the introduction of modern technology.

All three nations developed new forms of state. It was the goal of the modern Japanese to incorporate successful elements of the cultures and governments of the United States, Germany, France, and Great Britain along with the best of Japanese culture, thus creating a new form of society. The Russians, on the other hand, modeled the new state, formed after the 1917 revolution, on the theories of Karl Marx, which were largely untested in practical application. The United States, ninety years earlier than Japan and one hundred thirty years earlier than the Soviet Union, established a new form of state by developing the principles of democracy, then slowly emerging in Europe and graphically illustrated to the founders of the American nation by the governmental forms of some New World Indians. The Soviet Union and the United States both undertook experiments in new forms of government; their experiments are now respectively seven and twenty-one decades old. The Japanese chose to maintain their ancient heritage at the same time that they integrated into their society well-tested, beneficial elements of modern Western society.

There were historical differences between the three nations in the types of people making up the population. In Russia Lenin saw the proletariat at the time of the revolution as unable to develop enough self-consciousness to spark a revolution; his concern was an inbred passivity amongst the majority of people, largely the former serfs.[3] In 1917 the Russian population was 80 percent illiterate.

In Japan the social class of the samurai had great historical influence on the nature of the whole population. Samurai discipline was an individual undertaking, greatly respected by the whole populace, which produced qualities of strength, endurance, clarity of spirit, and aesthetic sensitivity. The samurai leaders, though deposed in 1868, set an example of individual development universally admired and aspired to by the Japanese. Zen discipline, the spiritual training of the samurai, is now part of Japanese national education; where the commoner of Japan was once excluded from the samurai caste, now the principles of Zen training are available to all. Historically, the Japanese have in the samurai tradition an established belief in and practice of individual inner development.

In American history there is a different variation on the tradition of individual achievement from that motivating the Japanese. All Americans, except American Indians, were originally immigrants. The courage, initiative, faith, and strength required to leave homelands in the hope of building a better life in a wilderness were the necessary personal qualities of large numbers of people in the early years of the new state. In turn, these new citizens taught their families their pioneer attitudes: work hard and deal with immediate problems in a straightforward, aggressive, and thorough manner in order to master nature and build a safe and prosperous home. The pioneer spirit has become part of the ideal American character.

The differing experiences these three nations have had of war over time has contributed to divergent world views. Aside from skirmishes with Indians, the early, distant Spanish-American war and the short Civil War, Americans have not seen war on their own soil. The Japanese and the Russians, on the other hand, have experienced much war. In the early centuries of its history, Japan experienced repeated invasions, which resulted, prior to the 1868 Restoration, in a two-hundred-year period of isolationist policy in which there was heavy emphasis on the development of defense. This defense depended on the fierceness of their individual warriors, the samurai. The samurai tradition led them to a natural primary emphasis on militarism, which created the conditions whereby they became a major power in the Second World War. In this war they were badly beaten, finally suffering the devastation of two cities by nuclear explosions. In the reconstruction following the war, the samurai discipline was turned away from militarism to the strategies of business, where warrior techniques were translated into financial strategy.[4]

The Russian experience with war has been equally devastating. For centuries the Mongols tyrannized the Russian people; the country was in a state of constant invasion during the thirteenth and fourteenth centuries. Sweeping across the continent, the Mongols pillaged, burned, and massacred. After the Russians had painfully rebuilt, the Mongols appeared again, fierce, clever, ruthless fighters that the Russians did not subdue until 1480. The repeated devastation and the lack of power to resist attack created the psychological pattern of passivity and fatalistic resignation, the character of the Russian peasant traditionally cited. The majority of the Russian populace continued to live under difficult circumstances during the subsequent years of tsarist reign and during the austere years of the Russian Revolution.

More recently, the Soviet Union suffered severely in World War II. The death of twenty million people, military and civilian, meant that every family suffered numerous losses. Thus there was personal impact of the war on every individual of the present population, through either the personal experience of the older people or through recent family history for the younger. In the Soviet Union pride was taken in the fact that the Allied victory in Europe was dependent on the staunch resistence of the Russian people against the German invasion. And as a result, the memory of the war was kept alive through the enormous impact of personal loss on the society and as a pledge to themselves that they had to maintain vigilance against such a war happening to them again.

Americans have a distinctly different perspective on World War II from either the Russians or the Japanese, since the war was not fought in the United States and our losses, 400,000, almost all military, were not as significant a proportion of the population as that of the Soviet Union; nor did we experience nuclear devastation as did the Japanese. Subsequent to the war, the Japanese turned away from war-making to peaceful enterprise. The Soviet Union chose to maintain vigilance against war. And the United States, having to face no reconstruction after the war, got on with becoming a great, powerful nation. The enterprise of Japan meshed well with the thrust of American industry. The Soviet Union, on the other hand, preoccupied with fear of recurrence of war and experiencing secret inner turmoil in their struggle to stabilize and rebuild, mystified and frightened the United States. In this way, increasing ideological distance was created as years passed. While the enemy status of Japan waned in America's eyes, that of the Soviet Union increased.

Here a few environmental factors and a few historical factors have been selected from the very complicated national patterns of three dominant countries and cursorily analyzed to illustrate elements that contribute to the development of significantly different world views of these nations that impact the international scene. Within the individual, subpersonalities develop in response to environmental and historical circumstances, finding through trial and error the best ways of fulfilling various functions. Likewise, national cultural groups of people find the best response they can to the unique environmental and historical circumstances that confront them, developing over time what are recognized as individual national "personalities."

Each of these three nations, having been powerful and influential in its own right, presents a different configuration of traits. Each as a subpersonality of the total world personality has been necessarily unique through the impact of varying developmental factors, and thus unique in its position, contribution, and expression. Within the total world unit each of these nations has been dominant and influential in its own way; the dominance and influence, the assertion of specific values, ideologies, and priorities, arose from developmental factors, just as it does in the subpersonalities of the individual.

NONDOMINANT NATIONS

Unlike dominant nations, the many nondominant nations have little power individually. They are like shadow subpersonalities in the individual. They do not expect their cultural or political values to be adopted by other countries as is the case with the dominant nations, just as shadow subpersonalities are subservient to dominant subpersonalities. Many nondominant nations need interaction with other countries, particularly dominant nations, for their well-being, even their survival, whereas the large, powerful nations can be nearly self-sufficient. Shadow subpersonalities initially have only limited expression in the total personality; until they are more comprehensively developed, they rely on dominant subpersonalities to do the major portion of the work.

Just as there are varieties of shadow subpersonalities, there are a number of different types of nondominant nations. In the Western world, there are small countries, notably the Scandinavian countries and Switzerland, that have a high standard of living, good internal management, adequate provisions for defense, but no significant military power aspirations or responsibilities. They represent a position of equanimity toward the problems of the world. These countries are quiet in the interplay of international affairs; they often play the role of spokespersons for objectivity and justice, remaining neutral in many tumultuous world situations.

Another group of nations have been dominant nations in the past. At various points in past history, Egypt, India, China, Greece, Italy, Spain, France, England, and Germany have represented the pinnacle of civilization. Their actions had strong impact on many other parts of the world. Their great past power affects their present world perspective and colors their current choice of action, even though they exert smaller actual influence today. Those nations that have been recently prominent are still honored with world respect and deference though their actual power is now limited.

Those nondominant nations that are referred to as Third World nations participate in the world community in a different way. Many are new nations struggling for their identity; their primary focus is on the well-being of their peoples. In this pursuit, they seek aid from richer, stronger nations. Some are subservient to the superpowers, realizing their potential gain, but also in awe and admiration of the true power of these nations, economically and militarily. Most of these small nations are undeveloped by Western standards; a poor standard of living, lack of adequate educational opportunity, and deficient agricultural practices are some of the major problems. Some of these nations exist on the edge of catastrophe due to such things as starvation, unending warfare, and extreme governmental instability. Anger and aggressive action on the part of Third World countries attracts international attention. Their military escapades have upset the tenuous balance of equanimity between the superpowers. Uncertainty about the belligerent intentions of small countries, both internally and externally, has created a burden for the governments of other countries, particularly the superpowers.

The development of Third World nations is an international concern. Initially seen as a project of the larger, affluent nations, in recent years development in many Third World countries has gone beyond the control of their benefactors.[5] It has been an assumption on the part of the superpowers that they could impose ideologies and governmental structures on the nations who received their aid, however, no country can automatically develop so complicated a governmental form as democracy or communism except through internal evolution.[6] Advanced stages of economic development cannot be transferred to undeveloped nations; there is an insufficient knowledge base in the society for sustaining the high level of expertise required for maintaining these advanced products of a highly developed society.[7]

Universal compulsory education is the first requirement of development. No nation that is literate has a poor standard of living. Through cultural education a national identity is forged, and the factors that foster the maintenance of a poverty mentality are countered. Then technical education is possible.[8]

The responsibility for development lies with the nations of the Third World themselves; instead of a passive interdependence, a position of active solidarity with dominant nations would affirm commitment to their own development.[9] There is no desire on the part of new nations to return to colonial status, but this position is held so strongly that it is hyperexaggerated.[10] Even more so then, it is necessary that internal commitment be made to national development.

NATIONS AND SUBPERSONALITIES

Subpersonalities within the individual are microcosmically equivalent to the nations of the world. Each is a distinct entity with more or less distinct boundaries. Each has an inner system of organization and management. All are contained inseparably together, subpersonalities in the individual, nations on planet Earth. No nation can depart for the moon; no subpersonality can leave a psyche for residence in another. Between subpersonalities there are differences that can lead to friction; the same is true between nations. In both cases the friction can become so intense that it creates war.

All human beings have the same biological needs. The subpersonalities, clusters of psychological patterns, form to get these needs met for the individual. In the same way clusters of people band together to efficiently provide for human needs. Each nation operates on the basis of one or more cultural patterns. The evolution of cultural groups has established the best thought and action for meeting survival needs, varied in form from group to group.

Each subpersonality within the individual develops its unique shape in response to external circumstances. The course of development proceeds with each momentary environmental stimulus eliciting choice or reflex in the embryonic subpersonality, choice when a new way must be forged, or reflex when the best way has been established. The uniqueness, the individual color, of the subpersonality arises through the series of choices made in fulfilling its functional role.

The development of nations proceeds in similar fashion. Each aspect of meeting survival needs on the planet forces a group of people living together to make choices in order to establish means for meeting these needs. Nations are aggregates of peoples who have initially banded together because of geographical proximity and similar survival pattern choices. Management of their living habits could thus be arranged conveniently. Time produces polished practices and ideologies that creates a unique color, a unique personality for each cultural group. Sometimes a nation has found the best way of fulfilling its peoples' varied survival needs, and sometimes circumstances prevent the development of the best way. As with subpersonalities, nations act in a mixture of best ways and inadequate ways.

Just as many factors, in fact all the conditions of a whole lifetime, contribute to the development of subpersonalities, there is also a great multiplicity of factors involved in the emergence of a nation. In the discussion of dominant nations, only four factors out of many—climate, land use, and the effects of feudalism and war—were discussed as variables in the development of unique national personality patterns. Yet in this brief example, the strongly significant effect of different experiences with these particular variables on national development and on the national world view is apparent.

The antagonism that arises between nations is like the antagonism that arises between subpersonalities. Fixed ideological positions, the controversial answers to survival questions, create blindness. Because the answers produced practical results and survival security at one time, they become sacred and inviolable over time within a cultural or national group. The survival solution may not be much different or much better than that of the next group, but emotional attachment and conviction of its power to provide safety through observance to the letter, creates barriers to dispassionate appraisal of another group's ideologies. Often there is rampant fear that even the appraisal of another group's position may lead to the erosion of safety. The traditional ideology may be undermined, and the group may fall into jeopardy.

The fixedness of the subpersonalities is related to this dilemma. Each subpersonality, answering in its own way the problem of safety for the individual, has difficulty objectively appraising the positions of other subpersonalities. Rivalry for expression of subpersonalities is basically the attempt on the part of each to prevent other functional modes from attaining dominance, for fear of instability and danger to the whole organism upon whom they all depend.

Alignment of nations is common in international politics. As nations with similar ideological positions band together for mutual support, so subpersonalities who agree on ways of functioning ally themselves with each other, trying to suppress elements that counter their security measures. Alignment, however, no matter the strength it gives to the process of growth and development in both cases of nations and of subpersonalities, also results in opposed camps. Alignment fosters the closed emotional position of "us against them," in which opportunity for evaluation of differing problem-solving techniques is lost. "Poor Brutus, with himself at war . . . The state of man, like to a little kingdom suffers . . . the nature of an insurrection."[11] Shakespeare's Brutus speaks of the analogy between the inner psyche and the outer dynamics within and between nations. The personality finds itself in a state of insurrection with warring factions, made up of "best ways" and anachronistic elements indiscriminately mixed, fighting tenaciously for dominant expression. Over and over in the world the same scenario is repeated between nations.

If one subpersonality changes slightly, immediately and automatically there is change in the whole personality. Even if elements continue to function as they did previously, there are new underlying dynamics that force change. Monitoring the international scene one sees the same process, as nations all over the globe react to change occurring in one nation. The network of international interdependency becomes denser with each passing year, so that nations that once had little contact with each other are now connected by many ties. The individual develops in the same way; subpersonalities initially operate autonomously, but as time passes, and each subpersonality becomes involved in more aspects of the individual's life, the interdependency between subpersonalities increases. In this network, change in one part reverberates throughout the psyche.

Ideological inflexibility leads to friction. Mounting friction can lead to war. For nations, this means destruction and death. For the individual, a war in the psyche can result in pain ranging in intensity from major discomfort to psychosis or suicide. In both the world and the individual, such extreme turbulence must be kept to a minimum. A way to avert open warfare is to engage in "shadow" warfare. Through espionage and sabotage, underlying pressure on other nations, on other subpersonalities, is exerted. It is less expensive to promote clandestine efforts to influence the internal affairs of other nations than it is to wage war.[12] Certainly, in the individual, sabotaging subpersonality action occurring at a subliminal level is cheaper than a psychic war that results in loss of control or mental illness.

Comparative study of developmental factors and dynamics of nations leads to the conclusion that it is absurd to expect that there should be uniformity of political ideology and cultural values. In many nations, the ideological stance is: "We are right and they are wrong." This is the same position expressed by some subpersonalities. "I am right and you are wrong; thus, you must conform to my point of view, my values, my way of doing things," is a typical statement of a dominant subpersonality in a psyche that is out of balance. The solution to the conflict in the individual is acknowledgement, acceptance, and, finally, celebration of difference; the result is balanced expression of the personality. Evolutionarily, it would appear, the nations of the world are for the most part presently at the stage of mutual isolation. The process of acknowledgement, acceptance, and celebration of difference has only begun.

THE DOWNING OF SOUTH KOREAN JETLINER KAL 007

In the individual psyche, an external event of consequence begins an inner dialogue between the subpersonalities: a discussion of the facts, accusations, blame and guilt, and proposed resolutions from the point of view of each subpersonality. Exactly like this inner process is the international dialogue in the face of crisis. Each nation has a set position that represents its own interests and ideologies. As with incensed subpersonalities, the international language is often inflammatory in nature, the attitudinal stance one of stylized posturing.

The accompanying table presents an international dialogue that happened a number of years ago. On September 1, 1983, a South Korean airliner carrying 269 passengers entered Soviet airspace and was shot down by the Soviet military. This international incident is particularly interesting to consider because of its worldwide impact rousing concern about safety in civilian airline travel. There was uncertainty of the facts surrounding the incident, an uncertainty that in part remains today. Articles with new information appeared in the press periodically for several years. This uncertainty highlights the confusion that is characteristic of international dialogue. Without firm facts upon which to negotiate, the international dialogue moves into ideology, accusation, and power play.

As you read the dialogue, let go of your particular political beliefs and biases, and listen to the words as you would the words of a set of conflicted subpersonalities. You will note that the process of international dialogue sounds exactly the same as that of inner dialogue. For the individual, if facts are uncertain in a crisis, the inner dialogue becomes a harangue with the dominant subpersonalities vying through the impact of their influence for the acceptance of their position, the nondominant subpersonalities making background comments.

This dialogue continued for many days beyond this point. Nearly two weeks subsequent, USSR Marshal Ogarkov appeared on television explaining that the convening of a State Commission of Inquiry had been necessary before the Soviets could make a complete statement about their understanding of the incident. The Soviet pilot who shot down the plane was also interviewed. The following day, the U.S. State Department issued a statement revising the original translation of the pilot tapes to indicate harmony with the USSR's original statement that the pilot had fired warning shots.

Reading the statements made by the disputing nations, it is impossible to objectively evaluate the accuracy of the claims. In fact, each heated statement followed by heated counterstatement, creates more confusion than clarity. There are interesting dynamics to note. Though the dispute was between South Korea and the Soviet Union, the first nation to speak was the United States. Was the superpower championing the cause of the small allied nondominant nation, South Korea, or seizing an opportunity to blast its rival where seeming scandalous error had been committed? Or indeed, as claimed by the USSR and some analysts, did the United States have something to hide in regard to espionage activity?

The great contrast in international style between the United States and the USSR in these statements was characteristic of the two nations at that time. The United States responded immediately with several villifying statements, later quietly retracting some of the original accusations. The Soviet Union, on the other hand, took six days to respond with a full statement of their view of the incident, leaving all nations mystified and angry in the meantime. It appeared to the world community that initially the USSR intended to use the fact that the actual circumstances of the event were difficult to ascertain to allow them to claim that they had nothing to do with the disappearance of the plane.

Statements made by other nations particularly in Scandinavia, were cool, clear, and dispassionate compared with the statements of the United States and the USSR, which are rife with ideologies and incendiary language, especially on the part of the United States, both of which tend to arouse emotion rather than rational thinking. This type of dialogue does not lead to resolution but to further argument since it engenders the festering of negative emotion. Inflammatory language is manipulative; in honest negotiation, angry inflammatory language should be replaced with equivalent words of different connotation, which will hopefully elicit a rational response.

DIALOGUE BETWEEN THE UNITED STATES
AND THE SOVIET UNION AFTER THE
DOWNING OF KAL 007

Quotations are from the *New York Times:* "U.S. says Soviet Downed Korean Airliner" by Robert D. McFadden, September 2, 1983, pp. 1, 5; "Shultz Denounces 'Coverup'" by Bernard Gwertzman, September 3, 1983, pp. 1, 4; "Moscow Response" by John F. Burns, September 3, 1983, pp. 1, 4; "Transcript of Reagan's Statement on Airliner," September 3, 1983, p. 4; "Tass Reports on a Soviet General's Comments about Airliner," September 5, 1983, p. 4; "U.S. Says Spy Plane Was in the Area of Korea Airliner," September 5, 1983, pp. 1, 6; "Reagan, Denouncing Soviet, Bars Series of Negotiations; Demands It Pay for Jet's Loss; Charges Massacre" by Steven R. Weisman, September 6, 1983, pp. 1, 14, 15; "Russians' Version" by John F. Burns, September 6, 1983, pp. 1, 16; "U.S. Says Soviet Continues 'to Lie to the World' on Jet" by Steven R. Weisman, September 7, 1983, p. 14; "A Soviet Downed Airliner" by John P. Burns, September 7, 1983, pp. 1, 16; "Gromyko Defends Actions in Plane Incident" by John Darnton, September 8, 1983, pp. 1, 10; "Korean Jetliner: What Is Known and What Isn't" by David Shribman, September 8, 1983, pp. 1, 12.

U.S.	USSR

SEPTEMBER 2, 1983

U.S. announces that a South Korean airliner was shot down in the Sea of Japan by a Soviet jet fighter. Requests UN Security Council Meeting. The incident is a "[f]lagrant violation of every form of civil aviation and international law."

President Reagan, "I speak for all Americans protesting the Soviet attack on an unarmed civilian plane. Words can scarcely express our revulsion at this horrifying act of violence. . . . The U.S. and international community demand full explanation for this appalling and wanton misdeed. . . . Soviet statements to this moment have totally failed to explain how or why this tragedy occurred."

After twenty-four hours' silence, TASS states that an unidentified plane twice entered Soviet airspace. The plane had no navigation lights, did not respond to query. Fighters tried to direct it to the nearest airfield, but the plane did not respond and continued its flight toward the Sea of Japan.

Foreign Minister Gromyko echoed this report adding there were "signs of a possible crash."

Secretary of State Shultz says the USSR is "continuing its effort to cover up the facts of the inhuman Soviet attack. They still will not admit to the truth that they shot down an unarmed civilian aircraft. . . . There is no indication that the Soviets tried to warn the plane by firing tracers. The Soviet Union is clearly engaged in an effort to divert attention from its own actions. . . . No cover-up however brazen and elaborate can change the reality or absolve the Soviet Union. . . . The world is waiting for the Soviet Union to tell the truth."

President Reagan: "In the wake of the barbaric act committed yesterday by the Soviet regime . . . the U.S. and many other countries made compelling statements expressing . . . outrage [and] demand for . . . facts. . . . While events in Afghanistan and elsewhere have left few illusions about the willingness of the Soviet Union to advance its interests through violence and intimidation . . . this event shocks the sensibilities of people everywhere. . . . Where human life is valued, extraordinary efforts are extended to preserve and protect it. . . . What can we think of a regime that so broadly trumpets its vision of peace and disarmament and yet so callously and quickly commits a terrorist act to sacrifice the lives of innocent human beings? What can

TASS announces that "an unidentified plane rudely violated the Soviet state border and intruded deep into the Soviet Union's airspace . . . 500 km into Soviet territory and 2 hours over Kamchatka Peninsula and Sakhalin Island. . . . Soviet anti-aircraft defence aircraft . . . repeatedly tried to establish contact [with] tracer shots and radio signals. The intruder plane ignored all this. Soon after this, the intruder plane left the limits of Soviet airspace and continued its flight toward the Sea of Japan. For 10 minutes it was within the observation zone of radio location means after which it was observed no more. Now a hullabaloo has been raised in the U.S.A. and some other countries around the disappearance of the South Korean plane. . . . It is indicative that now, post facto, on the American side [data have been cited] which indicates the relevant U.S. services followed the flight throughout its duration in the most attentive manner. Why American authorities, which now resort to . . . dirty insinuations about the USSR, did not . . . contact the Soviet side and provide it with data about the flight . . . (The USSR) recalls instances of deliberate violation of state frontiers . . . by American planes . . . (This) plane cannot be regarded in any other way than . . . (as having) special intelligence

be said about Soviet credibility when they so flagrantly lie about such a heinous act? What can be the scope of legitimate mutual discourse with a state whose values permit such atrocities?"

aims. . . . Those who organized this global provocation . . . strive to smear the Soviet Union, to sow hostility to it and to cast aspersions on [its] peace loving policy. This is illustrated by the impudent, slanderous statement in respect to the Soviet Union that was instantly made by President Reagan."

SEPTEMBER 5, 1983

Senator O'Neill: "Of course, this isn't the United States versus Russia, this is the world as opposed to Russia."

TASS: The intruding plane was a provocation . . . navigation and collision-prevention lights were switched off. The [fighter] pilot made attempts to lead the plane closer to Soviet airfield . . . no response, no radio signals. No response to radio signals. No response to wing rock. The interceptor flew with his lights on, flashing them in order to attract attention. The intruder plane's outline resembles that of the reconnaissance plane RC-135. The interceptor fired tracer shots. American planes have intruded in Soviet air space on nine occasions. This looked like a direct provocation. The 747 could also be confused with a U.S. EAB bomber.

SEPTEMBER 6, 1983

President Reagan addresses the nation: "My fellow Americans, I'm coming before you tonight about the Korean Air Line massacre, the attack by the Soviet Union against

TASS: Tracer bullets were fired only after the airliner changed course and altitude . . . in such a way as to carry it over a Soviet air base.

201

269 innocent men, women and children aboard an unarmed Korean passenger plane. This crime against humanity must never be forgotten, here or throughout the world. . . . This attack was not just against ourselves or the Republic of Korea. This was the Soviet Union against the world and the moral precepts which guide human relations among people everywhere. It was an act of barbarism born of a society which wantonly disregards individual rights and the value of human life and seeks constantly to expand and dominate other nations. . . If the massacre and their subsequent conduct is intended to intimidate, they have failed in their purpose. From every corner of the globe, the world is defiant in the face of this unspeakable act and defiant of the system which excuses it and tries to cover it up. . . [In response to the massacre] [w]e will not renew our bilateral agreement of cooperation in the field of transportation. We reaffirm the order that Aeroflot be denied right to fly to the U.S. We are cooperating with other countries to find better means to insure the safety of civil aviation and to join us in not accepting Aeroflot as a normal member of the international civil air community unless and until the Soviets satisfy the cries of humanity for justice. I ask Congress to pass a joint resolution of condemnation of this Soviet crime. We suspend negotiations on

Pravda: The airliner had previously flown over a Soviet naval base and had radioed air traffic control in Tokyo to report that it had "successfully" flown over Soviet territory. . . . Soviet forces had tracked 7 RC-135's between 3:45PM and 8:49PM,, Moscow time, on the day of the incident [2 hours before the KAL airliner was lost.] There were also 3 U.S. naval vessels outside Soviet territorial waters at the time.

The RC-135 and KAL liner were involved in the same American spying mission. The RC-135 flew parallel to and may have corrected the flight path of the KAL liner.

Mr. Reagan's attacks on the Kremlin in the wake of the incident were part of a broader effort "to put the world on the brink of a dangerous confrontation."

several bilateral arrangements under consideration. We called an emergency meeting of UN Security Council and ask for a meeting of the ICAO. We, with thirteen other countries seek reparations from the Soviet Union. We are redoubling efforts to stop the flow of military and strategic items. Shultz will demand facts from Gromyko."

USAF Lt. Col. Friend denied emphatically that seven RC-135's had been flying off the Soviet far east coast during the period in question.

An official statement on the intelligence aircraft then stated, "A U.S. RC-135 was in the vicinity of the Korean airliner on August 31 when the airliner was initially detected by Soviet radar. Both aircraft were then in international airspace. . . . The Soviets know that our aircraft do not enter their airspace. The Korean aircraft's inadvertent entry into Soviet territory should have been an early indication to them that the flight was not a U.S. reconnaissance aircraft. . . . The closest point of approach was 75 nautical miles . . . at the time the KAL was shot down, [the RC-135 in question] had been on the ground at its home base in Alaska for more than an hour."

SEPTEMBER 7, 1983

The U.S. State Department states that "today [September 6] the Soviet government at last admitted

The USSR government statement reiterates earlier TASS statements and adds, "The intruder plane en-

that its forces shot down KAL 007. ... [t]he Soviet government states flatly that it will take the same action in the future in similar circumstances. The international community is thus being asked to accept that the Soviet Union is not bound by the norms of international behavior and human decency to which virtually all other nations subscribe. ... The Soviet Union must accept the norms of civilized society in respecting the lives of innocent travelers. The world demands that the Soviet Union give assurances and takes specific steps to isure that the events of August 31 cannot occur again."

tered the airspace over Kamchatka in an area where a most important base of the strategic nuclear forces of the USSR is located. ... Contrary to the false contentions of the U.S. President, Soviet anti-aircraft defense fighter planes are fitted out with communication equipment in which the frequency is fixed. ... The Soviet radio control services picked up short coded radio signals transmitted from time to time, such signals that are usually used in transmitting intelligence information. ... The anti-aircraft defense fulfilled the order of the command post to stop the flight. ... The Soviet pilot in stopping the actions of the intruder plane, could not know that it was a civilian aircraft. It was flying without navigation lights at the height of night in conditions of bad visibility and was not answering signals. ... It is the sovereign right of every state to protect its borders, in particular its airspace. ... Can anyone imagine anything more cynical than Reagan's statement that no one will ever know how data was fed into the plane's computer?" (There follows much about the imperialist crimes of the United States.) "The Soviet government expresses regret over the death of innocent people and shares the sorrow of their bereaved relatives and friends. The entire responsibility for this tragedy rests wholly and fully with the leaders of the United States of America."

The White House says that the Japanese have tapes of some transmissions from Soviet ground control positions and it is up to the Japanese to make them public.

Shultz, in response to Gromyko states, "If the borders of the Soviet Union are sacred, the impression is if anyone strays over them, they're ready to shoot them down again. Now I think that illustrates the difference in allocation of weight to security, on the one hand, and human values on the other. He speaks of a dishonest juggling of facts and falsehoods. Falsehoods have been continuous and juggling of facts is too mild a word for the way the Soviet Union has responded."

Gromyko, at a Foreign Ministers' meeting in Madrid: "Pronouncements are being made from this rostrum about the South Korean aircraft. This incident—and this is well known—is being deliberately exploited by certain circles in the U.S. to exacerbate the international situation. They have unleashed a wave of slander and insinuations against the USSR and the socialist countries. . . . The basic question which arises is this: has anyone the right to violate with impunity foreign frontiers of another state? No, nobody has such a right. This major provision has been enshrined in the most authoritative international documents—in the very charter of the UN. . . . We state: Soviet territory, the borders of the Soviet Union are sacred . . . those who still give credence to the falsehoods will no doubt, at long last understand the true aim of this major provocation used by its instigators in the interests of their militaristic policy and of the inflation of military psychosis."

Ushakov, a top USSR academic lawyer, points to Sections of the 1944 Chicago Convention on International Civil Aviation: Article 1, the complete sovereignty of each nation over its airspace, and Article 6, all flights should take place through that airspace in accordance with the rules set down by the nation concerned.

A PERSONAL EXPERIENCE OF IDEOLOGY

The effects of negative ideology are insidious and are uprooted only by education and experience. In working with the structure of the psyche it is clear that once the subpersonalities are known in depth and breadth, there is much less power in the belief structures (ideologies) of dominant subpersonalities. Smear tactics against other subpersonalities are seen for what they are, because the genuine shapes of all the subpersonalities are known to the whole person.

I had the opportunity in 1985 to make a journey to the Soviet Union just after Gorbachev came to power. At the time there was no realization of Gorbachev's future impact and the Cold War yet raged. In the months preceding the trip, emotional questions came from deep in my mind, though logic tried to quell them. I was surprised at the fear that gripped me. Was it true the Russians were "the evil empire" who would at some slight, unknowing misdemeanor on my part secrete me away to prison in Siberia where I would remain, never to see my family again? Was there indeed something wrong with me that I wanted to visit a drab, gray country where the people are automatons and slaves? What would be the point of travel where I would be shown only what the Russians wanted me to see and my movements would be entirely circumscribed? Would my going to the USSR cause my neighbors to think of me as anti-American? How could I, being citizen of the "best" nation in the world, want to have anything to do with a rival nation who wanted to destroy our prosperity and our way of life? How could I, who lived and believed in democracy, open my inquiring mind in any way to communism and not be contaminated? These common ideologies of the American people preyed on my thinking; my ignorance about the Soviet Union and my lack of objectivity thoroughly amazed me.

When I arrived in the USSR, I did not find what I had expected. I traveled with forty Americans on a citizen diplomacy trip sponsored by the Institute of Noetic Science. Our leader, Sharon Tennison, provided opportunities for meetings with Soviet citizens, and she taught us how to meet people on the subways to expand our informal contacts. At no time in three weeks did any of the group members have a feeling that our activities were monitored in any way, although they probably were, nor were our actions within cities ever restricted. Special requests were granted; another group member and I made a trip to Tolstoy's home one hundred and twenty miles from Moscow. We were free to strike up acquaintances on the street and accompany people to their homes. The Russian hospitality and warmth were outstanding. Though people were quiet and drab on the street, in their homes I had no sense I was with subjugated slaves. The Russian people we met expressed pride in their accomplishment in greatly improving the standard of living for the whole population since the time of the revolution, a reality in that year that seems sad now in light of the country's present economic disaster.

Belying our ideologies, I found no one who hated Americans, though all were at odds with the American government. They expressed belief that the American government wanted to wage a nuclear war and would do so, but they did not see the American *people* as wanting war. Understanding that the Russians have been terror stricken at the thought of any more war hardship after their experience in World War II, I was appalled one day to hear the phrase "the coming war" in the middle of a sentence on another subject. The casual inclusion of this phrase indicated to me how deep has been the belief in the Russian people that war was impending, and it would be begun by the Americans.

After the months I spent in the U.S. prior to the trip fearing untoward events, only four times did I experience any fear in the Soviet Union:

1. The Moscow customs. There was nothing in the customs procedure or the place that was particularly frightening. It was the contagious fear in the Americans entering the Soviet Union.

2. The Moscow subway. The height and steepness of the fast-moving escalators were at first alarming. After a few days, however, the escalators became sport, and the focus of subway travel became the faces of the people and the interesting artwork in the stations.

3. A shriek in the night. It was my roommate waking me with a squeal of delight as she discovered hot water in our bathroom. The luxury of hot water is not always available in the Soviet Union.

4. Repeated cannon shots. I was on the wrong side of the hotel and missed a fireworks display over the river Neva in Leningrad. It was in honor of Border Guard Day. So important is the security of the Soviet Union that each year they have a national holiday honoring the border guards.

Rather than the expected fear, I was surprised to find I experienced a peaceful feeling even on crowded subways. My feeling seemed well explained by the fact that I was surrounded by people who have learned to endure. Because of a history of true hardship, they have learned to prevent their psyches from being buffeted by petty anxieties.

Perhaps the most distressing experience of the entire trip was returning to the United States with a different perspective of the Soviet Union than the one then common in our society. The sheer power of government and media to prey upon people's ignorance and create irrational ideological positions overwhelmed me. I could say that all I had learned from the media about the Soviet Union was perhaps true in some way, but there was much of a positive nature in the USSR that was not reported. In addition, in the context of Russian history and geography, many factors considered negative by Americans could be seen in a different light. From the Russian perspective, there was consistency in their actions and reason for even harsh governmental measures.

It is interesting that at the time I was there, Rajiv Gandhi was in Minsk, exploring trade arrangements with the USSR. Several weeks later, he went to the United States with the same mission. India's attempt to establish the best international arrangements for India, bypassing the obstacles of cloying political ideologies, was refreshing, since it focused on the real purpose of government, which is to serve the best interests of its people.

Brainwashed or mind-cleansed?[13] In analogy with subpersonalities, my experience in traveling to Russia was like leaving the security and isolation of a dominant subpersonality that functions well, and thus deems its behavior to be the only way for the well-being of the person. I journeyed many hours to stand in the shoes of the opposing subpersonality and found to my surprise that it was not vile as I had heard. In fact, standing in those shoes and returning to my own home, I found I could only wish that somehow the strengths of these two world subpersonalities could be coordinated for the benefit of the whole world.

THE DEVELOPMENT OF AN INTERNATIONAL CENTER

The resolution to the conflicts between subpersonalities comes about through the establishment of a Center to act as impartial director of the whole person's resources. Subpersonalities initially function as though their autonomy were possible, even preferable, to integration. In fact, it is normal for dominant subpersonalities to fight to retain their power.

As the establishment of Center is a developmental stage for the microcosm of the individual, so is the establishment of a Center for the macrocosm of the world a developmental stage, which is apparently upon us at the present time. Most nations have been fiercely independent until recent times; they are now, however, beginning to acknowledge their interdependence with other nations. Robert Muller, former assistant to secretaries general of the UN, says that this new world awareness is the "advent of an intricate and extremely dense network of worldwide interdependencies among societies which until recently were living in relative isolation from each other. Beyond nature's interdependencies which have characterized our planet (the water cycle, the oxygen cycle, the carbon cycle, the nitrogen cycle and many other internal links in the biosphere), the world has suddenly been seized in a rapidly growing web of man-made interdependencies. . . . These interdependencies have forced governments into new collective thinking and cooperative arrangements which would have been inconceivable only a few decades ago."[14]

There is willingness to cooperate with other nations when it is in a nation's own best interests, but there is often reluctance, and refusal is common, when issues involve the nation's denial of its own preferences, or even needs, in order to benefit other nations. There is little appreciation for world interests over national interests, though the life of the planet itself be at stake. Read any national history book for a picture of bias; "if you are the civilized nation and everyone else mere savages, it makes the history of your own land that much easier to write."[15] Each nation writes its own history as though it were the center of the universe; historians focus on the negative interaction with other nations as perceived in light of national ideologies, in order to justify and honor their own nation. As a matter of fact, however, it may be impossible for nations to have objective understanding of other nations' situations because of geographical difference and because they are immersed in their own business and their own ideologies.

In response to increasingly unavoidable interdependency, there is a growing drive on the part of the peoples of the world to establish a Center, a governmental principle of some sort, which would deal with the well-being of the whole planet. The UN, and its predecessor, the League of Nations, are to date the most comprehensive international endeavors that have functioned as a world Center. In addition, however, hundreds of international organizations deal with specific areas of international networking. These organizations, like subpersonalities closely linked to Center, approximate and experiment with activities that the Center of the world ideally would perform, and in fact support the establishment of a Center by networking around it.

Within the psyche, the main function of Center initially is objectivity and impartiality. Likewise, the first goal of a Center undertaking the well-being of the planet needs to be objectivity and impartiality. Of all international organizations, the UN has the most structural breadth for addressing and balancing the many concerns of all nations.

Developmentally, the UN is much like the developing Center in the individual. Initially, in identifying individual Center, there is great hope that it will be the salvation of all of the person's problems, and eventually it will be. But the usual developmental pattern experienced by the individual is that after a euphoric period of first finding Center, there follows a reassertion of old patterns in the subpersonalities, and the eclipsing of Center, and then its subsequent waxing again. This early instability produces an inevitable questioning of the usefulness of Center.

Likewise, the advent of the League of Nations was hailed as the answer to world problems, but it existed for only a short time and then disappeared. After World War II, the formation of the UN was hailed as the answer to world problems. It has survived forty years, but over and over again the question is asked: of what value is the UN since it is not strong enough to resolve international conflict? It is seen as having no teeth.[16] The consensus system of the Security Council (veto system) has kept the Security Council from enforcing its peacekeeping resolutions. Nations become frustrated in attempting to get their pressing concerns addressed in the cumbersome mechanics of the organization. Because the interminable work of international dialogue continues and the UN has not magically created universal peace, the expenditures for UN programs are questioned, and the resolutions and policy statements of the UN have been dismissed by the media with boredom and intolerance. More often than not, the media have suggested that the UN is an inferior, ineffectual entity, and in the world, the compelling action and important dynamics continue to be between the strong nations. Only very recently has the UN begun to be given some respect. In fact, there has been an enormous amount of international work done by the international agencies of the

UN that has received no publicity.[17] Western newspapers are sold primarily through dramatization of conflict. International development is not "sexy." As most of the Western press functions today, there would be little to write about if the world were truly at peace.

The UN actually functions well as an objective Center in a number of ways. First of all, in its charter, it sets itself apart from those very factors that have set nations at odds with each other. Each nation has vested interest in its geography, the sovereignty of its land and borders, and problems of climate and physical terrain that effect national productivity. The "thinking" of a nation is inevitably shaped by its relationship to the piece of planet that it inhabits. As has been discussed, it is in this way that the ideologies—the agreed-upon answers to survival questions—of a nation are developed.

The UN, on the other hand, has no geography. Its offices are located in cities all over the world. Though it follows the laws of the country in which it is situated, nonetheless, it is considered to have its own jurisdiction. Since it has no investment in geography, the UN can have more impartiality in questions involved in equitable living on the planet.

The working arms of the UN are agencies led by delegates from many nations. The agencies of the UN are involved in many projects that affect planetary well-being. The Secretariat of the UN consists of civil servants who take an oath of international impartiality. The chief responsibility of the Secretariat is to insure that the whole organization is coordinated and to monitor impartiality and overall progress, reporting their evaluation regularly to the General Assembly.

One of the most important organs of the UN is the World Court. Though its rulings are often seen as weak and ineffectual, the gradual definition of international law that has evolved through court action over time is significant. Its consistent statement of human rights and just forms of international interaction quietly erodes partisan national opinion. This court provides an international forum in which to sift and test wisdom that is not culturally biased, seeking consensus for the welfare of all peoples of the world. In the early days of the UN, when its popularity was high, a profound declaration of human rights was written. Except in the World Court, this declaration has fallen into obscurity. Unrealistically, the early UN enthusiasts thought that the principles of this document would automatically be acclaimed and incorporated into the governments of all nations; when the document was ignored, it was prematurely set aside. Nonetheless, this declaration is repeatedly tested in international disputes that come before the UN, proving its soundness in its continued applicability. Each ruling of the court that discusses basic human rights publicizes and increases awareness of the principles of this document.

Through the far-reaching, complicated mechanics of the operation of the UN, the same subtle international pressure exerted by the formal action of the World Court quietly moves in the world. Major issues of debate elicit response from many nations who repeat over and over in the assemblies of the international forum their opinions, censorship, blame, or praise. This may not immediately produce change in a delinquent nation's behavior, but a consensus is formed among dissenting nations as to what is correct action in light of the well-being of all world inhabitants. The diplomatic ritual of courtesy that preludes every delegate's speech is very important; if indeed in gesture only, there is in this action the embryonic expression of honor and respect for other nations, the beginning of the practice of equality.

Another important aspect of the work of the UN is the universal principle of respect for cultural identity. Where a superpower would move industry into a developing country because of economic motivation, defining the shape of that industry according to the superpower's national ideology, when the UN becomes involved in the economic development of a country it considers first the country's cultural system and then models economic improvement according to that. Within the working structure of the UN, all types of government are seen as practical experiment, and honored for true success in meeting

Diagram of a World Center
The United Nations

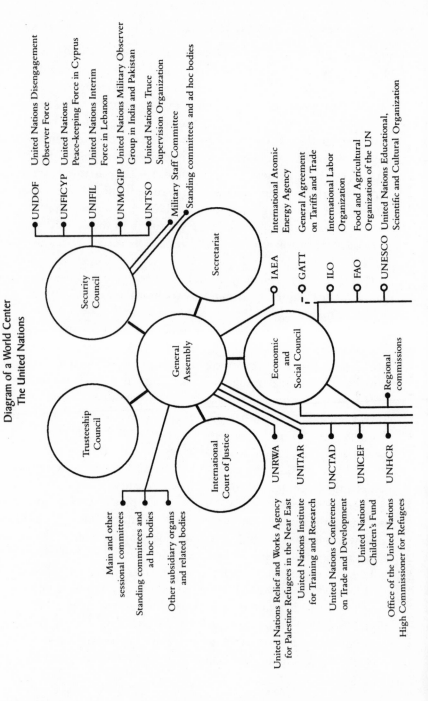

UNDOF   United Nations Disengagement Observer Force
UNFICYP United Nations Peace-keeping Force in Cyprus
UNIFIL United Nations Interim Force in Lebanon
UNMOGIP United Nations Military Observer Group in India and Pakistan
UNTSO   United Nations Truce Supervision Organization

Standing committees and ad hoc bodies

IAEA   International Atomic Energy Agency
GATT   General Agreement on Tariffs and Trade
ILO   International Labor Organization
FAO   Food and Agricultural Organization of the UN
UNESCO United Nations Educational, Scientific and Cultural Organization

Main and other sessional committees
Standing committees and ad hoc bodies
Other subsidiary organs and related bodies

UNRWA   United Nations Relief and Works Agency for Palestine Refugees in the Near East
UNITAR United Nations Institute for Training and Research
UNCTAD United Nations Conference on Trade and Development
UNICEF United Nations Children's Fund
UNHCR   Office of the United Nations High Commissioner for Refugees

Regional commissions

Security Council

Secretariat

Trusteeship Council

General Assembly

Economic and Social Council

International Court of Justice

Military Staff Committee

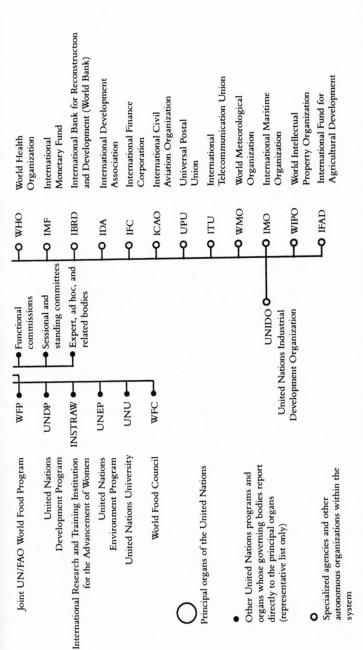

Figure 3. A world center, the United Nations. Adapted from *Basic Facts about the United Nations* (New York: UN, 1977), p. 58; updated from Robert E. Riggs and Jack C. Plano, *The United Nations: International Organization and World Politics* (Pacific Grove, Calif.: Brooks, 1988). Reproduced by permission.

peoples' needs; no ideology is considered sacred. It is the expressed philosophy of the UN that all cultures add richness to planetary society. In fact, under the umbrella of the UN, it is theoretically possible for nations who wish to do so to experiment with creative cultural change unhampered by aggravation of nations with differing ideologies. In this light, the UN can be a clearinghouse for the emigration of dissidents who do not fit into a particular governmental experiment—movement from East to West, or West to East, or movement from North to South, or South to North—without censure. Facilitated movement of population groups would stimulate development of all nations in that it is economically in their best interests to govern contented people.

UN DELIBERATION ON THE DOWNING OF JETLINER KAL 007

Earlier, the international dialogue of nation speaking to nation about the downing of the KAL jetliner was considered. The dialogue went on for many days, accusation rife on both sides, without any means of resolution. New to the world, only established now for forty years, is a forum for such problems—the Security Council of the UN.

The first meeting of the Security Council on the KAL disaster was called on September 2, 1983. Six meetings were held in which many nations beyond the five official members formally expressed regret in varying strong terms, but yet in diplomatic formality, about the events concerning the downing of the airliner. They asked many questions, but all continually emphasized the need for international civil aviation safety. The superpowers maintained their respective positions as presented in the press with little alteration. Jeane Kirkpatrick, representative for the United States, presented tapes of the Soviet pilots that illustrated the basis for the United States' position. (These tapes, which were indistinct, were later retranslated, giving support to Russian claims of having attempted to warn the aircraft, but this retranslation was little publicized.)[18] On

September 12, a resolution of censure toward the USSR was presented to the Council. It was not adopted because of the Soviet veto.

Here we have an example of the workings of the embryonic Center. In considering the matter in international forum, there is no resolution because of the lack of power in the Center, the UN. Nonetheless, the diplomatic statements of many nations of the world create a formal censure, a formal statement of world opinion, which places pressure on the USSR.

Despite the veto of the resolution, the investigation by the International Civil Aviation Organization (ICAO), a UN agency, was carried out as fact-finding. The results of this investigation were not publicized. Murray Sayles, a highly experienced journalist who had been asked by the British media to fully investigate the jetliner downing, found his results to be fully in harmony with the ICAO report. Examining the incident from a purely technical point of view, it can be explained on the basis of accident with no evidence of conspiratorial or evil intent on the part of any of the participants. Because Sayles found only evidence of accident, he was informed that no documentary (originally planned for the first anniversary of the downing) would be made. He was told "conspiracies are sexy; accidents are not."[19]

Basically, Sayles and the ICAO agreed that there was no problem with the plane's innertial navigation system, but there was an incorrect setting on the autopilot, which could account for a wrong flight path, the flight path traced by Russian radar. The incorrect setting was not caught because of a defective instrument that had in fact been detected and reported as malfunctioning before the flight.

The Soviets were particularly sensitive to airspace intrusion that night because of a scheduled missile test. It was assumed by them that there would be much reconnaissance activity on the part of the United States because of the missile launch. Reconnaissance activity is agreed upon as a part of the Salt II Treaty. At one point, two planes merged on the Russian radar screens, both assumed to be American military planes. One was traced as flying to an American military base, but the other headed across the Russian border straight for highly sensitive Russian military installations. The first scrambled Russian fighters were not able to catch up with the intruding plane. In a country ravaged by war, where duties of border guards are considered sacred, a mysterious plane assumed to be a hostile military presence could only be viewed as a threat. When the plane did not respond to the international signals of the Russian fighter, the crew of the airliner being at that very moment occupied by a regular radio transmission to Tokyo, a ground command followed military routine by shooting the plane down. Sayles writes in conclusion that the "deepest lesson is how easily an all too human mistake abetted by a conspiracy of circumstance can defeat all supposedly infallible safeguards which keep the superpowers balanced on their nuclear knife edge, and how easily our whole world, and not just one wretchedly unlucky airliner, could be shot down."[20]

The results of the ICAO investigation is an example of the careful but "unsexy" fact-finding characteristic of UN agencies and organizations. The UN, as Center of the world, plays a role of strong objectivity. The press, both West and East, did not publicize this work because the Western press, pandering to people's craving for excitement for the sake of sales, did not find this issue "sexy" enough, and the Soviet press, at that time, was forced to act under a policy of publishing what made their government seem infallible. In both cases, this is propaganda of dominant nations, just like the propaganda of the dominant subpersonalities, trying, on the one hand, to follow a particular practical agenda at the expense of reality, or, on the other hand, to appear all-powerful to the rest of the subpersonalities. In the case of the Western press's emphasis on excitement, one of the interesting parallels here is that when an individual first discovers Center, he finds it to be so quiet that it is boring and he returns to the excitement of conflict between the subpersonalities. There is indeed peace and quiet in the background work of the agencies of the UN that are seeking to establish well-being for all people. Like the world turning always to intrigue and conspiracy, and away from the peaceful work of the UN, the individual keeps returning from the quiet of Center to the strife and turbulence of the subpersonalities' interactions, until the pain is too great—or until he discovers a different kind of excitement in the work of Center. Hopefully, the world will soon discover the latter path.

THE UN AS A MODEL FOR
THE DEVELOPING INDIVIDUAL CENTER

The structure and functions of the UN suggest an array of practical models for increasing the effectiveness of Center in the individual. First of all, the UN has a central core agency, the Secretariat, which consists of a staff whose work is focused on world benefit without national bias. It is the job of the Secretariat to coordinate the efforts of the many UN agencies that are run by international delegates. Center in the individual has the same job, the coordination of the subpersonality efforts on behalf of the whole person. A frequent experience for the individual is that Center is indeed operating separately and impartially, but at the same time there is intrusive subpersonality input. The impulse is to fight subpersonality interference with Center. If the UN is considered as a projected model of the natural psychic process, the active participation of subpersonalities in the work of Center is illuminated. The Secretariat is central and impartial, but is surrounded by the strong activity of nationals working not for their countries but for the benefit of the world. So too can subpersonalities, separate from their routine functions, join the higher ventures of Center undertaken for the benefit of the whole person. The voice of Center with the accompanying subpersonality comment is a normal process. In the UN, there is awareness from time to time of strong national pressure; reorientation needs to be made that redirects efforts toward planetary benefit again.

219

In the individual, the intent is to focus through Center on the benefit for the whole person; in this way, there is a constant redirecting of the working subpersonalities toward Center.

The charter of the UN states that it has "no power to compel action but recommendations carry moral weight."[21] In similar fashion, Center begins to influence the individual through "recommendation." The subpersonalities, just like nations, are the actors and can defy the direction of Center. Over a period of time, however, the influence, the "moral weight" of Center's recommendation is felt in the whole psyche and shifts of attitude and behavior take place. "Fundamental changes in societies have always come from vast numbers of people changing their minds just a little."[22] Within the psyche, small shifts in the subpersonalities can create significant change in the whole personality. The UN pressure of recommendation is a distillation of the wisdom of national belief and action; it is an objective, ongoing search for an ideal model of planetary management. Center within the individual searches and pressures for the development of ever more evolved systems of use of an individual's resources, the product of dialogue between the active experimenters, the subpersonalities, and the objective distillation process of Center.

It was the intent of the UN to create a space separate from the jurisdiction of nations. The UN headquarters in New York and Geneva are not American or Swiss territory, but owned and governed by the UN. Likewise, Center, as it is conceptualized and as it is experienced, has its own psychological space. It actually feels separate from subpersonalities.

As the UN's work is ideally to monitor and direct all aspects of interdependent life on this planet, so it is the function of Center to monitor and direct the life of the individual. It has been repeatedly pointed out that the UN agencies are unsung heroes; their work represents huge benefit for the money invested.[23] In all agency work, there is education and awareness-raising about global issues; those nations who receive the largest proportion of their services benefit most. An individual Center that quietly directs small projects in a person's life creates a climate that increasingly fosters development of all the subpersonalities, all the individual resources. In the ideal of the UN, no political system is judged as right or wrong, but all are seen as experiments, which the test of time will prove valuable or not. In the individual, Center does not take the role of judge. The mode of function and the value system of each subpersonality can be viewed as an experiment, the best way to fulfill a need, which must prove itself over time. The UN hopes to foster healthy, productive alliances between nations. Center also does this job, suggesting from an overview new ways for subpersonalities to join in productive action.

The international forum of the General Assembly is comparable, in the individual, to subpersonalities meeting for dialogue. Within the confines of individual nations, foul accusations and epithets are often hurled at other nations with impunity. Likewise, subpersonalities say things in thought toward other subpersonalities that they would never say aloud, or even think of directing at other people. In the General Assembly, however, language is diplomatically formal and ideologies toned down. In the presence of Center, subpersonalities stop their usual chatter, become more reasonable, civil, and wise.

In the relationship between the UN and the nations, smaller, weaker nations highly respect the authority of the UN and its international forum. They see alliance with the UN and its resources as giving them strength and voice. The UN fosters the development of weak nations; it places value on all cultures and all national identities. Likewise, shadow subpersonalities welcome Center's intervention on their behalf with its encouragement and recognition of their development and valuing of their structures within the whole individual.

Dominant nations, on the other hand, accuse the UN of being ineffectual and weak. They resist UN direction and see UN action as interference. Dominant subpersonalities function the same way. They refuse at first, perhaps for a long period of time, to recognize the value of Center, much less accept any direction from it.

The record of the UN, however, in its forty-year history, is like that of the developing Center in the individual. A period of great enthusiasm at its advent was followed by disillusionment and detraction. Nonetheless, there is quiet steady development, pride in averting yet another great war, and genuine accomplishment in codification of international law (comparable to the rules affecting regulation of the whole person) and the principles of human rights (humane treatment of one's self). In the UN, as in the individual, there is frustration and sadness when too many world (or individual) resources are given over to the war machine (internal conflict) when there are so many situations where these resources could be better used.

CENTER AS A MODEL FOR THE DEVELOPING UN

Though knowledge of psychological Center is still far from complete, in many ways the present knowledge is instructive in considering the course of development of a world Center. World organization is a new process, but even in its very short history, it parallels the initial individual experience of Center. The League of Nations, formed after World War I, was not universally accepted, particularly not by Americans, an ironic historical note since the primary author of the League was Woodrow Wilson. When Center is first identified in the individual, subpersonalities cannot place trust in it; the defense systems of the psyche are threatened by the upset in realignment. So too, with the League of Nations the question of national sovereignty arose. The first identifications with Center in the individual are often aborted; high hopes are dashed.

Now that the second attempt at world organization, the UN, has been active for a number of years, another parallel with individual Center is evident. Hailed almost universally as the salvation of the world at its inception after World War II, the UN has been until recently dismissed as not living up to expectation and not worth the cost of supporting it. Step two in the establishment of the individual Center involves a fairly lengthy period of trial and error, experimentation, and simple practice, in which the psychic Center becomes an indispensable part of the person. Actually, the process of human growth and discipline involves the effort of many years, a fact fully understood in Eastern cultures but not in the West. Those who engage seriously in the discipline of their own development are aware of the enormous subtle refinement, first inner and then outer, that is necessary. The impatience with the UN reflects ignorance about human development, individual and institutional.

As the individual Center bears patiently with the slow development of shadow aspects of the personality, quietly supporting and allowing new exploration, so the UN today deals with the slow development of the many nations now moving into world participation. Only as these elements grow and are stable can Center move to higher levels of function in the person and in the world. As Center is the integration point for all psychological elements, so the UN seeks to integrate the millions of world entities, which is a huge task. In individual functioning it is expected that periodic imbalance will occur. The subpersonalities do not sit in a static circle around Center, but are always active; each set of life circumstances and each fresh initiative of developing subpersonalities makes new demands on the subpersonalities, and they are inevitably thrown out of balance. The pressure of the new creates disruption to which each subpersonality responds in its own way. If there is a well-functioning Center, however, there is rapid new alignment of subpersonality resources, and an inner balancing process that reestablishes equilibrium. In crisis, the well-established Center overrides the subpersonalities and structures a course of action for the individual's well-being.

Like the new psychological Center, the UN is not well enough established to intervene in crisis situations; it can only declare what is right and just and make recommendation for action. The Security Council's power is hobbled by the rule of veto. Yet, there is evidence in worldwide peacekeeping that the UN is a significant influence. Like early Center, the eroding

223

force of recommendation wears down old, ineffectual patterns, bringing openness to change.

The world knows a great deal about war, but not much about peace. In the individual who has been handicapped by warring subpersonalities, the quiet that comes in as war subsides seems at first lifeless and boring; actually, it is the quiet of healing. Just as the individual does not initially understand inner peace, so too at this time the peoples of the world do not understand peace. In both cases, there is longing for freedom from pain and suffering. In the individual's early development, however, returning to the inner war for a little excitement is common. And how often in history have wars been initiated simply for the glory of war? Another reason for the return to war in the individual is the belief or hope that a power-hungry subpersonality can once and for all vanquish other subpersonalities who threaten its identity and power. Likewise, a function of war has always been killing off other people in order that one's own people can live supreme, maintaining cultural identity and national power. [24]

The idea that peace is not the absence of tension but the presence of justice has been a truth cited by numerous international leaders. Like subpersonalities, nations will always be developing and changing, and new issues will arise that will create tension. Also, like subpersonalities, it is necessary to have a balance process that will realign national interests. The administration of international justice, a system only now being developed, is fragile and new. It is delayed by the rigorous requisites of codification of international law, so difficult because of cultural factors, but eventually it can become the international balance process. The central agency for the development of an international justice system is the World Court in the UN. This body is given small respect at the present time because its rulings are not binding; a nation may choose to ignore the court. As the voice of Center increases in pervasive impact on the individual, however, so the voice of the court carries ever increasing moral influence in the world.

As evolution continues in the individual, Center increasingly manages the functioning of the whole psyche. This process is extremely important particularly in life areas that represent novelty. When a new challenge presents itself, Center accesses deeper unconscious wisdom and then coordinates the action of the subpersonalities. The UN is beginning to assume this role in the preservation and coordination of resources, research, and compilation of knowledge in many areas, and rallying world wisdom in meeting emergency situations.

Yet, Center in the individual does not become judge or dictator. Subpersonalities are supported in their creative growth and in their unique contribution to the psyche. The evolution within each entity is honored. The pull of the balance process maintains the attunement of the developing entities. Likewise, in the UN, honor of every culture and respect for national sovereignty and jurisdiction is the same balance process begun on the world scene. It is a very important point that Center as a model for the UN does not suggest the development of a world government.

Most significant, perhaps, is the capacity of Center to envision and oversee higher development. Functionally, Center has easier access to higher levels of consciousness than the subpersonalities, which are primarily focused on response to and interaction with the environment. Thus, in this respect, Center is constantly influencing, even pressuring, the development of the subpersonalities to their highest level of functioning. In the same way, the UN, not being plagued with the mundane duties of nations, has space to be a philosophical agent of change. Not only does the UN experiment with ever better solutions to meet the balance requisites of all aspects of the planet, they seek the wisest thinking about the future, the wisest formulation for a functioning model of planetary peace and prosperity. Just as Center fosters the full development of subpersonalities, the UN can support each nation's development at the same time as fostering the preservation of the great diversity of cultural groups.

The macrocosmic planetary process mirrors the microcosmic psychic process. Each level has much to learn from the present dynamic developmental leaps of its twin. The stretching of the psyche toward full development and the evolution of a planetary society are now the most exciting processes happening on Earth.

EPILOGUE

As suddenly as an individual personality can change, so has the world recently changed. As of this writing (August 1991), the Cold War is ending. Communism as it has been practiced has proved itself economically unfeasible. The states that formerly made up the USSR and the Eastern European nations have begun to turn toward free-market strategies. Peace has begun to break out.

Suddenly, in the midst of this, we have the Gulf crisis. Here is yet another parallel with the human psyche. As previously warring subpersonalities are harmonized, conflicts that had been considered more minor come to the surface and assume major proportions.

Of further significance in the current world scene is the new respect for the UN, evidence of the emerging strength of a world Center. With changes in the relationship between the superpowers, nations are more able to work together and to influence the world through the auspices of the UN. There is an upcoming election for a new secretary general, a position now internationally acclaimed as an important world leadership role rather than one of a mere diplomat. And the work of the UN, until now largely ignored in the press of the powerful nations, currently appears daily.

Ongoing change in and between parts procedes, the subpersonalities in the individual, and the cultures and nations of the world, each in its own time, a continuous, compelling, and personal drama.

Notes

CHAPTER I. FACETS OF THE PSYCHE

1. After struggling with the question of the inadequacy of the English language in honoring both sexes equally—even inventing my own forms to mean both sexes, forms which would be only irritating to the reader—I opted for the most frequent current usage, an alternate use of the masculine and feminine pronouns.

2. *Synthesis Journal* was published between 1974 and 1976. Copies may be obtained from Psychosynthesis Distribution, 2561 Tioga Way, San Jose, CA 95124.

3. Henri F. Ellenberger, *The Discovery of the Unconscious* (New York: Basic Books, 1970), p. 669.

4. John-Raphael Staude, *The Adult Development of C. G. Jung* (Boston: Routledge & Kegan Paul, 1981), p. 23. Also Ellenberger, *The Discovery of the Unconscious.*

5. Staude, *The Adult Development of C. G. Jung,* p. 60.

6. Ken Wilber, *Up from Eden* (Boston: Shambhala Publications, 1986), p. 315.

7. Brendan O'Regan, "Multiple Personality—Mirrors of a New Model of Mind." *Investigations: Institute of Noetic Sciences,* 1, nos. 3–4 (Sausalito, Calif.: Institute of Noetic Sciences, 1985); Robert Ornstein, *Multimind* (Boston: Houghton Mifflin, 1986), pp. 130–141: John O. Baehrs, "Co-consciousness: A Common Denominator in Hypnosis, Multiple Personality and Normalcy." *American Journal of Clinical Hypnosis,* 26 (October 1983):100–112.

8. Philip M. Coons, "Psychophysiologic Aspects of Multiple Personality Disorder: A Review." *Dissociation,* 1 (March 1988):47–53.

CHAPTER 2. DISCOVERING SUBPERSONALITIES

1. Unfortunately, Roberto Assagioli, unlike Carl Jung, left no autobiographical material that describes his experience with subpersonalities.

2. Roberto Assagioli, "Per un nuovo umanesimo ariano," quoted in

Alessandro Berti, *Roberto Assagioli: profilo biografico degli anni di formazione* (Florence: Istituto di Psicosintesi, 1988), p. 17.

3. Ibid.

4. Ibid.

5. Ibid.

6. Roberto Assagioli, "La psicologia delle idee forze e la psicagogia," quoted in Alessandro Berti, *Roberto Assagioli*, p. 77.

7. Ibid., pp. 77, 78.

8. Massimo Rosselli, private communication.

9. Alessandro Berti, *Roberto Assagioli*, p. 17.

10. Ibid., p. 74.

11. Roberto Assagioli, *Psychosynthesis* (New York: Viking, 1965), p. 68.

12. Ibid., p. 75.

13. Ibid., p. 68.

14. Ibid., p. 75.

15. Ibid., p. 76.

16. Ibid., p. 22.

17. Ibid., p. 112.

18. Ibid., p. 75.

19. Ibid., p. 113.

20. Ibid.

21. Ibid., p. 20.

22. Ibid., p. 77.

23. Ibid., p. 72.

24. John-Raphael Staude, "Jung and Assagioli," unpublished talk presented at the International Psychosynthesis Conference, Sesto Pusteria, Italy, 1988.

25. A brief discussion of psychosynthesis is included at this point because of the relative unfamiliarity of this school of psychology. For a more complete introduction read: Assagioli, *Psychosynthesis*; Piero Ferrucci, *What We May Be* (Los Angeles: Tarcher, 1982); or Molly Y. Brown, *The Unfolding Self* (Los Angeles: Psychosynthesis Press, 1983).

26. Ferrucci, *What We May Be*, p. 131.

27. Piero Ferrucci has written a whole book about models: *Inevitable Grace, Breakthroughs in the Lives of Great Men and Women: Guides to Your Self-Realization* (Los Angeles: Tarcher, 1990).

28. Roberto Assagioli, *Lo sviluppo transpersonale* (Rome: Astrolabio, 1988),

chapter one. This is my rough translation of the Italian from Assagioli's last work, published in 1988. At this writing, an English translation has just become available: *Transpersonal Development: The Development Beyond Psychosynthesis* (London: Crucible/Harper Collins, 1991).

29. Assagioli, *Lo sviluppo transpersonale*, chap. 3, "Alpinismo psicologico," paras. 35, 36 (translation mine).

30. Ibid., para 40 (translation mine).

31. C. G. Jung, *Psychological Types* (Princeton, N.J.: Princeton University Press, 1971), p. 518.

32. C. G. Jung, *Mandala Symbolism* (Princeton, N.J.: Princeton University Press, 1972), p. 4.

33. Jung, *Psychological Types*, p. 480; Jolande Jacobi, *The Psychology of C. G. Jung* (New Haven, Conn.: Yale University Press, 1943), p. 127.

34. Jung, *The Structure and Dynamics of the Psyche, Collected Works*, vol. 8 (Princeton, N.J.: Princeton University Press, 1960), p. 96.

35. Ibid., p. 101.

36. Jung, *Two Essays on Analytical Psychology* (Princeton, N.J.: Princeton University Press, 1966), p. 177.

37. J. W. T. Redfearn, "Ego and Self: Terminology." *Journal of Analytical Psychology*, 28 (1983).

38. Jung, *The Structure and Dynamics of the Psyche*, p. 224.

39. Marie-Louise von Franz, "The Process of Individuation." In Jung, et al., *Man and His Symbols* (New York: Doubleday, 1964), p. 162.

40. Ferrucci, *What We May Be*, p. 44.

CHAPTER 3. ORDINARY GENIUS

1. In these case histories, a few facts about life circumstances have been changed by the choice of the individuals involved in order to protect their privacy. Otherwise, the presentation is exactly as it happened.

CHAPTER 4. THE CONTINUUM OF DEVELOPMENT

1. The concepts in the next several paragraphs are basic Piagetian theory.

2. Charles Tart, *Waking Up* (Boston: Shambhala Publications, 1986), p. 163.

3. Daniel Stern, *The Interpersonal World of the Infant* (New York: Basic Books, 1985).

Notes

4. Bennett Braun, *Treatment of Multiple Personality Disorder* (Washington: American Psychiatric Press, 1986), p. xii.

5. Roberto Assagioli, quoted in Vivian King, *Psychosynthesis* (unpublished manuscript).

6. Henry A. Murray, quoted in James Vargiu, et al., "Psychosynthesis Workbook," *Synthesis* 1 (1974), p. WB13.

7. Piero Ferrucci, *What We May Be* (Los Angeles: Tarcher, 1982), p. 47.

8. Keyserling, quoted in Vargiu, "Psychosynthesis Workbook," p. WB13.

9. Vargiu, "Psychosynthesis Workbook," p. WB14.

10. Marvin Minsky, *Society of Mind* (New York: Simon & Schuster, 1986), p. 9.

11. Pierre Janet, *Major Symptoms of Hysteria* (New York: Hafner Publishing, 1965), p. 92.

12. Ferrucci, *What We May Be*, p. 52.

13. Note here that William James's question about the elusive thought change process is addressed. *The Principles of Psychology*, vol. 1 (New York: Dover, 1950), p. 246.

14. Roberto Assagioli, *Psychosynthesis* (New York: Viking, 1965), p. 75.

15. Deeper physical change is suggested by the work of R. Cloninger and others. I have observed disease states and physical handicaps carried by only one subpersonality.

16. Stern, *The Interpersonal World of the Infant*, p. 227.

17. Edward Whitmont, *The Symbolic Quest* (Princeton, N.J.: Princeton University Press, 1978).

18. Vargiu, "Psychosynthesis Workbook," p. WB 19.

19. Ferrucci, *What We May Be*, p. 58.

20. Vivian King, *Psychosynthesis*, p. 101.

21. Mike Sayama, *Samadhi* (Albany: State University of New York, 1986), p. 93.

22. John G. Watkins and Rhonda J. Johnson, *We, the Divided Self* (New York: Irvington, 1982), p. 138.

23. Many branches of present-day psychological practice (for instance, Transactional Analysis, Gestalt, and so on) direct work with parts of the personality but fail to recognize the full scope of the potential of subpersonalities by not acknowledging their symbolic value.

24. Ferrucci, *What We May Be*, p. 58.

25. The Portuguese poet Fernando Pessoa, quoted in Ferrucci, *What We May Be*, p. 47.

26. *Center* is an experientially accurate term. Piero Ferrucci uses this term interchangably with *self* and *observer*. See *What We May Be* and *Vivere meglio oggi* (Florence, Italy: Centro Studi di Psicosintesi "Robert Assagioli," 1985). In some writings of Assagioli there is also the interchangable use of *Center* with *the I* and *self*. I consider Center to be the easiest term for lay people to understand.

27. Assagioli, *Psychosynthesis*, p. 111.

28. Centering as a specific technique that I practice is a variation of disidentification discussed by Assagioli in *Psychosynthesis*, p. 116, by Ferrucci in *What We May Be*, p. 49, and in other writings about psychosynthesis.

29. Assagioli, *Psychosynthesis*, p. 26.

30. Ferrucci, *Vivere meglio oggi*, p. 17.

31. Ferrucci, *What We May Be*, p. 53.

32. Assagioli, *Psychosynthesis: Height Psychology* (New York: Psychosynthesis Research Foundation, 1974), p. 218.

33. B. Marie Fay, private communication.

34. Assagioli, *Psychosynthesis*, p. 113.

35. Ken Wilber, *Up from Eden* (Boston: Shambhala Publications, 1981), p. 71.

36. In his work Marvin Minsky refers to the fact that developmental steps happen abruptly because of the largely unconscious preparation that must take place. The status quo functioning on the surface continues in order to maintain security. *Society of Mind* (New York: Simon & Schuster, 1986).

37. Quotation of Miyamoto Musashi in Victor Harris's introduction to Miyamoto Musashi, *A Book Of Five Rings* (Woodstock, N.Y.: Overlook, 1982), p. 22.

38. Eugen Herrigel, *Zen in the Art of Archery* (New York: Vintage, 1971), p. 7.

39. Ibid., p. 40.

40. Ibid., p. 69.

41. Ibid., p. 41.

42. Ibid., p. 6.

43. Assagioli, *Psychosynthesis*, p. 200.

CHAPTER 5. THE UNFOLDING PSYCHE OF HUMANKIND

1. Ken Wilber, *The Atman Project* (Wheaton, Ill.: Quest, 1980), pp. 30–36; Wilber, *Up from Eden* (Boston: Shambhala Publications, 1986), p. 179. This system of nomenclature for developmental stages fits subpersonality theory well. I am indebted to Ken Wilber's writing for the concepts that underpin the ideas of this chapter.

2. Wilber, *The Atman Project*, p. 32.

3. Ibid., pp. 7, 12, 22; Wilber, *Up from Eden*, pp. 21, 39, 87.

4. Wilber, *Up from Eden*, p. 315.

5. Ibid., pp. 71–72.

6. Wilber, *The Atman Project*, pp. 42–44, 67, 79–81.

7. Ibid., pp. 45–62; Wilber, *Up from Eden*, p. 319.

8. Wilber, *The Atman Project*, p. 45.

9. Ibid., pp. 63–70.

10. Wilber, *A Sociable God* (Boston: Shambhala Publications, 1983), pp. 27–29.

11. Wilber, *The Atman Project*, p. 70.

12. Ibid.

13. Wilber, *A Sociable God*, p. 29.

14. Wilber, *The Atman Project*, p. 71.

15. Wilber, *A Sociable God*, p. 31.

16. Lucy Menzies, Ronald A. Knox, and Ronald Selby Wright, "St. Margaret, Queen of Scotland" (Kirkcaldy, Scotland: St. Margaret Guild, 1957), p. 15.

17. Emery Kelen, *Hammarskjöld* (New York: Putnam, 1966), p. 42.

18. Ibid., p. 39.

19. Ibid., p. 46.

20. Ibid.

21. Ibid., p. 47.

22. Ibid., p. 95.

23. Ibid., p. 133.

24. Ibid., p. 59.

25. Dag Hammarskjöld, *Markings* (New York: Knopf, 1964), p. 81.

26. Kelen, *Hammarskjöld*, p. 119.

27. Charles M. Coffin, editor, *The Major Poets: English and American* (New York: Harcourt Brace, 1954), p. 124.

28. Alfred Kazin, editor, *The Portable Blake* (Harmondsworth, Middlesex, England: Penguin, 1977).

29. W. H. Gardner and N. H. MacKensie, editors, *The Poems of Gerard Manley Hopkins* (Oxford: Oxford University Press), p. 69.

30. Thomas H. Johnson, editor, *The Poems of Emily Dickinson* (Cambridge, Mass.: Harvard University Press, 1955). Reprinted by permission.

31. T. S. Eliot, *The Complete Poems and Plays: 1909–1950* (New York: Harcourt Brace, 1952), p. 63. Reprinted by permission.

32. Annie Dillard, *Pilgrim at Tinker Creek* (New York: Harper & Row, 1974), pp. 12–13.

33. James M. Cox, editor, *Robert Frost: A Collection of Critical Essays* (Englewood Cliffs, N.J.: Prentice Hall, 1962), p. 3.

34. Ben Shahn, *The Shape of Content* (New York: Vintage, 1960), p. 72.

35. Georgia O'Keeffe, *Georgia O'Keeffe* (New York: Viking, 1976), p. 71.

36. Ibid., p. 70.

37. Ibid., p. 63.

38. Ibid., p. 1.

39. Ibid., p. 11.

40. Ibid., p. 88.

41. Ibid.

42. Ibid., p. 51.

43. R. Hughes, *Time*, March 17, 1986.

44. Henry Moore, *Henry Moore at the British Museum* (New York: Abrams, 1981), p. 28.

45. Ibid., p. 37.

46. Ibid., p. 67.

47. Ibid., p. 81.

48. Ibid., p. 125.

49. Joel Funk, "Beethoven: A Transpersonal Analysis." *ReVision*, 5 (Spring 1982):29–41.

50. Robert Schauffler, *The Unknown Brahms* (New York: Dodd, Mead, 1936), pp. 177–179.

51. Funk, "Beethoven: A Transpersonal Analysis," pp. 29–41.

52. Ibid.

53. Thomas Hoover, *The Zen Experience* (New York: American Library, 1980); Wilber, *Up From Eden*, pp. 245–252.

54. Wilber, ibid., p. 242.

55. Elaine Pagels, *The Gnostic Gospels* (New York: Vintage, 1979).

56. Ibid.

57. This is an idea I derived from the teaching of John Lee, who runs the Denver program for the Guild of Psychological Studies, 2230 Divisadero Street, San Francisco, California 94115. This organization studies the historic Jesus in a Jungian context.

58. Nikos Kazantzakis, *The Saviors of God* (New York: Simon & Schuster, 1960), pp. 99–102.

59. Nikos Kazantzakis, *Report to Greco* (New York: Simon & Schuster, 1975).

60. Edward Whitmont, *The Symbolic Quest* (Princeton, N.J.: Princeton University Press, 1978), pp. 42, 235.

61. Wilber, *Up from Eden*, p. 152.

62. Kazantzakis, *Report to Greco*, 41.

CHAPTER 6. FAMILY AS A COMMUNITY OF SUBPERSONALITIES

1. Laura Dodson, *Family Counseling* (Muncie, Ind.: Accelerated Development, 1977).

2. Virginia Satir, *Conjoint Family Therapy* (Palo Alto: Science and Behavior Books, 1967), p. 185, and *Peoplemaking* (Palo Alto: Science and Behavior Books, 1972), pp. 112–122.

3. Dodson, *Family Counseling*, p. 20.

4. Ibid., p. 6. Dodson considers developmental levels in a somewhat different format than I do here.

5. J. Byng-Hall, "Re-editing Family Mythology During Family Therapy." *Journal of Family Therapy*, 1 (1979):105–116.

6. Paul Scott, *The Raj Quartet* (New York: Avon, 1966, 1968, 1971, 1975).

CHAPTER 7. CULTURE

1. Sue Walrond-Skinner, *Dictionary of Psychotherapy* (London: Routledge & Kegan Paul, 1986), p. 266.

2. Edward Hall, *The Silent Language* (New York: Premier, 1959).

3. In Figure 2, Hall's diagram is modified to include the biological basis of culture.

4. Ken Wilber, *Up from Eden* (Boston: Shambhala Publications, 1986), p. 80.

5. Hall, *The Silent Language.*

6. Erik Erikson, quoted in Philip Bock, *Continuities in Psychological Anthropology* (San Francisco: W. H. Freeman, 1980), p. 185.

7. Melford Spiro quoted in Bock, *Continuities in Psychological Anthropology*, p. 31.

8. Leo Tolstoy, quoted in introduction by Ronald Wilkes, translator, Maxim Gorky, *My Apprenticeship* (Hammondsworth, Middlesex, England: Penguin, 1974), p. 11.

9. Gorky, *My Apprenticeship*, p. 354.

10. Ronald Wilkes, quoting Soviet writer Konstantin Paustovsky in introduction to Gorky, *My Apprenticeship*, p. 10.

11. Ronald Wilkes in introduction to *My Apprenticeship*, p. 6.

12. Cliff Ishigaki teaches conflict resolution in an aikido and psychosynthesis framework nationally. For information, write: Clifford Ishigaki, 140 S. Flower, Suite 200, Orange, California 92668.

13. Clifford Geertz, *The Interpretation of Cultures* (New York: Basic Books, 1973), pp. 193–233. The ideas in the following discussion on ideologies are largely from this work.

14. Ibid., p. 207.

15. Frank H. Cushing, *Zuñi* (Lincoln, Neb.: University of Nebraska, 1979); Ruth Benedict, *Patterns of Culture* (Boston: Houghton Mifflin, [1934] 1959, pp. 57–129.

16. Information on Cushing's life is primarily from Jesse Green's introductory materials in Cushing's *Zuñi.*

17. Ibid., 408.

18. Margaret Mead, preface to Benedict, *Patterns of Culture*, p. ix.

CHAPTER 8. THIS SMALL PLANET

1. Roberto Assagioli, *Psychosynthesis* (New York: Viking, 1965), p. 29.

2. Astrid Koch, representative to the UN from Planetary Citizens, and I discovered in 1984 that we had been working, unbeknownst to each other, on the same analogy of the nations as subpersonalities of the world.

3. R. Kuttner, "Cultural Selection of Human Psychological Types." In M. F. Ashley Montagu, ed., *Culture: Man's Adaptive Dimension* (New York: Oxford University Press, 1968).

4. See Victor Harris, introduction to Miyamoto Musashi, *A Book of Five Rings* (Woodstock, N.Y.: Overlook, 1982).

5. Carl Marcy, "The Future of the Third World," *New York Times Book Review*, August 21, 1983.

6. Ibid. and John Kenneth Galbraith, *The Voice of the Poor* (Cambridge, Mass.: Harvard University Press, 1983).

7. Marcy, "The Future of the Third World," Galbraith, *The Voice of the Poor*, and Kuttner, "Cultural Selection."

8. Galbraith, Ibid.

9. Marcy, "The Future of the Third World."

10. Galbraith, *The Voice of the Poor*.

11. William Shakespeare, *Julius Caesar*.

12. Philip Taubman, "War by Other Means," *New York Times Book Review*, August 21, 1983.

13. Willis Harmon, "Report from the Soviet Union" (Institute of Noetic Sciences, 1985).

14. Robert Muller, *New Genesis* (New York: Doubleday, 1982), p. 5.

15. Goeffrey Anderson, from a sermon presented at St. John's Episcopal Church, Boulder, Colorado, June 23, 1985.

16. John V. Logue and Robert B. Rosenstock, "Reforming, Restructuring and Strengthening the United Nations," World Affairs Conference, University of Colorado, Boulder, Colorado, April 12, 1985.

17. Muller, *New Genesis*.

18. Murray Sayles, "SK 007—A Conspiracy of Circumstances," *New York Times Book Review*, April 25, 1985.

19. Ibid.

20. Ibid.

21. UN Charter, *United Nations Yearbook, 1947–48* (Lake Success, N.Y.: United Nations, 1949).

22. Willis Harmon, "Report from the Soviet Union" (Institute of Noetic Sciences, 1985).

23. Logue and Rosenstock, "Reforming, Restructuring and Strengthening the United Nations."

24. Ken Wilber, *Up From Eden* (Boston: Shambhala Publications, 1986).

BIBLIOGRAPHY

Psychosynthesis books and pamphlets may be obtained from Psychosynthesis Distribution, 2561 Tioga Way, San Jose, California 95124.

Adler, Gerald. "Hospital Treatment of Borderline Patients." *American Journal of Psychology*, 130 (1973):1, 32–36.

Allport, Gordon W. *Pattern and Growth in Personality*. New York: Holt, Rinehart & Winston, 1937.

Anthony, Dick, Bruce Ecker, and Ken Wilber, editors. *Spiritual Choices: The Problem of Recognizing Authentic Paths to Inner Transformation*. New York: Paragon House, 1987.

Ardell, Donald B. *High Level Wellness*. New York: Bantam, 1979.

Arnheim, Rudolph. "Review of Proportion." In *Module, Proportion, Symmetry, Rhythm*, Gyorgy Kepes, editor. New York: George Braziller, 1966, pp. 218–230.

Assagioli, Roberto. *The Act of Will*. Baltimore: Penguin, 1973.

_____. *The Balancing and Synthesis of Opposites*. New York: Psychosynthesis Research Foundation, 1972.

_____. "Cheerfulness: A Psychosynthesis Technique." Pasadena, Calif.: Psychosynthesis Training Center, 1983.

_____. "Dynamic Psychology and Psychosynthesis." New York Psychosynthesis Research Foundation, 1959.

_____. *The Education of Gifted and Super-gifted Children*. New York: Psychosynthesis Research Foundation, 1960.

_____. *Interviste 1972–74*. Florence: Centro Studi di Psicosintesi, 1974.

_____. "Jung and Psychosynthesis," a series of three lectures given in 1966 at the Istituto di Psicosintesi, Florence. New York: Psychosynthesis Research Foundation, 1966.

_____. Letters to Carl Jung. ETH—Bibliothek, History of Science Collection, Zurich, 1946.

_____. "Life as a Game and Stage Performance (Role Playing)." Pasadena, Calif.: Psychosynthesis Training Center, 1983.

_____. *Lo sviluppo transpersonale*, M. L. Girelli, editor. Rome: Astrolabio, 1988. In English translation: *Transpersonal Development: The Development Beyond Psychosynthesis*. London: Crucible/HarperCollins, 1991.

_____. "Psychosomatic Medicine and Bio-psychosynthesis." New York: Psychosynthesis Research Foundation, 1967.

_____. *Psychosynthesis*. New York: Viking, 1965.

_____. "Psychosynthesis: Height Psychology, Discovering the 'self' and the 'Self.' " New York: Psychosynthesis Research Foundation, 1974.

_____. "Psychosynthesis: Individual and Social (Some Suggested Lines of Research)." New York: Psychosynthesis Research Foundation, 1965.

_____. "Psychosynthesis: Typology." London: Institute of Psychosynthesis, 1983.

_____. "The Resolution of Conflicts and Spiritual Conflicts and Crises." New York: Psychosynthesis Research Foundation, 1975.

_____. "Self-Realization and Psychological Disturbances." New York: Psychosynthesis Research Foundation, 1961.

_____. "Symbols of Transpersonal Experiences." New York: Psychosynthesis Research Foundation, 1969.

_____. "The Technique of Evocative Words." New York: Psychosynthesis Research Foundation, 1970.

Augustine. *Confessions. Great Books of the Western World*, vol. 18. Chicago: Encyclopedia Britannica, 1952.

Bandler, Richard, and John Grinder. *The Structure of Magic: A Book About Language and Therapy*. Palo Alto, Calif.: Science and Behavior Books, 1975.

Barnes, Kenneth. "The Creative Imagination." Swarthmore Lecture Series. London: Friends Home Service Committee, 1960.

Barnouw, Victor. *An Introduction to Anthropology: Ethnology*. Homewood, Ill.: Dorsey, 1971.

Beahrs, John O. "Co-Consciousness: A Common Denominator in Hypnosis, Multiple Personality, and Normalcy." *American Journal of Clinical Hypnosis*, 26 (October 1983):100–112.

Benedict, Ruth. *Patterns of Culture*. Boston: Houghton Mifflin, [1934] 1959.

Berne, Eric. *Games People Play*. New York: Grove, 1964.

Berreman, T., et al. *Cultural Anthropology Today*. Del Mar, Calif.: Communications Research, 1971.

Berti, Alessandro. *Roberto Assagioli: Profilo biographico degli anni di formazione*. FLorence: Istituto di Psicosintesi, 1988.

Bingham, June. *U Thant: The Search for Peace*. New York: Knopf, 1966.

Bibliography

Bion, W. R. "Notes on Memory and Desire." *Psychoanalytic Forum*, 2 (1967):271–280.

Bliss, Eugene. "A Re-examination of Freud's Basic Concept from Studies of Multiple Personality Disorder." *Dissociation*, 1 (September 1988):36–40.

Bliss, Jonathan, and Eugene Bliss. *Prism: Andrea's World*. New York: Stein and Day, 1985.

Bly, Robert. *News of the Universe: Poems of Twofold Consciousness*. San Francisco: Sierra Club Books, 1980.

Bock, Philip K. *Continuities in Psychological Anthropology*. San Francisco: W. H. Freeman, 1980.

Bolitho, William. *Twelve against the Gods*. New York: Simon & Schuster, 1929.

Boraiko, Allen A. "Lasers: A Splendid Light." *National Geographic*, 165 (March 1984):335–363.

Boulding, Elise. "Children and Solitude." Pendle Hill pamphlet no. 125. Lebanon, Penn.: Pendle Hill, 1962.

Brain/Mind Bulletin. 9(13)–13(1) (July 1984–October 1987), 13(11), 11(12).

Braun, Bennett G. "The BASK (Behavior, Affect, Sensation, Knowledge) Model of Dissociation." *Dissociation*, 1:1 (1988):4–23.

————. "The BASK Model of Dissociation: Clinical Applications." *Dissociation*, 1:2 (1988):16–23.

————, editor. *Newsletter of the International Society for the Study of Multiple Personality and Dissociation*. Smyrna, Ga.: Ridgeview Institute. 6:1, 5:1, 5:3, 1988.

————. "Neurophysiologic Changes in Multiple Personality Due to Interaction: A Preliminary Report." *American Journal of Clinical Hypnosis*, 26 (October 1983):84–91.

————. "Psychophysiologic Phenomena in Multiple Personality and Hypnosis." *American Journal of Clinical Hypnosis*, 26 (October 1983):124–134.

————, editor. *Treatment of Multiple Personality Disorder*. Washington, D.C.: American Psychiatric Press, 1986.

Bronfenbrenner, Urie. *Two Worlds of Childhood*. New York: Russell Sage, 1970.

Brown, Barbara B. *Supermind: The Ultimate Energy*. New York: Harper & Row, 1980.

Brown, Molly Y. *The Unfolding Self*. Los Angeles: Psychosynthesis Press, 1983.

Bibliography

Byng-Hall, J. "Family Myths Used in Defense in Conjoint Family Therapy." *British Journal of Medical Psychology*, 46 (1973):239–250.

_____. "Re-editing Family Mythology During Family Therapy." *Journal of Family Therapy*, 1 (1979):103–116.

Calder, Nigel. *The Mind of Man*. New York: Viking, 1970.

Calverton, V. F. editor. *The Making of Man*. New York: Modern Library, 1931.

Campbell, Joseph. *The Inner Reaches of Outer Space: Metaphor as Myth and as Religion*. New York: Alfred van der Marck, 1985.

_____. *The Masks of God: Creative Mythology*. Harmondsworth, Middlesex: Penguin, 1968.

_____. *The Masks of God: Occidental Mythology*. Harmondsworth, Middlesex: Penguin, 1964.

_____. *The Masks of God: Oriental Mythology*. Harmondsworth, Middlesex: Penguin, 1962.

_____. *The Masks of God: Primitive Mythology*. Harmondsworth, Middlesex: Penguin, 1959.

Campbell, Susan M. *The Couple's Journey*. San Luis Obispo, Calif.: Impact Publishers, 1980.

Capote, Truman. "Nocturnal Turnings." In *Music for Chameleons*. New York: New American Library, 1981, pp. 246–265.

Carter-Haar, Betsie. "Identity and Personal Freedom." *Synthesis*, 1 (1975):56–108.

Churchill, Winston. *The Birth of Britain*. New York: Dodd, Mead, 1956.

Clayre, A. *The Heart of the Dragon*. Boston: Houghton Mifflin, 1985.

Cloninger, R. "Three Brain Systems May Hold Key to Personality." *Brain/Mind Bulletin*, 12 (1986).

Coan, Richard W. *Hero, Artist, Sage, or Saint: A Survey of Views on What Is Variously Called Mental Health, Normality, Maturity, Self-Actualization and Human Fulfillment*. New York: Columbia University Press, 1977.

_____. *The Optimal Personality: An Empirical and Theoretical Analysis*. New York: Columbia University Press, 1974.

Coffin, Charles M., editor. *The Major Poets: English and American*. New York: Harcourt, 1954.

Cole, Michael, and Sylvia Scribner. *Culture and Thought: A Psychological Introduction*. New York: Wiley, 1974.

Coons, Philip M. "Psychophysiologic Aspects of Multiple Personality Disorder: A Review." *Dissociation*, 1 (1988):47–53.

Bibliography

Corning, Peter A. *The Synergism Hypothesis*. New York: McGraw-Hill, 1983.

Cox, James M., editor. *Robert Frost: A Collection of Critical Essays*. Englewood Cliffs, N.J.: Prentice Hall, 1962.

Cushing, Frank H. *Zuñi*. Lincoln, Neb.: University of Nebraska Press, 1979.

Dante Alighieri. *The Divine Comedy, 1: Hell; 2: Purgatory; 3: Paradise*. New York: Penguin Books, [1308] 1962.

DeBono, Edward. *Newthink: The Use of Lateral Thinking in the Generation of New Ideas*. New York: Basic Books, 1968.

de Castillejo, Irene Claremont. *Knowing Woman: A Feminine Psychology*. New York: Harper & Row, 1973.

Dickens, Charles. *Bleak House*. Harmondsworth, Middlesex: Penguin, [1852] 1986.

————. *Nicholas Nickleby*. Harmondsworth, Middlesex: Penguin, [1838] 1979.

————. *Oliver Twist*. London: Oxford University Press, [1837] 1963.

Dillard, Annie. *Pilgrim at Tinker Creek*. New York: Harper & Row, 1974.

Dodson, Laura S. *Family Counseling: A Systems Approach*. Muncie, Ind.: Accelerated Development, 1977.

————. "World Distress from a Jungian Perspective." Unpublished paper, 1982.

Drever, James. *A Dictionary of Psychology*. Baltimore, Md.: Penguin Books, 1964.

Eliade, Mircea. *Myths, Dreams, and Mysteries*. New York: Harper, 1960.

Eliot, T. S. *The Complete Poems and Plays, 1909–1952*. New York: Harcourt Brace, 1952.

Ellenberger, Henri F. *The Discovery of the Unconscious: The History and the Evolution of Dynamic Psychiatry*. New York: Basic Books, 1970.

Encyclopedia Britannica. Chicago: Encyclopedia Britannica, 1982.

Erikson, Erik H. *Childhood and Society*. New York: Norton, 1950.

————. *Identity and the Life Cycle*. New York: Norton, 1980.

————. *Identity: Youth and Crisis*. New York: Norton, 1968.

Escalona, Sibylle K. *The Roots of Individuality*. Chicago: Aldine, 1968.

Europa Yearbook 1985. London: Europa Publications, 1985.

Fairbank, J. K., Edwin O. Reischauer, and A. M. Craig. *East Asia Tradition and Transformation*. Boston: Houghton Mifflin, 1973.

Farb, P. *Humankind*. Boston: Houghton Mifflin, 1978.

Bibliography

Fay, B. Marie. *The Dream Guide*. Los Angeles: Center for the Healing Arts, 1978.

Fenichel, Otto. *The Psychoanalytic Theory of Neurosis*. New York: Norton, 1945.

Ferguson, George. *Signs and Symbols in Christian Art*. New York: Oxford University, 1961.

Ferrucci, Piero. *Inevitable Grace, Breakthroughs in the Lives of Great Men and Women: Guides to Your Self-Realization*. Los Angeles: Tarcher, 1990.

_____. *Vivere meglio oggi: Introduzione al psicosintesi*. Florence: Centro Studi di Psicosintesi "Roberto Assagioli," 1985.

_____. *What We May Be: Techniques for Psychological and Spiritual Growth*. Los Angeles: Tarcher, 1982.

Fink, David L. "The Core Self: A Developmental Perspective on the Dissociative Disorders." *Dissociation*, 1 (1988):43–47.

Fitzgerald, C. P. *History of China*. New York: American Heritage Publications, 1969.

Flavell, J. H. *The Developmental Psychology of Jean Piaget*. Princeton, N.J.: Van Nostrand, 1963.

Fox, Matthew, editor. *Western Spirituality: Historical Roots, Ecumenical Routes*. Santa Fe, N.M.: Bear and Company, 1981.

Funk, Joel. "Beethoven: A Transpersonal Analysis." *ReVision*, 5 (Spring 1982):29–41.

Galbraith, John Kenneth. *The Anatomy of Power*. Boston: Houghton Mifflin, 1983.

_____. *The Voice of the Poor: Essays in Economic and Political Persuasion*. Cambridge: Harvard University Press, 1983.

Gardner, Howard. *Frames of Mind: The Theory of Multiple Intelligences*. New York: Basic Books, 1983.

Gavshon, Arthur. *The Mysterious Death of Dag Hammarskjöld*. New York: Walker & Company, 1962.

Geetz, Clifford. *The Interpretation of Cultures*. New York: Basic Books, 1973.

_____. *Works and Lives: The Anthropologist as Author*. Palo Alto, Calif.: Stanford University, 1988.

Gerard, Robert. *Psychosynthesis: A Psychotherapy for the Whole Man*. New York: Psychosynthesis Foundation, 1964.

Gorky, Maxim. *My Apprenticeship*. Harmondsworth, Middlesex: Penguin, [1915] 1974.

Gould, Glenn. "Glenn Gould Interviews Himself About Beethoven." *Glenn Gould Reader*. New York: Knopf, 1985, pp. 43–50.

Gowan, John C. *Development of the Creative Individual*. San Diego: Knapp, 1972.

Greenberg, Jay R., and Stephen A. Mitchell. *Object Relations in Psychoanalytic Theory*. Cambridge: Harvard University Press, 1983.

Greene, Mary. "Working with Repressed and Dissociated Memories." Unpublished paper, 1988.

Grof, Stanislav, editor. *Ancient Wisdom and Modern Science*. Albany: State University of New York, 1984.

Grohman, Will. *The Art of Henry Moore*. New York: Abrams, 1960.

Gruber, L. F. *Famous Portraits*. New York: Ziff-Davis, 1960.

Guggenbühl-Craig, Adolf. *Marriage Dead or Alive*. Dallas: Spring Publications, 1977.

Guilford, J. P. *The Nature of Human Intelligence*. New York: McGraw-Hill, 1967.

Hall, Edward T. *The Dance of Life: The Other Dimension of Time*. Garden City, N.Y.: Anchor, 1983.

_____. *Beyond Culture*. Garden City, N.Y.: Anchor, 1976.

_____. *The Silent Language*. New York: Premier, 1959.

Hamel, Peter Michael. *Through Music to the Self*. Boulder, Colo.: Shambhala Publications, 1976.

Hammarskjöld, Dag. *Markings*. New York: Knopf, 1964.

Hampden-Turner, Charles. *Maps of the Mind*. New York: Macmillan, 1981.

Hardy, Jean. *A Psychology with a Soul: Psychosynthesis in Evolutionary Context*. London: Routledge & Kegan Paul, 1987.

Harmon, Willis, and Howard Rheingold. *Higher Creativity*. Los Angeles: Tarcher, 1984.

_____. "Report from the Soviet Union: The President's Letter." Institute of Noetic Sciences, 1985.

Hastings, A. C., J. Fadiman, and J. S. Gordon, editors. *Health for the Whole Person: The Complete Guide to Holistic Medicine*. Boulder, Colo.: Westview, 1980.

Hayward, Jeremy W. *Perceiving Ordinary Magic: Science and Intuitive Wisdom*. Boston: Shambhala Publications, 1984.

_____. *Shifting Worlds, Changing Minds: Where the Sciences and Buddhism Meet*. Boston: Shambhala Publications, 1987.

Herrigel, Eugen. *Zen in the Art of Archery*. Translated by R. F. C. Hull. New York: Vintage, 1951, 1971.

Hodgen, Margaret T. *Anthropology, History, and Cultural Change*. Tucson, Ariz.: University of Arizona Press, 1974.

Hoover, Thomas. *The Zen Experience*. New York: New American Library, 1980.

Horowitz, Mardi J. *States of Mind: Configurational Analysis of Individual Psychology*. New York: Plenum, [1934] 1987.

Howes, Elizabeth B., and Sheila Moon. *Man the Choicemaker*. Philadelphia: Westminster, 1973.

Hughes, R. "Georgia O'Keefe." *Time*, March 17, 1986.

Huxley, Aldous. *The Perennial Philosophy*. New York: Harper, 1944.

James, Muriel, and Dorothy Jongeward. *Born to Win: Transactional Analysis with Gestalt Experiments*. Reading, Mass.: Addison-Wesley, 1971.

James, William. *The Principles of Psychology*, vols. 1 and 2. New York: Dover, [1890] 1950.

_____. *The Varieties of Religious Experience*. Harmondsworth, Middlesex, England: Penguin, [1902] 1982.

Janet, Pierre. *The Major Symptoms of Hysteria: Fifteen Lectures Given in the Medical School of Harvard*. New York: Hafner Publishing, [1907] 1965.

Jersey, Bill, director. "The First Fifty Years: Reflections on United States–Soviet Relations." Documentary film for television, 1985.

Johnson, Robert A. *He: Understanding Masculine Psychology*. New York: Harper & Row, 1974.

_____. *She: Understanding Feminine Psychology*. New York: Harper & Row, 1976.

Jung, C. G. *Aion. Collected Works* 9, part 2. Princeton, N.J.: Princeton University Press, [1951] 1959.

_____. *The Archetypes and the Collective Unconscious. CW* 9, part 1. Princeton, N.J.: Princeton University Press, [1959] 1968.

_____. *Mandala Symbolism*. Princeton, N.J.: Princeton University Press, 1972.

_____. *Memories, Dreams, Reflections*. New York: Random House, [1961] 1965.

_____. *Modern Man in Search of a Soul*. New York: Harcourt Brace, 1933.

_____. *The Practice of Psychotherapy. CW* 16. Princeton, N.J.: Princeton University Press, 1954.

_____. *Psychological Types*. *CW* 6. Princeton, N.J.: Princeton University Press, [1921] 1976.

_____. *Psychology and Alchemy*. *CW* 12. Princeton, N.J.: Princeton University Press, [1953] 1977.

_____. *Psychology and Religion: West and East*. *CW* 11. Princeton, N.J.: Princeton University Press, 1958.

_____. *The Structure and Dynamics of the Psyche*. *CW* 8. Princeton, N.J.: Princeton University Press, 1960.

_____. *Two Essays on Analytical Psychology*. *CW* 7. Princeton, N.J. Princeton University Press, 1966.

Jung, C. G., et al. *Man and His Symbols*. London: Aldus, 1964.

Jung, Emma. *Animus and Anima*. Zurich: Spring Publications, 1957.

Katz, Michael, William P. Marsh, and Gail G. Thompson, editors. *Earth's Answer: Explorations of Planetary Culture at the Lindisfarne Conferences*. New York: Harper & Row, 1977.

Kazantzakis, Nikos. *Report to Greco*. New York: Simon & Schuster, 1975.

_____. *The Saviors of God: Spiritual Exercises*. New York: Simon & Schuster, 1960.

Keating, Thomas. *Open Heart, Open Mind: The Contemplative Dimension of the Gospel*. Amity, N.Y.: Amity, 1986.

Keen, Sam. "The Golden Mean of Roberto Assagioli." *Psychology Today*, (December 1974):97–107.

Keleman, Stanley. *Your Body Speaks Its Mind*. Berkeley: Center Press, 1981.

Kelen, Emery. *Hammarskjöld*. New York: Putnam, 1966.

Kernberg, Otto. *Object Relations Theory and Clinical Psychoanalysis*. Northvale, N.J.: Jason Aronson, 1984.

Kierkegaard, Søren. *Purity of Heart Is to Will One Thing*. New York: Harper, [1938] 1956.

King, Vivian. "Psychosynthesis: A Therapeutic-Educational Guide Toward the Realization of the Self." Unpublished manuscript, 1989.

Kluckhohn, Clyde. *Mirror for Man: The Relation of Anthropology to Modern Life*. Tucson, Ariz.: University of Arizona Press, [1949] 1985.

Kluft, Richard P. *Childhood Antecedents of Multiple Personality*. Washington, D.C.: American Psychiatric Press, 1985.

Koch, Astrid. "Towards National and Planetary Synthesis." Talk presented at the International Psychosynthesis Conference, Sesto Pusteria, Italy, 1988.

Kohut, Heinz, and Ernest S. Wolf. "The Disorders of the Self and Their Treatment: An Outline." *International Journal of Psychoanalysis*, 59 (1978):413–424.

Kolb, Lawrence C. *Modern Clinical Psychology*. Philadelphia: W. B. Saunders, 1977.

Kramer, Sheldon Z. *Psychosynthesis and Integrative Family Therapy*. San Diego: Mission Valley Psychosynthesis Center, 1987.

Kull, Steven. *Minds at War: Nuclear Reality and The Inner Conflicts of Defense Policy Makers*. New York: Basic Books, 1982.

Kushel, Gerard. *Centering*. New York: Pinnacle Books, 1979.

Lagerkvist, Pär. *The Dwarf*. New York: Hill & Wang, [1945] 1986.

Lasswell, H. D. "Man the Social Animal." *Encyclopedia Britannica*, volume guide, 1974, pp. 280–288.

Lessing, Doris. *The Marriages of Zones Three, Four, and Five*. New York: Random, 1981.

Lévi-Strauss, Claude. *The Elementary Structures of Kinship*. Boston: Beacon Press, [1949] 1969.

Lewis, C. S. *The Screwtape Letters*. New York: Macmillan, 1956.

Logue, John V., and Robert B. Rosenstock. "Reforming, Restructuring and Strengthening the United Nations." Talk presented at the World Affairs Conference, University of Colorado, April 12, 1985.

Ludwig, Arnold M. "The Psychobiological Functions of Dissociation." *American Journal of Hypnosis*, 26 (October 1983):93–99.

Luria, A. R. *The Making of Mind*. Cambridge: Harvard University Press, 1979.

Manchester, William. *The Last Lion, Winston Spencer Churchill: Visions of Glory*. Boston: Little, Brown, 1983.

————. *Alone*. Boston: Little, Brown, 1988.

Mandelbaum, D. *Language, Culture, and Personality*. Berkeley: University of California Press, 1968.

Manley, Michael. "Why Non-aligned Is Not Neutral." *Nation* 236 (April 1983).

Marcy, Carl. "Future of the Third World." *New York Times Book Review*, August 21, 1983, p. 11.

Marsh, Caryl. "A Framework for Describing Subjective States of Consciousness." In *Alternate States of Consciousness*, Norman E. Zinberg, editor. New York: Free Press, 1977.

Martin, P. W. *Experiment in Depth: A Study of the Work of Jung, Eliot, and Toynbee*. Boston: Routledge & Kegan Paul, [1955] 1978.

Marx, Melvin H., and William A. Hillix. *Systems and Theories of Psychology.* New York: McGraw-Hill, 1963.

Maslow, Abraham H. *The Farther Reaches of Human Nature.* New York: Viking, 1971.

_____. "Psychological Data and Value Theory." In *New Knowledge in Human Values,* Abraham H. Maslow, editor. New York: Harper & Row, 1959.

_____. *Toward a Psychology of Being.* Princeton, N.J.: Van Nostrand, 1968.

Mathias, Charles M. "Habitual Hatred—Unsound Policy." *Foreign Affairs* 1983:1017–1030.

May, Rollo. *The Courage to Create.* New York: Bantam, 1975.

Mayer, Kurt B. *Class and Society.* New York: Random House, 1955.

Menzies, Lucy, Ronald A. Knox, and Ronald Selby Wright. "St. Margaret, Queen of Scotland and Her Chapel." Kirkcaldy, Scotland: St. Margaret's Guild, 1957.

Minsky, Marvin. *The Society of Mind.* New York: Simon & Schuster, 1986.

Montagu, M. F. Ashley. *Culture: Man's Adaptive Dimension.* New York: Oxford University Press, 1968.

Moon, Sheila. *Changing Woman and Her Sisters.* San Francisco: Guild for Psychological Studies Publishing House, 1984.

Moore, Henry. *Henry Moore at the British Museum.* New York: Abrams, 1981.

Morrison, Philip. "The Modularity of Knowing." In *Module, Proportion, Symmetry, Rhythm,* Gyorgy Kepes, editor. New York: George Braziller, 1966.

Moustakas, Clark E., editor. *The Self: Explorations in Personal Growth.* New York: Harper & Row, 1956.

Muller, Robert. *New Genesis.* New York: Doubleday, 1982.

Musashi, Miyamoto. *A Book of Five Things* [1645]. Translated by Victor Harris. Woodstock, N.Y.: Overlook Press, 1982.

Neumann, Erich. *The Origins and History of Consciousness.* Princeton, N.J.: Princeton University Press, 1954.

New York Times, September 1–13, 1983. All articles concerning the downing of KAL 007.

O'Keeffe, Georgia. *Georgia O'Keeffe.* New York: Viking, 1976.

O'Regan, Brendan. "Multiple Personality: Mirrors of a New Model of Mind?" *Investigations: Institute of Noetic Sciences,* 1, nos. 3–4 (1985).

Ornstein, Robert. *Multimind*. Boston: Houghton Mifflin, 1986.

_____. *The Psychology of Consciousness*. Harmondsworth, Middlesex: Penguin, 1972.

Ornstein, Robert, and Paul Ehrlich. *New World, New Mind: Moving Toward Conscious Evolution*. New York: Doubleday, 1989.

Ouspensky, P. D. *In Search of the Miraculous*. New York: Harcourt Brace, 1949.

Pagels, Elaine. *The Gnostic Gospels*. New York: Vintage Books, 1979.

Parabola ("Wholeness"), 10, no. 1 (1985).

Perls, Frederick, Ralph Hefferline, and Paul Goodman. *Gestalt Therapy*. New York: Bantam, 1951.

Pfeiffer, Carl C. *Nutrition and Mental Illness*. Rochester, Vt.: Healing Arts Press, 1987.

Piaget, Jean. *The Origins of Intelligence in Children*. New York: Norton, [1952] 1963.

Pozner, Vladimir. Interview. Institute of Noetic Sciences, 1985.

Progoff, Ira. *Jung, Synchronicity, and Human Destiny: Noncausal Dimensions of Human Experience*. New York: Dell Publishing, 1973.

Protopapadakis, Irini. "Socrates and Psychosynthesis." Unpublished paper presented at the International Psychosynthesis Conference, Sesto Pusteria, Italy, 1988.

Putnam, Frank W. "The Switch Process in Multiple Personality Disorder." *Dissociation*, 1 (1988):24–32.

Redfearn, J. W. T. "Ego and Self: Terminology." *Journal of Analytical Psychology*, 28 (1983):91–106.

Reischauer, Edwin O. *Towards the Twenty-First Century: Education for a Changing World*. New York: Knopf, 1974.

Reynolds, David K. *Playing Ball on Running Water: Living Morita Psychotherapy*. New York: Quill, 1984.

Ristad, Eloise. *A Soprano on Her Head*. Moab, Utah: Real People Press, 1982.

Roberts, Bernadette. *The Experience of No-Self: A Contemplative Journey*. Boston: Shambhala Publications, 1982.

_____. *The Path to No-Self: Life at the Center*. Boston: Shambhala Publications, 1985.

Rolland, Romain. *Jean-Christophe*. New York: Random House, 1913.

Romano, Catharine. "A Psycho-spiritual History of Teresa of Avila." In

Western Spirituality: Historical Roots, Ecumenical Routes, edited by Matthew Fox. Sante Fe: Bear and Co., 1981.

Roth, Sheldon. *Psychotherapy: The Art of Wooing Nature*. Northvale, N.J.: Jason Aronson, 1987.

Rowan, John. *Subpersonalities: The People Inside Us*. New York: Routledge, 1990.

Samples, Bob. *The Metaphoric Mind: A Celebration of Creative Consciousness*. Reading, Mass.: Addison-Wesley, 1976.

Sarana, Gopala. *The Methodology of Anthropological Comparisons*. Tucson, Ariz.: University of Arizona, 1975.

Satir, Virginia. *Conjoint Family Therapy*. Palo Alto, Calif.: Science and Behavior Books, 1967.

—————. *Peoplemaking*. Palo Alto, Calif.: Science and Behavior Books, 1972.

—————. *Your Many Faces: The First Step to Being Loved*. Berkeley: Celestial Arts, 1978.

Sayama, Mike. *Samadhi: Self-Development and Zen, Swordsmanship, and Psychotherapy*. Albany: State University of New York, 1986.

Sayles, Murray. "SK 007—A Conspiracy of Circumstances." *New York Times Book Review*, April 25, 1985.

Schauffler, Robert. *The Unknown Brahms*. New York: Dodd, Mead, 1936.

Schenk, Gustav. *The History of Man*. Philadelphia: Chilton, 1961.

Scott, Paul. *The Raj Quartet*. 4 vols. New York: Avon, 1966, 1968, 1971, 1975.

Segalen, Martine. *Historical Anthropology of the Family*. Cambridge: Cambridge University Press, 1986.

Shah, Idries. *A Perfumed Scorpion*. San Francisco: Harper & Row, 1978.

Shahn, Ben. *The Shape of Content*. New York: Vintage, 1960.

Shaplen, Robert. "The Paradox of Non-Alignment." *The New Yorker* 59 (May 1983):82–102.

Simonsen, Thordis, editor. *You May Plow Here: The Narrative of Sara Brooks*. New York: Norton, 1986.

Simonton, O. Carl, Stephanie Matthews-Simonton, and J. Creighton. *Getting Well Again*. Los Angeles: Tarcher, 1978.

Singer, June. *Boundaries of the Soul: The Practice of Jung's Psychology*. New York: Anchor, 1953.

Sliker, Gretchen. "Creativity of Adults in Light of Piagetian Theory." Ph.D. dissertation. Case Western Reserve University, Cleveland, 1972.

Bibliography

_____. "Facets of the Psyche." Unpublished manuscript, 1990.

Smith, W. John. *The Behavior of Communicating: An Ethological Approach.* Cambridge: Harvard University Press, 1977.

Staude, John-Raphael. *The Adult Development of C. G. Jung.* Boston: Routledge & Kegan Paul, 1981.

_____. "Jung and Assagioli." Unpublished talk presented at the International Psychosynthesis Conference, Venice and Sesto Pusteria, Italy, 1988.

Stern, Daniel N. *The Interpersonal World of the Infant: A View from Psychoanalysis and Developmental Psychology.* New York: Basic Books, 1985.

Stevens, John O. *Awareness.* Moab, Utah: Real People Press, 1971.

Sutherland, John O. "The British Object Relations Theorists: Balint, Winnicott, Fairbairn, Guntrip." *Journal of the American Psychoanalytic Association,* 28 (1980):829–860.

Synthesis: The Realization of the Self. 1 (1–4) (1975–77). Redwood City, Calif.: Synthesis Press.

Tart, Charles T. *Altered States of Consciousness.* New York: John Wiley, 1969.

_____. "Putting the Pieces Together: A Conceptual Framework for Understanding Discrete States of Consciousness." In *Alternate States of Consciousness,* edited by Norman E. Zinberg. New York: Free Press, 1979.

_____. *Waking Up: Overcoming the Obstacles to Human Potential.* Boston: Shambhala Publications, 1986.

Taubman, Philip. "War by Other Means." *New York Times Book Review,* August 21, 1983.

Taylor, Gregg. "Hagi: Where Japan's Revolution Began." *National Geographic,* 165:750–773.

Thant, U. *View from the UN: The Memoirs of U Thant.* New York: Doubleday, 1978.

Trungpa, Chögyam. *Shambhala: The Sacred Path of the Warrior.* Boston: Shambhala Publications, 1988.

United Nations. Record of the Meeting of the Security Council S15966, September 8, 1983, and other transactions of UN concerning the downing of KAL 007.

_____. *United Nations Yearbook, 1947–48.* Lake Success, N.Y.: United Nations, 1949.

van der Post, Laurens. *The Heart of the Hunter: Customs and Myths of the African Bushman.* New York: Harcourt Brace, 1961.

_____. *Journey into Russia.* Covelo, Calif.: Island Press, 1964.

_____. *Jung and the Story of Our Time.* New York: Vintage Books, 1975.

Vargiu, James. "Global Education and Psychosynthesis." San Francisco: Psychosynthesis Institute, 1971.

Vargiu, James, et al. "Psychosynthesis Workbook." *Synthesis*, 1 (1974):WB1–WB74.

von Franz, Marie-Louise. *The Feminine in Fairytales*. New York: Spring Publications, 1972.

_____. "The Process of Individuation." In *Man and his Symbols*, C. G. Jung, et al. New York: Doubleday, 1964.

_____. *Puer Aeternus*. Santa Monica, Calif.: Sigo Press, 1981.

von Franz, Marie-Louise, and James Hillman. *Jung's Typology*. Irving, Tex.: Spring Publications, 1979.

Waddington, C. H. 1966. "The Modular Principle and Biological Form." In *Module, Proportion, Symmetry, Rhythm*, Gyorgy Kepes, editor. New York: George Braziller, 1966, pp. 20–37.

Walrond-Skinner, Sue. *Dictionary of Psychotherapy*. London: Routledge & Kegan Paul, 1986.

Walsh, Roger N., and Frances Vaughan, editors. *Beyond Ego: Transpersonal Dimensions of Psychology*. Los Angeles: Tarcher, 1980.

Ware, Caroline F., K. M. Panikkar, and J. M. Romein, editors. *Cultural and Scientific Developments: History of Mankind, the Twentieth Century*. New York: Harper & Row, 1966.

Watkins, John G., and Helen Watkins. "The Management of Malevolent Ego States." *Dissociation*, 1 (1988):67–72.

Watkins, John G., and Rhonda J. Johnson. *We, the Divided Self*. New York: Irvington Publishers, 1982.

Watkins, Mary. *Waking Dreams*. Dallas: Spring Publications, 1984.

Wehr, Gerhard. *Jung: A Biography*. Boston: Shambhala Publications, 1987.

Weiser, John, and Thomas Yeomans (eds.). *Psychosynthesis—The Helping Professions: Now and For the Future*. Toronto: Ontario Institute for Studies in Education, 1984.

_____. *Readings in Psychosynthesis: Theory, Process, and Practice*, vols. 1 and 2. Toronto: Ontario Institute for Studies in Education, 1985.

Whitmont, Edward C. *The Symbolic Quest*. Princeton, N.J.: Princeton University Press, 1978.

Whitmore, Diana. *Psychosynthesis in Education*. Wellingborough, Northamptonshire, England: Turnstone Press, 1986.

Wickes, Frances G. *The Inner World of Childhood*. Englewood Cliffs, N.J.: Prentice Hall, 1927.

_____. *The Inner World of Choice.* Englewood Cliffs, N.J.: Prentice Hall, 1963.

Wilber, Ken. *The Atman Project: A Transpersonal View of Human Development.* Wheaton, Ill.: Quest, 1980.

_____. *Eye to Eye: The Quest for the New Paradigm.* New York: Anchor, 1983.

_____. *No Boundary: Eastern and Western Approaches to Personal Growth.* Boulder, Colo.: Shambhala Publications, 1981.

_____. *A Sociable God: Towards a New Understanding of Religion.* Boulder, Colo.: Shambhala Publications, 1983.

_____. *Up from Eden: A Transpersonal View of Human Evolution.* Boston: Shambhala Publications, 1986.

Wilber, Ken, Jack Engler, and Daniel P. Brown. *Transformations in Consciousness.* Boston: Shambhala Publications, 1986.

Williams, Donald L. *Border Crossings: A Psychological Perspective on Carlos Castaneda's Path of Knowledge.* Toronto: Inner City Books, 1981.

Winston, Jonathan. *Brain and Psyche: The Biology of the Unconscious.* New York: Vintage Books, 1986.

Yeomans, Thomas. *The Three Dimensions of Psychosynthesis.* Boston: Concord Institute, 1989.

_____. "World Awakening: Psychosynthesis and Geosynthesis." Talk presented at the International Psychosynthesis Conference, Sesto Pusteria, Italy, July 1, 1988.

Young, Walter C. "Psychodynamics and Dissociation: All That Switches Is Not Split." *Dissociation,* 1 (1988):33–38.

Zimbardo, Philip G., and Floyd L. Ruch. *Psychology and Life.* Glenview, Ill.: Scott, Foresman, 1975.

Zinberg, Norman E., editor. *Alternate States of Consciousness: Multiple Perspectives on the Study of Consciousness.* New York: Free Press, 1977.

INDEX